Christian Isobel Johnstone

Early English Voyagers

Or, The Adventures and Discoveries of Drake, Cavendish, and Dampier

Christian Isobel Johnstone

Early English Voyagers
Or, The Adventures and Discoveries of Drake, Cavendish, and Dampier

ISBN/EAN: 9783337176525

Printed in Europe, USA, Canada, Australia, Japan

Cover: Foto ©ninafisch / pixelio.de

More available books at **www.hansebooks.com**

Early English Voyagers.

DUTCH MEDAL ON THE OVERTHROW OF THE ARMADA.

Thomas Nelson and Sons,
LONDON, EDINBURGH, AND NEW YORK.

EARLY ENGLISH VOYAGERS;

OR,

The Adventures and Discoveries

OF

Drake, Cavendish, and Dampier.

"The spirits of your fathers
Shall start from every wave;
For the deck it was their field of fame,
And ocean was their grave."
                              CAMPBELL.

London:
T. NELSON AND SONS, PATERNOSTER ROW.
EDINBURGH; AND NEW YORK.

1892.

Contents.

DRAKE.

I. SIR FRANCIS DRAKE, ... 11
II. DRAKE'S CIRCUMNAVIGATION, ... 30
III. EXPEDITIONS TO THE WEST INDIES, ... 108

CAVENDISH.

I. VOYAGE ROUND THE WORLD, ... 133
II. SECOND VOYAGE TO THE SOUTH SEA, ... 172

DAMPIER.

I. THE BUCCANEERS OF AMERICA, ... 197
II. ADVENTURES AMONG THE WOOD-CUTTERS AND BUCCANEERS, 261
III. ADVENTURES WITH THE BUCCANEERS, ... 302
IV. CIRCUMNAVIGATION OF THE GLOBE, ... 325
V. VOYAGE TO NEW HOLLAND, 420

List of Illustrations.

ATTACKING THE ARMADA IN THE CHANNEL, … …	*Frontispiece*
DUTCH MEDAL ON THE OVERTHROW OF THE ARMADA, …	*Vignette*
SIR FRANCIS DRAKE, … … … … … …	13
SIR JOHN HAWKINS, … … … … … …	17
QUEEN ELIZABETH, … … … … … …	31
PENGUINS OF THE SOUTH SEAS, … … …	57
QUEEN ELIZABETH KNIGHTING DRAKE, …	101
DRAKE'S CHAIR IN THE UNIVERSITY OF OXFORD, … …	105
DRAKE FIGHTING WITH THE SPANIARDS, …	119
DRAKE'S FUNERAL, … … …	127
THOMAS CAVENDISH, … … … … …	135
WILLIAM DAMPIER, … … … …	199
INDIANS BUCCANING A TAPIR, … … … … …	203
INDIANS OF DARIEN, … … … … …	313
SEA LIONS, … … … … …	335
MALAY PROA, … … … …	367

DRAKE.

DRAKE.

CHAPTER I.

SIR FRANCIS DRAKE.

FRANCIS DRAKE, in common with many of the great men whose names impart lustre to the annals of England, may be termed the son of his own brave deeds. His family, and the rank of his father, have, however, been made the subject of much unprofitable discussion. In the heroic ages, the birth of so illustrious a man, if at all obscure, would at once have been derived from the gods,—an origin of extreme convenience to such biographers as, influenced by the prejudices of descent, disdain to relate the history of a poor man's son. Modern scepticism and coldness of imagination making this no longer possible, a struggle is nevertheless made for distinguished origin of some kind. The godfather of Drake was Sir Francis Russell of Tavistock, afterwards Earl of Bedford; and though various authorities are given for his father having been in orders, there remains no doubt that he was an honest mariner belonging to the same place. An attempt has been made to reconcile the contradictory accounts of Camden and Stowe, by assuming that the father of Drake, originally a seaman, was converted to the Reformed faith in the reign of Henry VIII., fell under the cognizance of some of his capricious and arbitrary edicts, and, fleeing into Kent, obtained orders, first read prayers to the fleet, and afterwards was appointed vicar of Upnore on the Medway, in which river the royal fleet then usually rode. Though Johnson, following Camden, without hesitation assumes the fact of the elder Drake being a clergyman, it is superfluous to cite the dates and accurate authority which disprove what both the annalist and the sage had a strong inclination to believe. Stowe, and the "Biographia Britannica," restore to the "honest mariner of Tavistock" the son of whom he had been innocently deprived by the real or imaginary vicar of Upnore; and Burney, in later times, though searching and accurate, does not even advert to a claim of birth which could add nothing to the renown of Francis Drake. The credit of having had Sir Francis Russell for his godfather is also disputed; and with this too Drake could dispense, especially as he is allowed to have gained nothing by this distinction save the Christian name which he bore.

But, whatever were his ancestry, it is clearly ascertained that Francis was the eldest of twelve sons, who, with few exceptions, went to sea. It is said that he was brought up and educated by Sir John Hawkins,

who was his kinsman. The degree or existence of the relationship is not clearly made out; and it is certain that young Drake was not long a charge upon any patron; for at a very tender age, his father, having a large family, put him apprentice to a neighbour who traded to Zealand and France. Here he speedily acquired that practical knowledge of his profession which made him early in life as experienced and expert a seaman as he afterwards became an able commander. His fidelity and diligence in this service gained the goodwill and regard of his master, who, dying a bachelor, bequeathed his vessel to young Drake; and thus, in the active and vigilant discharge of his first humble duties, was laid the sure foundation of future eminence and prosperity. At the early age of eighteen, Drake was made purser of a ship trading to Biscay, and soon afterwards engaged in the Guinea trade, which had lately been opened by the enterprise of his reputed relation Captain John Hawkins. The cruelty and injustice of this traffic were the discovery of a much later age.

The regular course of the trade, the most lucrative in which England had ever been engaged, was for ships to repair first to the Guinea coast for the human cargo, obtained by fraud, violence, and the most inhuman means, and then to the Spanish islands and the colonies on the Main, where the Africans were bartered for silver, sugar, hides, etc., etc. The history of the first voyage to the Guinea coast is that of every succeeding one,—"Master John Hawkins coming upon the coast of Sierra Leone, stayed for some time, and partly by the sword, and partly by other means, got into his possession three hundred negroes at the least."

Few voyages had been made from England to this new El Dorado, when Drake, at the age of twenty, desirous of extending his professional knowledge and participating in the gains of the slave-trade, embarked for Guinea in the squadron of Captain John Hawkins. Though Hawkins, for his exploits on the Guinea coast, had already obtained for his coat-of-arms, by patent from the Herald's Office, "a demi-Moor, in his proper colour, bound with a cord," he was not knighted till after he had obtained distinction in the public service. Whether Drake sailed from Plymouth captain of the *Judith*, one of the smallest ships of Hawkins's squadron, in the expedition undertaken to Guinea in 1567, or obtained this honour during the voyage, or in the harbour of St. Juan de Ulloa, is not clear; though it is asserted, in the relation of Miles Philip, that he went out captain. It is sufficient that, in the desperate encounter at St. Juan de Ulloa, between the Spaniards and the English squadron, he held a command, and honourably distinguished himself. But this somewhat anticipates the order of events in the first remarkable period of Drake's history.

Having completed his cargo of slaves, Hawkins and his company took the usual course to the Canaries and Spanish America, to exchange the Africans for other

SIR JOHN HAWKINS. *Page 16.*

wares more valued in England. In passing, he took the town of Rio de la Hacha, because the governor did not choose to trade with him. This circumstance is noticed, as it affords the only shadow of palliation for the subsequent treachery displayed by the Spaniards in the port of St. Juan de Ulloa, whither Hawkins was driven in to obtain shelter and refreshments by the severe gales which, on his way to England, were encountered off the coast of Florida. When the squadron of six ships entered the port, they were believed by the inhabitants to be a Spanish fleet, then hourly expected; and those who came on board were in some consternation on discovering the mistake. Hawkins, who from the first professed that he came in peace and friendship, to obtain shelter from stress of weather, and provisions for his money and merchandise, treated them with civility, but thought it prudent to detain two persons of consequence as hostages till assured of the terms on which he was to be received. The temptation of twelve merchant ships lying in the port, with cargoes estimated at £200,000, did not shake his integrity, though he was aware that they might easily be overmastered by his force. It is indeed candidly confessed by Hawkins that he dreaded the displeasure of the queen. A messenger was despatched to the Viceroy of Mexico; but before any answer could be returned to the demand of Hawkins, the expected fleet appeared, and his situation became uneasy and critical. The Spanish fleet had on board a cargo valued at six or seven million. If Hawkins prevented them from entering the harbour, they ran imminent risk of destruction; and if admitted, his own safety was put in jeopardy,—the port being confined, the town populous, and the Spaniards ready, he believed, and fatally experienced, to practise any treachery. At last the fleet was admitted, the Governor of Mexico agreeing to the terms stipulated, which were the exchange of hostages, a supply of provisions on fair terms, and that a fortified island, which lay across and commanded the port, should be given up to the English till their departure. On the faith of this treaty the Spanish fleet was allowed to sail in; mutual salutations were fired by the ships of both nations, and visits and civilities exchanged between the officers and the seamen.

Save for embroiling England in war, and thereby incurring the wrath of Elizabeth, and perhaps endangering his own neck, Hawkins, dissatisfied and rendered suspicious by the tardiness of the late negotiation, would certainly have put all to the hazard of a fight, and have gained glory and the seven million, or have lost himself; but he was now lulled into temporary security, on the faith of a treaty which the Spaniards had never meant to observe longer than until they were able to violate it with impunity. Their fleet was reinforced by a thousand men secretly conveyed from the land. An unusual bustle and shifting of men and weapons from ship to ship were noticed by the English; and their demand for explanation of these symptoms was answered by an instant attack on all sides. The *Minion*, and the *Judith*, the small vessel commanded by Drake, were the only English ships that escaped, and their safety was owing to the valour and conduct of the commanders, and only insured after a desperate though short conflict. The other four vessels were destroyed, and many of the seamen were rather butchered in cold blood than killed in action. The English who held the fortress, struck with alarm, fled to reach the ships at the beginning of the fight; and in the attempt were massacred without mercy. Such an engagement in a narrow port, each of the English vessels surrounded and attacked by three or four of those of Spain, presents a scene of havoc and confusion unparalleled in the records of maritime warfare. By the desperate valour of the English in this unequal combat, the *Admiral* and several more of the Spanish ships were burnt and sunk.

Placed between the fortress and the still numerous fleet, it was by miracle that even one English vessel got away. Hawkins reached England in the *Minion*, which suffered incredible hardships in the homeward voyage. She left the port without provisions or water, and crowded with seamen who had escaped the general slaughter, many of them wounded. The relation of their hardships, produced as they were by the basest treachery, must have made an indelible impression in England, where the Spaniards were already in bad odour. The details given by Miles Philip of the hardships of the voyage are too revolting to be transferred to this narrative, but may be imagined from the words of Hawkins:—"If all the miseries and troublesome affairs of this voyage be thoroughly written, there would need a painful man with his pen, and as great a time as he that wrote the 'Lives of the Martyrs.'" The *Judith*, Drake's vessel, which parted from the *Minion* on the fatal night—("forsook us in our great misery," are the words of Hawkins)—made the homeward voyage with less hardship and difficulty than the *Minion*.

Here Drake had lost his all, and here was laid the foundation of that hatred and distrust of the Spaniards which must have palliated many of his subsequent actions, and reconciled his countrymen to conduct they might not so readily have pardoned in one less sinned against. The chaplain of the fleet obtains the credit of expounding the justice of making reprisals on all Spaniards for the wrong inflicted by a few; but this might well be a spontaneous feeling, in a brave young man burning with resentment at the perfidy by which his comrades had been murdered, and himself betrayed and beggared. It has been quaintly said, "that in sea-divinity the case was clear. The King of Spain's subjects had undone Mr. Drake, and therefore Mr. Drake was entitled to take the best satisfaction he could on the subjects of the King of Spain."

This doctrine was very taking in England, where "the good old rule, the simple plan," was still followed,—

"That they should take who have the power,
And those should keep who can."

The scheme of Drake, for a new expedition to the Spanish American colonies, was accordingly no sooner made public than he found numbers of volunteers and friends ready to promote so praiseworthy a design as that which he was presumed to entertain, and who, having no personal quarrel of their own, were quite ready to adopt his, if the issue promised any share of those treasures with the fame of which Europe rung. But Drake was not yet prepared for the full development of his projects, and in all probability it was but gradually that they arose in his own mind.

The infamous transaction of St. Juan de Ulloa took place in September 1568, and in 1570 Drake undertook his first voyage with two ships, the *Dragon* and the *Swan*. In the following year he sailed with the *Swan* alone. That the means of undertaking any voyage were placed in the hands of a man still so young, is highly creditable to his character and good conduct. These might be called preparatory or experimental voyages, in which he cautiously and carefully reconnoitred the scene of future exploits; and, improving his acquaintance with the islands and coasts of South America, on the only side hitherto supposed accessible to Englishmen, amassed the wealth which enabled him to extend his sphere of enterprise, and enrich himself and his owners, while paying back part of his old debt to Spain.

Drake's first bold and daring attempt at reprisal was made in 1572. His squadron consisted of two vessels of small weight,—and this kind of light bark he seemed always to prefer,—the *Pacha* of seventy tons burden, which he commanded; and the *Swan*, once again afloat, a vessel of twenty-five tons, in which he placed his brother, Mr. John Drake. His whole force consisted of seventy-three men and boys. Instead of setting out, as has been alleged, with so slender a force as twenty-three men and boys, to take ships and storm towns, it is probable that Drake, after leaving England, recruited his numbers from vessels with which he fell in among the islands, as Lopez Vaz relates that at Nombre de Dios he landed one hundred and fifty men. This town was at that time what Porto Bello, a much more convenient station, afterwards became,—the *entrepôt* between the commodities of Old Spain and the wealth of India and Peru, and in riches imagined to be inferior only to Panama on the western shore. It was, however, merely a stage in the transmission of treasure and merchandise, and not their abiding place; and at particular seasons the town, which did not at any time exceed thirty houses, was almost deserted.

On the 24th March, Drake sailed from Plymouth, and on the 22nd July, in the night, made the attack on the town. A relation of this adventure, written by Philip Nicols, preacher, and afterwards published by Sir Francis Drake, nephew, heir, and godson of the navigator, is both less accurate and circumstantial than the narrative of Lopez Vaz, who, if not an eye-witness, was near the spot, and conversant with the actors and spectators. Drake's force is estimated at one hundred and fifty men, half of which he left at a small fort, and with the other division advanced in cautious silence to the market-place, when he ordered the calivers to be discharged, and the trumpet to be loudly sounded, the trumpeter in the fort replying, and the men firing at the same time, which made the alarmed Spaniards, startled out of their sleep, believe the place was attacked on all sides. Some, scarcely awake, fled to the mountains; but a band of fourteen or fifteen rallied, and, armed with harquebusses, repaired to the scene of action. Discovering the small number of the assailants, they took courage, fired and killed the trumpeter, and wounded one of the leaders of the party,—Drake was also wounded. The men in the fort, hearing the trumpet silenced, which had been the preconcerted signal, while the firing continued more briskly than before, became alarmed, and fled to their pinnaces.

Lopez Vaz relates that Drake's followers, retiring on the fort and finding it evacuated, shared in the panic, hastened to the shore, leaving their equipments behind, and by wading and swimming reached the pinnaces. One Spaniard, looking out at a window, was accidentally killed.

Disappointed of the rich booty expected in the town, Drake, on information obtained from the Symerons, a tribe of Indians in the Darien who lived in constant hostility with the Spaniards, resolved to intercept the mules employed to carry treasure from Panama to Nombre de Dios. Leaving his small squadron moored within the Sound of Darien, he set out, with a hundred men and a number of Indians, to attack and plunder this caravan of the New World. The plan, so well laid, was in the first instance frustrated by a drunken seaman.

It was in this expedition across the Isthmus that Drake, from the first sight of the Pacific, received that inspiration which, in the words of Camden, "left him no rest in his own mind till he had accomplished his purpose of sailing an English ship in those seas." The account of this adventure is in one original history so interesting and picturesque that we transfer it without mutilation:—" On the twelfth day we came to the height of the desired hill (lying east and west like a ridge between the two seas) about ten of the clock; where the chiefest of the Symerons took our captain by the hand and prayed him to follow him. Here was that goodly and great high tree, in which they had cut, and made divers steps to ascend near the top, where they had made a convenient bower, wherein ten or twelve men might easily sit; and from thence we might see the Atlantic Ocean we came from, and the South Atlantic so much desired. South and north of this tree they had felled certain trees, that the prospect might be the clearer.

" After our captain had ascended to this bower with

the chief Symeron, and having, as it pleased God at this time by reason of the breeze, a very fair day, had seen that sea of which he had heard such golden reports, he besought of Almighty God of his goodness to give him life and leave to sail once in an English ship in that sea, and then, calling up all the rest of our men, acquainted John Oxnam especially with this his petition and purpose, if it should please God to grant him that happiness."

This enthusiasm of a noble ambition did not, however, divert the thoughts of the adventurer from enterprises of a more questionable kind. Disappointed at Nombre de Dios, and again of intercepting the mules, he stormed Venta Cruz, a half-way station for the lodgment of goods and refreshment of travellers making their way through the difficult and fatiguing passes of the Isthmus. According to Lopez Vaz, six or seven merchants were killed; and as no gold or silver was obtained to satiate the thirst of the English seamen, goods were wantonly destroyed to the amount of two thousand ducats. It is, however, not easy to say whether it was before or after this outrage that a string of treasure-mules was by accident surprised. The gold was carried off, and as much silver as it was possible to bear away. The rest was buried till a new voyage should be undertaken, and Drake and his company regained their ships just in time to escape the Spaniards. "Fortune so favoured his proceedings," says Vaz, "that he had not been above half an hour on board when there came to the seaside above three hundred soldiers, which were sent of purpose to take him; but God suffered him to escape their hands to be a further plague unto the Spaniards." In this expedition a trait of Drake's character is recorded which at once marks his generosity and enlightened policy. To the cacique of the friendly Symerons he had presented his own cutlass, for which the chief had discovered a true Indian longing. In return the Indian gave him four large wedges of gold, which, declining to appropriate, Drake threw into the common stock, saying "he thought it but just that such as bore the charge of so uncertain a voyage on his credit should share the utmost advantage that voyage produced." And now, "God suffering him to be a further plague to the Spanish nation, he sailed away with his treasure." This was considerable, and good fortune attended Drake to the end of his voyage; for, leaving Florida, in twenty-three days he reached the Scilly Isles—probably the quickest passage that had yet been made. It was in time of public service, on Sunday the 9th August, 1573, that he returned to Plymouth; and "news of Captain Drake's return being carried to church, there remained few or no people with the preacher; all running out to observe the blessing of God upon the dangerous adventures of the captain, who had spent one year two months and some odd days in this voyage."

The next undertaking of Drake was of a more ambitious character. With the wealth acquired thus gallantly, and in the opinion of his contemporaries fairly and honourably, though the means may not stand the test of the morality of a more enlightened and philosophic age, Drake fitted out three stout frigates, which, with himself as a volunteer, he placed at the disposal of Walter, Earl of Essex, father of the unfortunate favourite of Elizabeth. Of these he was, as a matter of course, appointed commander, and performed good service in subduing the rebellion in Ireland. His former reputation and his late exploits had now acquired for Drake high fame and noble patronage. He became known to the queen through the introduction of her favourite and privy-councillor, Sir Christopher Hatton—a distinction doubly desirable as it promised assistance in "that haughty design which every day and night lay next his heart, pricking him forwards to the performance."

Though, in the enthusiasm of the moment of inspiration, Drake had betrayed his project, when the time came for its accomplishment he maintained an almost suspicious reserve, meditating his great design without "confiding it to any one." His character through life was that of a man who listens to every one's counsel, but follows his own; and doubtless in the purpose he meditated there was no judgment so well-informed and ripe.

CHAPTER II.

DRAKE'S CIRCUMNAVIGATION.

SPAIN and England were still nominally at peace, though the national animosity was continually breaking out in fits of aggression and violence; and if Elizabeth did not absolutely discountenance, her policy forbade open approbation of a project so equivocal as that which Drake contemplated. It is, however, certain that the plan of his voyage was laid before the queen; and her majesty, once convinced of its importance and the glory and advantage which might be derived to her kingdom from its prosperous issue, was easily reconciled to the justice of what appeared so expedient. The plan accordingly at last received her decided though secret approbation. In one relation of the voyage it is even affirmed that Drake held the royal commission, though this is not probable. What follows is more true to the character of Elizabeth, subtle at once and bold. At a parting interview she is said to have presented Drake with a sword, delivered with this emphatic speech,— "We do account that he who striketh at thee, Drake, striketh at us." Even this verbal commission saves

Drake from the charge of having made a piratical voyage, or divides the shame with his sovereign.

The high estimation in which Drake was now held may be gathered from the readiness with which friends and admirers placed in his hands their ships, and the means of equipping a squadron to go on some expedition of which the destination lay hid in his own bosom. Nor, though the horrible sufferings of Hawkins's crew and more recent disasters were still fresh in the public memory, did he lack both officers and seamen, from among the most bold, able, and active of that age, who were ready to follow him blindfold to the end of the world. Some of the more sordid might from afar smell the spoils of the Spaniards, but many were actuated by nobler motives.

The squadron was ostensibly fitted out for a trading voyage to Alexandria, though the pretence deceived no one, and least of all the watchful Spaniards. It consisted of five vessels of light burden, the largest being only one hundred tons. This was named the *Pelican*, and was the captain-general's ship. The others were, the *Elizabeth*, a bark of eighty tons belonging to London, and commanded by Captain John Winter; the *Swan*, a fly-boat of fifty tons burden, Captain John Chester; the *Christopher*, a pinnace of fifteen tons, Captain Thomas Moone; and the *Marigold*, a bark of thirty tons, Captain John Thomas. The *Benedict*, a pinnace of twelve tons, accompanied the *Elizabeth*. The frames of four pinnaces were taken out, to be set up as they were wanted. The anxiety displayed for the proper outfit of the squadron, the extent of preparations in provisioning the ships, and laying in arms and stores equal to a very long voyage, and the improbability of Drake, after his late exploits, undertaking a peaceful expedition for traffic, had betrayed in part his design before the fleet left England; but when, out of sight of the land, the captain-general, in case of separation, appointed a rendezvous at the island of Mogadore on the Barbary coast, there was no remaining doubt that his enterprise pointed to a place more distant and important than Alexandria.

Though it is probable that traversing the Pacific was a subsequent idea arising from the condition in which we shall find him after leaving the coast of New Albion, Drake is not the less entitled to the praise he has often received for attempting an enterprise like that of passing the Strait of Magellan with so small a force, and adventuring into wild, stormy, and unknown seas with ships of so little weight. The passage of the Strait, even to a man not so obnoxious to the Spanish nation, was a project which could only rationally be entertained by a bold and commanding genius relying implicitly on its own resources. The dangers and difficulties of Magellan Strait had made it be for a long period of years almost abandoned by the Spaniards, and it was come to be a saying among them that the passage had closed up. A superstitious prejudice was conceived against all further attempts in the SOUTH SEA, which, it was asserted, had proved fatal to every one who had been celebrated as a discoverer there,—as if Providence had a controversy with those who were so daring as to pass the insuperable barriers placed between the known and the unknown world. Magellan had been killed by the heathen in this new region, which Europeans had no sanction to approach; Vasco Nunez de Balboa, the European who first saw the South Sea, had been put to death by his countrymen; and De Solis was cruelly murdered by the natives of Rio de la Plata when proceeding to the Strait. Most of the commanders had successively perished of diseases produced by the hardships and anxiety attending the voyage. The mariner De Lope, who from the topmast of a ship of Magellan's fleet first saw the Strait, had a fate still more dreadful in the eyes of the good Catholics of Castile, as he had turned a renegade and Mohammedan. None of these real and imaginary dangers deterred Drake; and he, who at all times preferred vessels of light burden, as of greater utility in threading narrow and intricate channels and coasting unknown shores than ships of large and unwieldy size, selected those mentioned above.

Besides the cargoes usually exported for trading, both with civilized and savage nations, Drake, who knew the full value of shows and pageants, and whatever strikes the senses, had taken care to equip himself with many elegancies seldom thought of by early navigators. His own furniture and equipage were splendid, and his silver cooking utensils and the plate of his table of rich and curious workmanship. He also carried out a band of musicians, and studied everything that could impress the natives in the lands he was to visit or discover with the magnificence, and the high state of refinement and of the arts in his own country.

On the 15th November, 1577, the squadron sailed from Plymouth, but encountering a violent gale on the same night, were forced to put back into Falmouth: the mainmast of the *Pelican* was cut away, and the *Marigold* was driven on shore and shattered. This was a disheartening outset; but after refitting at Plymouth, they sailed once more on the 13th December, and proceeded prosperously.

On Christmas-day they reached Cape Cantin on the coast of Barbary, and, on the 27th, Mogadore,—an island lying about a mile from the mainland, between which and it they found a safe and convenient harbour. Mogadore is an island of moderate height; it is about a league in circuit. Having sent out a boat to sound, they entered by the north approach to the port, the southern access being found rocky and shallow. Here Drake halted to fit up one of the pinnaces for service; and while thus engaged, some of the Barbary Moors appeared on the shore, displaying a flag of truce, and making signals to be taken on board. Two of superior condition were brought to the ships, an English hostage being left on shore for their safe return. The strangers were courteously received and hospitably regaled by the captain-general, who presented them with linen, shoes, and a javelin. When sent on shore, the hostage was restored; and next day, as several loaded camels were seen approaching, it was naturally presumed their burdens were provisions and merchandise, and the English sent off a boat to trade. On the boat reaching the shore, a seaman, more alert than his neighbours, leapt among the Moors, and was instantly snatched up, thrown across a horse, and the whole party set off at a round gallop. The boat's crew, instead of attempting to rescue their companion, consulted their personal safety by an immediate retreat to the ships. Indignant at the treachery of the Moors, Drake landed with a party to recover the Englishman and take vengeance, but was compelled to return without accomplishing his object. Time, which cleared up the mystery, also partly exculpated the Moors. It was ascertained that the seaman had been seized to be examined by the king, the famous Muley Moloch, respecting an armament then fitting out by the Portuguese to invade his territory,—an invasion which soon afterwards took place, and of which the results are well known. Before the prisoner was dismissed the fleet had sailed; but he was well treated, and permitted to return to England by the first ship that offered.

The fleet having taken in wood, sailed on the 31st December, and on the 17th January, 1578, reached Cape Blanco, having on the cruise captured three caunters, as the Spanish fishing-boats were called, and two or else three caravels,—the accounts on this, as on several other minor points, being often contradictory. A ship, which was surprised in the harbour with only two men on board, shared the same fate. At Cape Blanco they halted for five days' fishing: while on shore Drake exercised his company in arms, thus studying both their health and the maintenance of good discipline. From the stores of the fishermen they helped themselves to such commodities as they wanted, and sailed on the 22nd, carrying off also a caunter of forty tons burden, for which the owner received, as a slight indemnification, the pinnace *Christopher*. At Cape Blanco fresh water was at this season so scarce that, instead of obtaining a supply, Drake, compassionating the condition of the natives, who came down from the heights offering ambergris and gums in exchange for it, generally filled their leathern bags without accepting any recompense, and otherwise treated them humanely and hospitably. Four of the prizes were released here. After six days' sailing they came to anchor on the 28th at the west part of Mayo,—an island where, according to the information of the master of the caravel, dried goat's flesh might be had in plenty, the inhabitants preparing a store annually for the use of the king's ships. The people on the island, mostly herdsmen and husbandmen belonging to the Portuguese of the island of St. Jago, would have no intercourse with the ships, having probably been warned of danger. Next day a party of sixty men landed, commanded by Captain Winter and Mr. Doughty,—a name with which, in the sequel, the reader will become but too familiar. They repaired to what was described as the capital of the island, by which must be understood the principal aggregation of cabins or huts, but found it deserted. The inhabitants had fled, and had previously salted the springs. The country appeared fertile, especially in the valleys; and in the depth of the winter of Great Britain they feasted on ripe and delicious grapes. The island also produced cocoa-nuts, and they saw abundance of goats and wild hens; though these good things, and the fresh springs, were unfortunately too far distant from the ships to be available. Salt produced by the heat of the sun formed here an article of commerce, and one of the prizes made was a caravel bound to St. Jago for salt.

Leaving Mayo on the 30th, on the south-west side of St. Jago they fell in with a prize of more value,—a Portuguese * ship bound to Brazil laden with wine, cloth, and general merchandise, and having a good many passengers on board. The command of this prize was given to Doughty, who was, however, soon afterwards superseded by Mr. Thomas Drake, the brother of the general. This is the first time we hear of offences being charged against the unfortunate Doughty. It is said he appropriated to his own use presents, probably given as bribes to obtain good usage, by the Portuguese prisoners. These captives Drake

* Portugal was at this time annexed to the crown of Spain, which enabled the English navigators to reconcile an attack on the Portuguese ships, to consciences not, however, particularly scrupulous.

generously dismissed at the first safe and convenient place, giving every passenger his wearing apparel, and presenting them with a butt of wine, provisions, and the pinnace he had set up at Mogadore. Only the pilot was detained, Nuno de Silva, who was acquainted with the coast of Brazil, and who afterwards published a minute and accurate account of Drake's voyage.

Here, near the island named by the Portuguese Isla del Fogo or the Burning Island, where, says the " Famous Voyage," " on the north side is a consuming fire, the matter whereof is said to be sulphur," lies Brava, described in the early narratives as a terrestrial paradise,—" a most sweet and pleasant island, the trees whereof are always green, and fair to look upon ; in respect of which they call it Isla Brava, that is, The Brave Island." The " soil was almost full of trees ; so that it was a storehouse of many fruits and commodities, as figs, always ripe, cocoas, plantains, oranges, lemons, citrons, and cotton. From the brooks into the sea do run in many places silver streams of sweet and wholesome water," with which ships may easily be supplied. There was, however, no convenient harbour nor anchoring found at this " sweet and pleasant" island,— the volcanic tops of Del Fogo " not burning higher in the air" than the foundations of Brava dipped sheer into the sea.

The squadron now approached the equinoctial line, sometimes becalmed, and at other times beaten about with tempests and heavy seas. In their progress they were indebted to the copious rains for a seasonable supply of water. They also caught dolphins, bonitos, and flying-fish, which fell on the decks, and could not rise again "for lack of moisture on their wings." They had left the shore of Brava on the 2nd February. On the 28th March, their valuable Portuguese prize, which was their wine-cellar and store, was separated in a tempest, but afterwards rejoined at a place which, in commemoration of the event, was called Cape Joy. The coast of Brazil was now seen in $31\frac{1}{2}°$* south. On the 5th April the natives, having discovered the ships on the coast, made great fires, went through various incantations, and offered sacrifices, as was imagined, to the devil, that the prince of the powers of the air might raise storms to sink the strangers. To these diabolical arts the mariners doubtless attributed the violent lightning, thunder, and rain, which they encountered in this latitude.

About Cape Joy the air was mild and salubrious, the soil rich and fertile. Troops of wild deer, "large and mighty," were the only living creatures seen on this part of the coast, though the foot-prints of men of large stature were traced on the ground. Some seals were killed here, fresh provisions of any kind never being neglected. On the 14th of April, Drake anchored within the entrance of Rio de la Plata, where he had

* Another account says 38° south. In determining the latitude or longitude, the authority of Burney is generally followed in this volume, as his eminent practical skill makes his observations on the discrepancies in the different accounts of great value.

appointed a rendezvous in case of separation after leaving the Cape de Verd Islands; and here the caunter, which had separated in a gale on the 7th, rejoined, when the expedition sailed eighteen leagues further into the river, where they killed sea-wolves (seals),—"wholesome but not pleasant food." Still further in, they rode in fresh water; but finding no good harbour, and having taken in water, the fleet, on the 27th, stood out, and afterwards southward. The *Swan* lost them on the first night, and the caunter, ever apt to go astray, was separated ten days afterwards. In 47°·south a headland was seen, within which was a bay that promised safe harbourage ; and having, on the 12th May, entered and anchored, Drake, who seldom devolved the duty of examination on an inferior officer, went off in the boat next morning to explore the bay. Before he made land, a thick fog came on, and was followed by bad weather, which took from him the sight of the fleet. The company became alarmed for their protector and general, in whom all their hopes of fortune, fame, and even of preservation, were placed. The *Marigold*, a bark of light weight, stood in for the bay, picked up the captain-general, and came to anchor. In the meanwhile the other ships, as the gale increased, had been compelled to stand out to sea. The fog which had fallen between Drake and the fleet also took from his sight an Indian, who, loudly shaking a rattle, danced in time to the discordant music he made, and by his gestures seemed to invite the strangers on shore. Next day Drake landed, and several Indians came in sight, to whom a white flag was waved in token of amity, and as a signal to approach. The natives acknowledged the symbol of peace, but still kept at a wary distance.

Drake now ordered fires to be lighted as signals to the ships; and they all rejoined, save the two vessels formerly separated.

In a sort of storehouse here, above fifty dried ostriches were found, besides other birds laid up, dry or drying for provision, by the Indians. It was believed by some of the English that these had been left as a present; and Drake, whether believing or not in so rare an instance of hospitality, appropriated the dried birds to the use of his company. It is a charitable conjecture that some of his own wares were left in return. The manner in which these ostriches, whose flesh supplied food while their feathers furnished ornaments, were snared deserves notice. Plumes of feathers were affixed to a stick, made to resemble the head and neck of the bird. Behind these decoys the hunter concealed himself, and, moving onwards, drove the ostriches into some narrow tongue of land, across which strong nets were placed to intercept the return of the bird, which runs, but cannot fly.* Dogs were then set upon the prey, which was thus taken.

The choice of the place in which the fleet now lay

* It is to be understood that in this volume objects of natural history are often described according to the notions of early voyagers, and not as further research and observation, and the discoveries and classifications of science, warrant.

had been dictated by necessity alone. On the 15th it was abandoned, and on the 17th they anchored in a good port, in 47½° south. Here seals were so plentiful that upwards of two hundred were killed in an hour. While the crews were filling the water-butts, killing seals, and salting birds for future provision, Drake in the *Pelican*, and Captain Winter in the *Elizabeth*, set out on different courses in quest of the *Swan* and the Portuguese prize. On the same day Drake fell in with the *Swan*, and before attempting the Strait, formed the prudent resolution of diminishing the cares and hazards of the voyage by reducing the number of his ships. The *Swan* was accordingly broken up for firewood, after all her materials and stores had been removed.

When the ships had lain here a few days, a party of the natives came to the shore, dancing, leaping, and making signs of invitation to a few of the seamen then on a small island, which at low water communicated with the mainland. They were a handsome, strong, agile race, lively and alert. Their only covering was the skin of an animal, which, worn about their middle when walking, was wrapped round their shoulders while they squatted or lay on the ground. They were painted over the whole body after a grotesque fashion. Though fancy and ingenuity were displayed in the figures and patterns, and in the contrast and variety of colours, it is reasonable to conclude that the practice had its origin in utility, and was adopted as a defence against cold, ornament being at first only a secondary consideration, though, as in more refined regions, it sometimes usurped the place of the principal object. These Indians being first painted all over, on this ground-work many freaks of fancy were displayed: white full-moons were exhibited to advantage on a black ground, and black suns on a white one. Some had one shoulder black and the other white; but these were probably persons who carried the mode to the extreme.

On seeing that the signals made were interpreted in a friendly way, Drake sent a boat to the shore with bells, cutlery, and such small wares as were likely to be attractive and acceptable to the tastes of the natives. As the boat neared the shore, two of the group, who had been standing on a height, moved swiftly down, but stopped short at a little distance. The presents were fastened to a pole, and left on the beach; and after the boat put off they were removed, and in return such feathers as the natives wore, and the carved bones which they used as ornaments, were deposited near or fastened to the same pole. Thus a friendly, if not profitable or useful, traffic was established. For such trifles as the English bestowed, they gave in return the only articles they possessed to which value was attached. These were bows, arrows made of reeds and pointed with flint, feathers, and carved bones. Their mode of exchange was to have everything placed on the ground, from whence the goods were removed, and the article bartered for substituted. By some of the voyagers these people are described as of gigantic stature. They were of a gay and cheerful disposition; the sound of the trumpets delighted them; and they danced merrily with the sailors. One of their number who had tasted wine, and became, it is stated, intoxicated with the mere smell before the glass reached his lips, always afterwards approached the tents crying, " Wine, wine !" Their principal article of food was seals, and sometimes the flesh of other animals; all of which they roasted, or rather scorched for a few minutes, in large lumps of six pounds weight, and then devoured nearly raw,— "men and women tearing it with their teeth like lions."

The fleet sailed from Seal Bay, as this place was named, on the 3rd June, and on the 12th came to anchor in a bay where they remained for two days, during which they stripped the caunter and allowed it to drift. Drake had thus reduced his force to a more compact and manageable form. The place from which this vessel was sent adrift is sometimes called the Cape of Good Hope, but seems to have been named Cape Hope. From the 14th to the 17th May the fleet cruised about in search of the *Mary*, the Portuguese prize, and then came to anchor in a bay 50° 20′ south. On the 19th the missing vessel was found, and next day the whole squadron anchored in the Port St. Julian of Magellan in 40° 30′ south; where, says one relation, "we found the gibbet still standing on the Main where Magellan did execute justice upon some of his rebellious and discontented company." So soon as the ships were safely moored, Drake and some of his officers went off in a boat to examine the capabilities of this part of the coast, and on landing met two men of immense stature, who appeared to give them welcome. These were of the Patagonian tribes of Magellan. A few trifles presented to them were accepted with pleasure, and they were apparently delighted by the dexterity with which the gunner used the English bow in a trial of skill, sending his arrows so far beyond their best aim. Nothing, however, can be more fickle and capricious than the friendship of most savage tribes. An Indian of less amiable disposition than his companions approached, and with menacing gestures signified to the crew to be gone. Mr. Winter, an English gentleman, displeased with the interruption given to their pastime by this churlish fellow, between jest and earnest drew a shaft partly in intimidation, but also to prove the superiority of the English bow and skill. The bow-string unfortunately snapped; and while he was repairing it a sudden shower of arrows wounded him in the shoulder and the side. Oliver, the gunner, instantly levelled his piece; but it missed fire, and the attempt proved the signal for his destruction. He was pierced through with an arrow, and immediately dropped. At this critical moment Drake ordered the rest of the party to cover themselves with their targets, and advance upon the Indians, who were fast mustering. With ready presence of mind, he directed his men, at the same time, to break every arrow aimed at them, as the assailants must thus soon expend their stock. The captain-general might at this juncture have remembered that, in the *mêlée* where Magellan lost his life, the same arrows were picked up by the people of Matan, and repeatedly shot, as they drove the Spaniards into the water. At the same instant in which he gave the order, Drake seized the gunner's piece, and taking aim at the man who had killed Oliver and begun the affray, he shot him in the belly. This turned the fate of the hour, and probably prevented the massacre of the whole party of English; for many more of the Patagonians were seen hastening from the woods to support their countrymen, when the hideous bellowing of the wounded man struck with panic those already engaged, and the whole fled. It was not thought prudent to pursue them, nor even to tarry on shore. Mr. Winter was therefore borne off to the ships; but in the haste of embarkation the body of the gunner was left. Next day, when looked after, the body was found uninjured, save that an English arrow had been thrust into the left eye. The clothes were in part stripped off, and formed into a pillow or truss, which was placed under the head of the corpse. Winter soon afterwards died of his wounds.

This unfortunate affray appears to have been more the consequence of misunderstanding than design; and the usage of the dead body, and subsequent conduct of the natives, evince a less revengeful and ferocious disposition than is usually displayed even among the mildest savage tribes when inflamed by recent battle. During the remainder of the time that the fleet lay here no further molestation was offered to the English.

The stature of these tribes, and of those in the Strait, has been the subject of dispute among navigators from the voyage of Magellan to our own times, each succeeding band being unwilling to yield an inch to their precursors, or to meet with "giants" less formidable than those which had been previously seen. Cliffe, however, says "they were of ordinary height, and that he had seen Englishmen taller than any of them;" and then, like a true seaman of the period, he imputes their exaggerated stature to the "lies" of the Spaniards, from whom no good thing could come, and who, in the imaginary impunity of escaping detection from the navigators of other nations, related these marvellous tales. "The World Encompassed" makes the height of these people seven feet and a half. It is not unlikely that the mists, haze, and storms, through which the natives were often partially seen in the Strait, or on those wild coasts, perched on a rock or grovelling on the ground, may be the origin of the pigmies and giants of the early navigators; but that tribes of tall though not gigantic stature were seen in the South Sea islands, and also on the western coasts of the continent of America, from its southern extremity as far north as was then explored, does not admit of doubt.

While the fleet lay at Port St. Julian an event occurred, which, as the contradictory evidence is viewed, must either be termed the most heroic or the most questionable act in the life of Admiral Drake. Mr. Thomas Doughty, a man of talent, and too probably of ill-regulated ambition, had served as an officer in the fleet, and it is said enjoyed in a high degree the affection and confidence of the captain-general, who must voluntarily have selected him as one of his company. Doughty was at this place accused of conspiracy and mutiny; of a plan to massacre Drake and the principal officers, and thus defeat the whole expedition,—as if the first-imagined crime did not constitute sufficient guilt. The details of this singular affair are scanty, obscure, and perplexed; and no contemporary writer notices any specific fact or ground of charge. The offence of Doughty is purely constructive. Cliffe dismisses the subject in one seaman-like sentence, merely saying, "Mr. Thomas Doughty was brought to his answer,— accused, convicted, and beheaded." The account in "The World Encompassed" is more elaborate, and for Drake apologetic, but not much more satisfactory. It contains strong general charges, but no record of facts, nor a shadow of proof of the general allegations. These early chroniclers appear either thoroughly convinced of the guilt of the culprit, or indifferent to the propriety of convincing others of the justice and necessity of their captain's sentence, or they were fully convinced that the accused merited his fate. Doughty had previously been called in question for his conduct in accepting gifts or bribes while in the Portuguese prize, and he had afterwards strayed once or twice with the same vessel, which was burnt to prevent like accidents. According to one account his treason was of old date; and before the fleet left Plymouth, he had been hatching plots against his commander, who refused to believe "that one he so dearly loved would conceive evil against him, till perceiving that lenity and favour did little good, he thought it high time to call those practices in question, and therefore, setting good watch over him, and assembling all his captains and gentlemen of his company together, he propounded to them the good parts that were in this gentleman, and the great good-will and inward affection, more than brotherly, which he had ever since his first acquaintance borne him, and afterwards delivered the letters which were written to him (Drake), with the particulars from time to time, which had been observed not so much by himself as by his good friends; not only at sea, but even at Plymouth; not bare words, but writings; not writings, but actions tending to the overthrow of the service in hand, and making away his person. Proofs were required, and alleged so many and so evident that the gentleman himself, stricken with remorse, acknowledged himself to have deserved death, yea, many deaths; for that he conspired not only the overthrow of the action, but of the principal actor also." The account continues in the same strain, asserting that forty of the principal men of Drake's band adjudged the culprit to deserve death, and gave this judgment under their hand and seal, leaving the manner to the general, who allowed the unfortunate man the choice of being either abandoned on the coast, taken back to England to answer to the lords of the queen's council, or executed here. He chose the last, requesting, it is said, that he might "once more receive the holy communion with the captain-general before his death, and that he might not die other than the death of a gentleman." The circumstances of the execution are striking. Mr. Fletcher celebrated the communion on the next day. Drake received the sacrament with the condemned man, and afterwards they dined together "at the same table, as cheerfully in sobriety as ever in their lives they had done; and taking their leaves, by drinking to each other, as if some short journey only had been in hand." Without further delay, all things being in readiness, Doughty walked forth, requested the bystanders to pray for him, and submitted his neck to the executioner.

Camden's version of this transaction does not differ materially from the above. The chaplain of the fleet, Mr. Francis Fletcher, left a manuscript journal of the voyage, now deposited in the British Museum, which contradicts many of the important statements in the other relations. He asserts that the criminal utterly denied the truth of the charges against him, upon his salvation, at the time of communicating, and at the hour and moment of his death. Mr. Fletcher likewise affirms that no choice of life or death was given him upon any conditions. It is evident that, in the opinion of the chaplain, Doughty was an innocent and a murdered man; the victim of a conspiracy not rigidly sifted by the general, and in which the actors too probably consulted his secret wishes.

The fleet had not long left England when the affair of the Portuguese prisoners, in which there might be dishonour, but no crime deserving severity of punishment, and still less death, was brought against him. But in Port St. Julian, Fletcher remarks, "more dangerous matter is laid to his charge, and by the same persons (John Brewer, Edward Bright, and others of their friends)—namely, for words spoken by him to them in the general's garden at Plymouth, which it had been their part and duty to have discovered them at the time, and not have concealed them for a time and place not so fitting." Besides the vague charges made of plots and mutinous conduct, and the anomalous offence of being "an emulator of the glory of his commander," another cause is assigned for the death of Doughty, which, if it were supported by reasonable proof, would fix a deeper stigma on the character of Drake than all his other questionable deeds put together. In England the age of dark iniquitous intrigue had succeeded the times of ferocity and open violence; but the dependants and partisans of the leading men in the state were still as criminally subservient to the flagitious designs of their patrons as when their daggers had been freely drawn in their service. It was alleged that Captain Drake had carried this man to sea to rid the powerful Earl of Leicester of a dangerous prater, and in time and place convenient to revenge his quarrel.

It is probable that the intimacy of Doughty with Captain Drake had commenced in Ireland, as both had served under Essex; and it is affirmed that the real crime of the former was accusing Leicester of plotting the secret murder of his noble rival, of which few men in England believed him wholly guiltless. On the other hand, Essex was the patron of Drake, who, it is reasonably urged, was thus much more likely to protect than punish a friend brought into trouble for freedom of speech on an occasion that would have moved stocks or stones. It may be further pleaded on behalf of Drake, that, with the exception of the chaplain, whose relation has, however, every mark of sincerity and good faith, no man nor officer in the fleet has left any record or surmise of objection to the justice of the execution, though the affair, after the return of the expedition, was keenly canvassed in England. In his whole course of life Drake maintained the character of integrity and humanity; nor did he lack generosity in fitting season. He at all times discovered a strong sense of religion, and of moral obligation, save in the case of the Spaniards and "Portugals," for which, however, "sea-divinity" afforded an especial exception. That he could have put an innocent man to death to conceal the crimes or to execute the vengeance of Leicester, is too monstrous for belief; and that, conscious of the deepest injustice, he should have gone through the solemn religious observances which preceded the perpetration of his crime, presents a picture of odious hypocrisy and cold-blooded cruelty more worthy of a demon than a brave man. The case resolves itself into the simple necessity of maintaining discipline in the fleet, and sustaining that personal authority which, in a commander, is a duty even more important than self-preservation. Drake's notions of authority might have been somewhat overstrained; nor is it unlikely that he unconsciously imbibed slight feelings of jealousy of "this emulator of his glory." Every one who mentions Doughty speaks of him as a man of great endowments. Mr. Fletcher is warm in his praise. "An industrious and stout man," says Camden, even when relating his crimes, and one, it appears, of sufficient consequence to be imagined the cause of disquiet to the still all-powerful Leicester.

Immediately after the execution, Drake, who to his other qualities added the gift of a bold natural eloquence, addressed his whole company, "persuading us to unity, obedience, love, and regard of our voyage; and, for the better confirmation thereof, wished every man the next Sunday following to prepare himself to receive the communion as Christian brethren and friends ought to do; which was done in very reverent sort, and so with good contentment every man went about his business."

Doubt and darkness will, however, always hang over this transaction, though probably only from the simple reason of no formal record being kept of the proceedings. Doughty was buried with Mr. Winter and the gunner on an island in the harbour, and the chaplain relates that he erected a stone, and on it cut the names of these unfortunate Englishmen, and the date of their burial.

The ships, by the breaking up of the Portuguese prize, were now reduced to three; and being "trimmed" and supplied with wood and water, and such other necessaries as could be obtained, they sailed from this "port accursed" on the 17th August. Cliffe relates that while they lay here the weather, though in July and August, was as cold as at midwinter in England. On the 20th they made Cape de las Virgines, entered the Strait, and on the 24th anchored thirty leagues within it.

There is a considerable variation in the relations of Drake's passage of the Strait. The statements are even absolutely contradictory on some points, though the disagreements, when the facts are sifted, are more apparent than real, every narrator noting only what he had himself witnessed or casually gathered from the information of others. The original narrative of the passage by the Portuguese pilot Nuno de Silva is among the most interesting and accurate; but in the present account an attempt is made to combine whatever appears most striking and important in the different relations. The eastern mouth of the Strait was found about a league broad; the land bare and flat. On the north side Indians were seen making great fires; but on the south no inhabitants appeared. The

PENGUINS OF THE SOUTH SEAS. *Page 59.*

length was computed at one hundred and ten leagues. The tide was seen to rise (setting in from both sides) about fifteen feet. It met about the middle, or rather nearer the western entrance. The medium breadth was one league. Where the ships came to anchor on the 24th were three small islands, on which they killed three thousand " of birds (penguins) having no wings, but short pinions which serve their turn in swimming." They were as " fat as an English goose."

"The land on both sides was very huge and mountainous; the lower mountains whereof, although they be very monstrous to look upon for their height, yet there are others which in height exceed them in a strange manner, reaching themselves above their followers so high that between them did appear three regions of clouds. These mountains are covered with snow at both the southerly and easterly parts of the Strait. There are islands among which the sea hath his indraught into the Strait even as it hath at the main entrance. The Strait is extreme cold, with frost and snow continually. The trees seem to stoop with the burden of the weather, and yet are green continually, and many good and sweet herbs do very plentifully increase and grow under them."

Such are the natural appearances described. Near the western entrance a number of narrow channels, with which the whole of that side abounds, occasioned some difficulty in the navigation; and Drake, with his usual caution, brought the fleet to anchor near an island, while he went out in his boat to explore these various openings to the South Sea. In this expedition Indians of the pigmy race, attributed to a region abounding in all monstrous things, were seen; though both the gigantic and the diminutive size of these tribes are brought in question even by contemporary relations. Yet these pigmy Indians were seen close at hand, in a canoe ingeniously constructed of the bark of trees, of which material the people also formed vessels for domestic use. The canoe was semicircular, being high in the prow and the stern. The seams were secured by a lacing of thongs of seal-skin, and fitted so nicely that there was little leakage. The tools of these ingenious small folks were formed of the shell of a very large species of mussel, containing seed-pearls, which was found in the Strait. These shells they tempered, if the word may be used, so skilfully that they cut the hardest wood, and even bone. One of their dwellings, which might, however, be but a fishing-hut, was seen rudely formed of sticks stuck in the ground, over which skins were stretched.

Early in September the western entrance was reached; and on the 6th of the same month, Drake attained the long-desired happiness of sailing an English ship on the South Sea.

The passage of Drake was the quickest[*] and easiest

---

[*] Lopez Vaz makes the time spent in passing the Strait only twelve days, and it could not be above fifteen, where months had been occupied by less fortunate or skilful navigators.

that had yet been made, fortune favouring him here as at every other point of this voyage. The temperature was also much milder than had been experienced by former navigators, or the English seamen might probably be more hardy and enduring than those of Spain.

One main object of Drake in leaving England was undoubtedly the discovery of a North-west Passage, by following the bold and novel track his genius chalked out, and in which he might still hope to anticipate all other adventurers, whether their career commenced from the east or the west. On clearing the Strait he accordingly held a north-west course, and in two days the fleet had advanced seventy leagues. Here it was overtaken by a violent and steady gale from the north-east, which drove them into 57° south latitude, and two hundred leagues to the west of Magellan Strait. While still driving before the wind, under bare poles, the moon was eclipsed at five o'clock in the afternoon of the 15th, but produced neither abatement nor change of the wind. "Neither did the ecliptical conflict of the moon improve our state, nor her clearing again mend us a whit, but the accustomed eclipse of the sea continued in his force, we being darkened more than the moon sevenfold."

On the 24th the weather became more moderate, the wind shifted, and they partly retraced their course, for seven days standing to the north-east, during which land was seen, near which a vain attempt was made to anchor. Their troubles did not end here: once more the wind got back to its old quarter, and with great violence; and on the 30th the *Marigold* was separated from the *Elizabeth* and the *Golden Hind*, as Drake on entering the South Sea had named his ship, in compliment, it is said, to his patron Sir Christopher Hatton. They made the land; but the *Marigold* was borne to sea by the stress of the gale, and was never heard of more. We do not even find a conjecture breathed about the fate of this ship. On the evening of the 7th October the *Golden Hind* and *Elizabeth* made a bay near the western entrance of Magellan Strait, which was afterwards named the Bay of Parting Friends; and here they intended to lie by till the weather improved. During the night the cable of the *Hind* broke, and she drove to sea; nor did Captain Winter, in the *Elizabeth*, make any attempt to follow his commander. Heartily tired of a voyage of which he had just had so unpleasant a specimen, he next day entered the Strait, secretly purposing to return home. Edward Cliffe, who sailed in the *Elizabeth*, and whose relation stops with her return to England, stoutly denies for the seamen the craven intention of abandoning their commander, Captain Drake; and even asserts that some efforts were made to find the admiral's ship, though of a very passive kind. Anchoring in a bay within the Strait, fires were kindled on the shore; so that, if Drake sought them in this direction and on that day, there was a chance of his finding them. This duty discharged, they went into secure harbourage in a place which they named Port Health, from the rapid recovery of the crew, who had lately suffered so much from cold, wet, and fatigue. In the large mussels and other shell-fish found here they obtained pleasant and restorative food; and they remained till the beginning of November, when the voyage was formally abandoned, "on Mr. Winter's compulsion, and full sore against the mariners' minds." Winter alleged that he now despaired of the captain-general's safety, or of being able to hold his course with the *Elizabeth* for the imagined Ophir of New Spain.

It was the 11th of November before the *Elizabeth* got clear of the Strait—an eastward voyage that had only been once performed, and by a Spanish navigator, Ladrilleros, twenty years before, and believed to be next to impossible—and June in the following year before Winter returned to England, with the credit of having made the passage of the Strait eastward, and the shame of having deserted his commander, while his company, with nobler spirit, showed unshaken fidelity and unabated ardour.

There is more interest in following the fortunes of the *Hind*, which we left tossed about in the misnamed Pacific. Drake was once more carried back to 55° south, when he judged it expedient to run in among the islands or broken land of Tierra del Fuego, where, together with a supply of seals and fresh water, a season of repose was found from the continual fatigues of the last month. But this interval of ease was of short duration: they were once more driven to sea in a gale, and suffered the further calamity of being parted from the shallop, in which were eight seamen with almost no provisions. While the *Hind* drove further and further south, the shallop was in the first instance so far fortunate as to regain the Strait, where the men salted and stored penguins for future supply. They soon lost all hope of rejoining the captain-general; so, passing the Strait, they contrived to make, in their frail bark, first for Port St. Julian, and afterwards Rio de la Plata, where six of them, wandering into the woods in quest of food, were attacked by a party of Indians. All were wounded with arrows; but while four were made prisoners, two escaped, and joined their two comrades left in charge of the boat. The Indians pursued, and the whole four were wounded before the natives were beaten back and the shallop got off. The Englishmen made for a small island at three leagues' distance, where two of their number died of their wounds. Nor was this the last calamity they were to endure: the shallop was dashed to pieces in a storm.

A melancholy interest is connected with this fragment of Drake's original company. On the desolate island in which they remained for two months no fresh water was to be found; and though they obtained food from eels, small crabs, and a species of fruit resembling an orange, their sufferings from intense thirst came to an extremity too painful and revolting to be made the subject of narrative. At the end of two months a plank ten feet long, which had drifted from Rio de la Plata, was picked up, smaller sticks were fastened to it, and a store of provision was laid in; then committing themselves to God, paddling and clinging to this ark, they in three days and two nights made the mainland which had so long tantalized their sight. In relating the issue of this adventure, the words of Peter Carder the survivor are adopted:—" At our first coming on land we found a little river of sweet and pleasant water, where William Pitcher, my only comfort and companion, although I dissuaded him to the contrary, overdrank himself, being perished before with extreme thirst; and, to my unspeakable grief and discomfort, died half an hour after in my presence, whom I buried as well as I could in the sand."

The subsequent adventures of Peter Carder among the savages on the coast of Brazil, and his captivity among the Portuguese of Bahia de Todos los Santos, form an amusing and interesting section of Purchas's Pilgrims. After a nine years' absence he got back to England, and had the honour of relating his adventures before Queen Elizabeth, who presented him with twenty-two angels, and recommended him to her lord-high-admiral, Howard.

To return to Drake. His ship, now driven southward further than before, again ran in among the islands. This is an important stage in the navigation of Drake as a voyage of discovery. He had reached the southern extremity of the American continent, and been driven round it; for "here no land was seen, but the Atlantic and South Sea meeting in a large free scope."

On the 28th October, the weather, which since the 6th September, when they entered the Pacific, had been nearly one continued hurricane, became moderate, and the *Golden Hind* came to anchor in twenty fathoms water, though within a gunshot of the land, in a harbour of an island of which the southern point has long been known as Cape Horn.

Sir Richard Hawkins, the son of Sir John, and the reputed kinsman of Admiral Drake, relates that he was informed by the navigator himself that, "at the end of the great storm, he found himself in 50° S.," which was sufficient proof that he had been beaten round without the Strait; and, moreover, that from the change of the wind not being able to double the southernmost island, he anchored under the lee of it, cast himself down upon the extreme point, and reached over as far as was safe; and, after the ship sailed, told his company that he had been "upon the southernmost point of land in the world, known or likely to be known, and further than any man had ever before ventured."

Mr. Fletcher, the chaplain, also landed here. He found this island three parts of a degree further south than any of the other islands.

To all the islands discovered here Drake gave the general name of the *Elizabethides*, in compliment to his royal mistress. They were inhabited, and the natives were frequently seen, though little appears to have been learned of their character or customs.

Having thus discovered and landed on the southernmost part of the continent, Drake changed the *Terra Incognita* of the Spanish geographers into the *Terra bene nunc Cognita* of his chaplain, and on the 30th October, with a fair wind from the south, he held a course north-west; but, being bent on exploring, afterwards kept east, not to lose the coast. On the 25th November they anchored at the island of Mocha, off the coast of Chili, where the captain-general landed. Cattle and sheep were seen here, and also maize and potatoes. Presents were exchanged with the Indians, and next day a watering-party, which Drake accompanied, rowed towards the shore, in full security of their pacific dispositions. Two seamen, who landed to fill the water-casks, were instantly killed, and the rest of the party narrowly escaped an ambush laid for them in case they should come to the assistance of their countrymen. They were fiercely assailed with arrows and stones, and every one was wounded more or less severely. The general was wounded both in the face and on the head; and the attack was continued so warmly and close that the Indians seized four of the oars. This unprovoked attack was imputed by the ship's company to the hatred which the inhabitants of Chili bore the Spaniards, whom, it was presumed, they had not yet learned to distinguish from other Europeans. In this view it was forgiven by men whose prejudices and animosity were equally strong with those of the Indians.

Sailing along the coast with the wind at south, on the 30th November they anchored in a bay about 32° S., and sent out a boat to examine the shores, which captured and brought before the captain an Indian found fishing in his canoe. This man was kindly treated. A present of linen and a chopping-knife gained his affections; and he bore the message of Drake to his countrymen, who, induced by the hope of like gifts, brought to the ship's side a fat hog and poultry. It was at this time of more consequence to one main object of the voyagers, who, doing much for the glory of England and Elizabeth, wished at the same time to do a little for themselves, that an intelligent Indian repaired to the ship who spoke the Spanish language, and, believing them mariners of that nation, unwittingly gave them much valuable information. From him they learned that they had by six leagues oversailed Valparaiso, the port of St. Jago, where a Spanish vessel then lay at anchor. The innocent offer of Felipe, when he saw their disappointment, to pilot them back, was eagerly accepted. On the 4th December they sailed from Philip's Bay, as they named this harbour in honour of their Indian pilot, and next day, without any difficulty, captured the ship the *Grand Captain of the South Seas*, in which was found sixty thousand pesos of gold, besides jewels, merchandise, and one thousand seven hundred and seventy jars of Chili wine.

This was a joyful beginning: each peso was reckoned worth eight shillings. The people of the town, which consisted of only nine families, fled; and Drake's followers revelled in the unforbidden luxury of a general pillage of wine, bread, bacon, and other things most acceptable to men who had been so long at sea, both for present refreshment and also for storing the ship. In every new Spanish settlement, however small, a church rose as it were simultaneously. The small chapel of Valparaiso was plundered of a silver chalice, two cruets, and its altar-cloth, which, to prevent their desecration, and to obtain a blessing on the voyage, were presented to Fletcher, the pastor of this ocean-flock. They sailed on the 8th with their prize, taking, however, only one of the crew, a Greek named Juan Griego, who was capable of piloting them to Lima. Their Indian guide, Felipe, was rewarded, and sent on shore near his own home. From the most southern point of this coasting voyage Drake had been continually on the outlook for the *Marigold* and *Elizabeth;* and the *Hind* being too unwieldy to keep in near the coast in the search, a pinnace was intended to be built for this duty as well as for other operations which the captain-general kept in view. A convenient place for this purpose had been found at Coquimbo. Near the spot selected the Spaniards had raised or collected a considerable force; and a watering-party of fourteen of the English were here surprised, and with some difficulty escaped from a body of three hundred horse and two hundred foot. One seaman was killed, owing, however, to his own braggart temerity.

In a quieter and safer bay the pinnace was set up, and Drake himself embarked in it to look after the strayed ships; but the wind becoming adverse, he soon returned. They quitted this harbour on the 19th January 1579, invigorated by a season of repose, by the refreshments and booty obtained, and by the hopes of richer plunder and more glorious conquest. With few adventures they sailed along the coast, till, accidentally landing at Tarapaza, they found a Spaniard asleep on the shore with thirteen bars of silver lying beside him, as if waiting their arrival. Advancing a little further, on landing to procure water they fell in with a Spaniard and an Indian boy driving eight llamas, each of which was laden with two leathern bags containing fifty pounds of silver, or eight hundred pounds in all. The llamas, or Peruvian sheep, are described by the old voyagers as of the size of an ass, with a neck like a camel, and of great strength and steadiness, forming the beast of burden of these countries. They were indeed the mules of the New World; but a much more valuable animal, as the wool is fine and the flesh good. The credulity of the most credulous of the family of John Bull—his sons of the ocean—was here amusingly displayed. If the coast of Peru was not literally strewed with gold, pure silver was found so richly mixed with the soil that every hundredweight of common earth yielded, on a moderate calculation, five ounces.

The eight llamas and their precious burden being brought on board, the *Golden Hind* next entered the port of Arica, where two or three small barks then lay. These, when rifled, were found perfectly unprotected, the crews being on shore, unable to imagine danger on this coast. Arica is described as a beautiful and fertile valley. The town contained about twenty houses, which, the "Famous Voyage" states, "we would have ransacked, if our company had been better and more numerous; but our general, contented with the spoil of the ships, put to sea, and sailed for Lima" in pursuit of a vessel very richly laden, of which they had obtained intelligence. The ship, of which they were now in hot pursuit, got notice of her danger in time to land the treasure with which she was freighted,—eight hundred bars of silver, the property of the King of Spain. Drake, now preparing for active measures, rid himself of every encumbrance by setting all the sails of his prizes, and turning them adrift whithersoever the winds might carry them. The arrival of these tenantless barks on some wild coast or lonely island may yet form the theme of Indian tradition, though more probably they must all have been dashed to pieces.

Tidings of the English being upon the coast had by this time been despatched overland to the governor at Lima; but the difficulty of travelling in these still tangled and trackless regions enabled Drake to outstrip the messenger, and on the 13th September to surprise the Spanish ships lying in Callao, the port of Lima. The spoil was trifling for the number of vessels. In boarding a ship from Panama, which was just then entering the port, an Englishman was killed. Another account says he was shot from a boat while pursuing the crew, who were abandoning the vessel. In one ship a chest of ryals of plate, and a considerable store of linens, silks, and general merchandise, were obtained. From the prisoners Drake learned that ten days before (Lopez Vaz makes it but three) the *Cacafuego*, laden with treasure, had sailed for Panama, the point from whence all goods were carried across the Isthmus. This information at once determined the course of our navigator; and as ships from Callao to Panama were in the habit of touching at intermediate places, he reckoned the *Cacafuego* already his prize. As a measure of precaution, the mainmasts of the two largest prizes found here were cut away, the cables of the smaller ones were severed, and the goods and people being previously removed, the whole were abandoned to the mercy of the winds and waves; while Drake bore northward in full sail, or, when the wind slackened, was towed on by the boats, each man straining to reach the golden goal. But this rather anticipates the course of the narrative.

When intelligence of Drake's ship at last reached Lima, it was presumed some of the Spanish crews had mutinied, and that the *Golden Hind* was a Spanish vessel turned pirate, so little was an attack by the

English on this side of the continent deemed possible, or that the ships of any nation, save Spain, could pass the intricate and fatal Strait of Magellan. On being apprised of the real fact, and of the danger impending, Don Francisco de Toledo, the viceroy at Lima, immediately repaired to the port with a force estimated by Lopez Vaz at two thousand horse and foot. The *Golden Hind* still remained in sight of the port, and nearly becalmed. Two vessels, in each of which two hundred fighting men were embarked, were equipped in all haste, and the capture of Drake the pirate-heretic was already confidently reckoned upon. At the same hour in which they left the port to make the attack a fresh gale sprung up, and the English ship pressed onward. The flight and pursuit were continued for some time, as it was not the policy of Drake, with his very inferior force, to risk an action. By an oversight, most fortunate for the English, the Spaniards, in their eagerness and confidence of an easy conquest, had neglected to take provisions on board. Famine compelled them to abandon the pursuit, but Don Francisco lost no time in remedying this inadvertence. A force of three ships, fully equipped, was despatched under the command of Pedro Sarmiento de Gamboa, but arrived too late. The same commander afterwards long watched, and waited in vain, the return of Drake by the Strait. On his recommendation they were afterwards fortified, and a colony planted,—an abortive attempt which cost Spain much treasure and many lives.

Near Payti, a small vessel, in which some silver ornaments were found, was rifled and dismissed; and on passing Payti, from the crew of a vessel which was searched they learned that the *Cacafuego* had the start of them now only by two days. Every nerve was fresh-braced for pursuit; but the future advantage hoped for did not lead them, in the meantime, to despise present small gains. Two more vessels were intercepted, rifled, and turned adrift—the crews being first landed. In one of these some silver and eighty pounds of gold were found, and a golden crucifix in which was set "a goodly and great emerald." They also found a good supply of useful stores and a large quantity of cordage, which made most part of the cargo. On the 24th February they crossed the Line, the *Cacafuego* still ahead and unseen; and Drake, to animate the hopes and quicken the vigilance of his company, offered as a reward to whoever should first descry the prize the gold chain which he usually wore. The reward was gained by Mr. John Drake, who, at three o'clock in the afternoon of the 1st March, from the mast-head discerned the prize, which by six o'clock was boarded and taken. This capture was made off Cape Francisco. The captain, a Biscayan named Juan de Anton, was so little aware of his danger, that seeing a vessel coming up to him under a press of sail, he concluded that the viceroy had sent some important message, and struck his sails to await the approach of the *Golden Hind*. When aware, from closer inspection, of his mistake, he tried to escape; but he was already within reach of Drake's guns, and possessed no defensive weapons of any kind. Yet, with the brave spirit of his province, the Biscayan refused to strike till his mizzenmast was shot away, and he himself wounded by an arrow.

This ship proved to be a prize worth gaining. It contained twenty-six tons of silver, thirteen chests of ryals of plate, and eighty pounds of gold, besides diamonds and inferior gems,—the whole estimated at three hundred and sixty thousand pesos.

Among the spoils were two very handsome silver gilt bowls belonging to the pilot, of which Drake demanded one; which the doughty Spaniard surrendering, presented the other to the steward, as if he disdained to hold anything by the favour of the English. The "Famous Voyage" records some capital salt-water jests made on this occasion at the expense of the Spaniards. It must be owned that the laugh was wholly on the side of the English.

Had Drake, thus richly laden, now been assured of a safe and an easy passage to England, it is probable that the *Golden Hind* might not on this voyage have encompassed the globe. The advanced season, however, and the outlook which he was aware the Spaniards would keep for his return, forbade the attempt of repassing the Strait; while the glory of discovery, and the hope of taking his immense treasure safely to England, determined him in the resolution of seeking a north-west passage homeward. Though not in general communicative, his plans were no sooner formed than he unfolded them to the ship's company, with the persuasive eloquence of a man eminently fitted for command. The crew were now in high spirits, and full of confidence in their skilful, bold, and successful leader. His counsel, which carried all the weight of command, was "to seek out some convenient place to trim the ship, and store it with wood, water, and such provisions as could be found, and thenceforward to hasten our intended journey for the discovery of the said passage, through which we might with joy return to our longed homes."

With this resolution they steered for Nicaragua, and on the 16th March anchored in a small bay of the island of Canno, which proved a good station to water and refit. The pinnace was once more on active duty, and a prize was brought in laden with honey, butter, sarsaparilla, and other commodities. Among the papers of the prize were letters from the King of Spain to the governor of the Philippines, and sea-charts which afterwards proved of use to the English. While Drake lay here, a violent shock of an earthquake was felt. From Canno they sailed on the 24th March, the captain-general never loitering in any port beyond the time absolutely necessary to repair the ship and take in water. On the 6th April they made another valuable prize. Being already well supplied with stores, their choice was become more nice and difficult; and selecting only silks, linen, delicate porcelain, and a falcon of finely-wrought gold, in the breast of which a large emerald was set, the vessel was dismissed, and of her crew only a negro and the pilot detained, who steered them into the harbour of Guatalco. Landing, according to their approved good practice, to ransack the town, it is related in the " Famous Voyage" that they surprised a council then holding on certain negroes accused of a plot to burn the place. To their mutual astonishment, judges and culprits were hurried on board in company, and the chief men were compelled to write to the townspeople to make no resistance to the English. The only plunder found in ransacking this small place, in which there were but fourteen persons belonging to Old Spain, consisted of about a bushel of ryals of plate. One of the party, Mr. John Winter, seeing a Spaniard taking flight, pursued and took from the fugitive a chain of gold and some jewels. This is related with great exultation, as a feat of peculiar dexterity and merit. All the Spaniards on board the *Golden Hind* were now set at liberty. The Portuguese pilot, Nuno Silva, who had been brought from the Cape de Verd Islands, was also dismissed, and probably at this place wrote the relation of the voyage from which quotations have been made in this memoir. Silva's account was sent to the Portuguese viceroy in India, and long afterwards fell into the hands of the English.

Satiated with plunder on sea and shore, Drake, on

the 16th April, sailed on that bold project of discovery formerly communicated to his company, and by the 3rd of June had gone over one thousand four hundred leagues, in different courses, without seeing land. They had now reached 43° north; the cold was become very severe, and, on advancing two or three degrees further, so intense, that meat froze the instant it was removed from the fire, and the ropes and tackling of the ship became rigid from the influence of the frost. On the 5th, being driven in by the winds, land was seen, and they anchored in a small bay, too unsheltered, however, to permit of their remaining. Drake had not expected to find the coast stretching so far westward. The wind was now become adverse to holding a northerly course, although the extreme cold, and the chill, raw, unwholesome fogs which surrounded them had made such a track desirable. The land seen here was in general low; but wherever a height appeared it was found covered with snow, though now almost midsummer. The land seen was the western coast of California. On the 17th June they anchored in a good harbour, on an inhabited coast. As the *Hind* drew near the shore the natives approached, and an ambassador or spokesman put off in a canoe, who made a formal harangue, accompanied with much gesticulation. When the oration was concluded, he made a profound obeisance and retired to the land. A second and a third time he returned in the same manner, bringing, as a gift or tribute, a bunch of feathers neatly trimmed and stuck together, and a basket made of rushes. Of these rushes it was afterwards found that the natives fabricated several useful and pretty things. The females, though the men were entirely naked, wore a sort of petticoat composed of rushes, previously stripped into long threads resembling hemp. They also wore deer-skins round their shoulders; and some of the men occasionally used furs as a covering. It was remarked that the Indians appeared as sensible to the extreme severity of the weather as the English seamen,—cowering, shivering, and keeping huddled together, even when wrapped up in their furs. The basket brought by the Indian ambassador or orator was filled with an herb which, in some of the original relations of the voyage, is called *tabah*, the native name, and in others tobacco. The Indian was either afraid or unwilling to accept of any present from the English in return for this simple tribute, but picked up a hat which was sent afloat towards him. The kindness of Drake ultimately gained the confidence of these people.

The ship had some time before sprung a leak, and it was here found necessary to land the goods and stores, that she might be repaired. On the 21st this was done, though the natives appeared to view the movement with suspicion and dissatisfaction. They, however, laid aside their bows and arrows when requested to do so, and an exchange of presents further cemented the growing friendship. They retired apparently satisfied; but had no sooner reached their huts, which stood at a considerable distance, than a general howling and lamentation commenced, which lasted all night. The females especially continued shrieking in a wild and doleful manner, which, if not absolutely appalling to the English, was yet to the last degree painful. Drake, whose presence of mind never forsook him, and who was seldom lulled into false security by appearances of friendship, mistrusting the state of excitement into which the Indians were raised, took the precaution of intrenching the tents into which the goods and the crew had been removed while the repairs of the ship were in progress. For the two days following "the night of lamentation" no native appeared. At the end of that time a great number seemed to have joined the party first seen; and the whole assembled on a height overlooking the fortified station of the ship's company, and appeared desirous of approaching the strangers. The ceremonies were opened by an orator or herald making a long speech or proclamation, with which the audience were understood to express assent, by bowing their bodies at the conclusion, and groaning in chorus—*Oh!* or *Oh! oh!* After this friendly demonstration—for as such it was intended—a deputation of the assembly stuck their bows into the earth, and bearing gifts of feathers and rush-baskets with *tabah*, descended towards the fort. While this was passing below, the women, mixed with the group on the height, began to shriek and howl as on the "night of lamentation," to tear their flesh with their nails, and dash themselves on the ground, till the blood sprung from their bodies. This is said, in the "Famous Voyage," to have been part of the orgies of their idol or demon worship. Drake, it is said, struck with grief and horror, and probably not without a tincture of superstition, ordered divine service to be solemnized. The natives sat silent and attentive, at proper pauses breathing their expressive "Oh!" in token of assent or approbation. With the psalms, sung probably to one of the simple solemn chants of the Old Church, they appeared affected and charmed; and they repeatedly afterwards requested their visitors to sing. On taking leave they declined the gifts tendered, either from superstitious dread, or as probably on the same principle which makes a clown at a fair afraid to accept the tempting shilling offered by a recruiting-sergeant,—from no dislike to the coin, or reluctance to drink the king's health, but from great distrust of the motives of the giver. The voyagers, with amusing self-complaisance, ascribe this fear or delicacy to the deep veneration of the natives, and to their thinking "themselves sufficiently enriched and happy that they had free access to see us."

The Indians here managed their foreign relations with ceremonial that might have sufficed for more refined societies. The news of the arrival of the English having spread, on the 26th two heralds or pursuivants arrived at headquarters, craving an audience of the captain-general on the part of their *hioh* or king. The precursor of majesty harangued a full half-hour, his associate dictating to or prompting him, and concluded by demanding tokens of friendship and safe-conduct for the chief. These were cheerfully given.

The approach of the *hioh* was well arranged, and imposing in effect. First came the sceptre or mace bearer, as he is called, though club-bearer would be the more correct phrase. This officer was a tall and handsome man, of noble presence. His staff or club of office was about five feet in length, and made of a dark wood. To this were attached two pieces of net-work or chain-work, curiously and delicately wrought, of a bony substance, minute, thin, and burnished, and consisting of innumerable links. He had also a basket of *tabah*. These net-cauls or chains were supposed to be insignia of personal rank and dignity, akin to the crosses, stars, and ribbons of civilized nations,—the number of them worn denoting the degree of consequence, as the importance of a pasha is signified by the number of his tails. The king followed his minister, and in his turn was succeeded by a man of tall stature, with an air of natural grandeur and majesty which struck the English visitors. The royal-guard came next in order. It was formed of one hundred picked men, tall and martial-looking, and clothed in skins. Some of them wore ornamental head-dresses made of feathers, or of a feathery-down which grew upon a plant of the country. The king wore about his shoulders a robe made of the skins of the species of marmot afterwards described.

Next in place in this national procession came the common people, every one painted, though in a variety of patterns, and with feathers stuck in the club of hair drawn up at the crown of their heads. The women and children brought up the rear, carrying each, as a propitiatory gift, a basket, in which was either *tabah*, broiled fish, or a root that the natives ate both raw and baked.

Drake, seeing them so numerous, drew up his men in order, and under arms, within his fortification or blockhouse. At a few paces' distance the procession halted, and deep silence was observed, while the sceptre-bearer, prompted as before by another official, harangued for a full half-hour. His eloquent address, whatever it might import, received the concurrent "*Oh*" of the national assembly. The same orator commenced a song or chant, keeping time in a slow, solemn dance, performed with a stately air, the king and all the warriors joining both in the measure and the chorus. The females also moved in the dance, but silently. Drake could no longer doubt of their amicable feelings and peaceful intentions. They were admitted, still singing and moving in a choral dance, within the fort. The orations and songs were renewed and prolonged; and the chief, placing one of his crowns upon the head of the captain-general, and investing him with the other imagined insignia of royalty, courteously tendered him his whole dominions, and hailed him king! Songs of triumph were raised, as if in confirmation of this solemn cession of territory and sovereignty. Such is the interpretation which the old voyagers put upon a ceremony that has been more rationally conjectured to resemble the interchange or exchange of names, which in the South Sea islands seals the bonds of friendship; or as something equivalent to a European host telling his visitor that he is master of the house. "The admiral," it is shrewdly observed, "accepted of this new-offered dignity in her majesty's name, and for her use; it being probable that, from this donation, whether made in jest or earnest by these Indians, some real advantage might hereafter redound to the English nation and interest in these parts." We are expressly informed that the natives afterwards actually worshipped their guests, and that it was necessary to check their idolatrous homage. They roamed about among the tents, admiring all they saw, and expressing attachment to the English in their own peculiar fashion. It was for the youngest of the company these fondnesses were imbibed. To express affection, the Indians surrounded and gazed upon them, and then began to howl and tear their flesh till they streamed in their own blood, to demonstrate the liveliness and strength of their affection. The same unnatural and uncouth shows of regard continued to be made while the English remained on the coast; and obeisances and homage were rendered which, being considered as approaching to sacrifice or worship, were strenuously and piously disclaimed. These people are described as an amiable race; of a free, tractable, kindly nature, without guile or treachery. To mark their esteem of the English, and confidence in their skill and superiority, it may be noticed that they applied for medicaments for their wounds and sores.

The men, as has been noticed, were generally naked; but the women, besides the short petticoat woven of peeled bulrushes, wore deer-skins, with the hair on, round their shoulders. They were remarked to be good wives,—very obedient and serviceable to their husbands. The men were so robust and powerful that a burden which could hardly be borne by two of the seamen, a single native would with ease carry up and down hill for a mile together. Their weapons were bows and arrows, but of a feeble, useless kind. Their dwellings were constructed in a round form, built of earth, and roofed with pieces of wood joined together at a common centre, somewhat in form of a spire. Being partly under ground, they were close and warm. The fire was placed in the middle, and beds of rushes were spread on the floor.

Before sailing, Drake made an excursion into the interior. Immense herds of deer were seen, large and fat; and the country seemed one immense warren of a species of cony of the size of a Barbary rat, "their heads and faces like rabbits in England, their paws like a mole, their tails like a rat. Under their chin on each side was a pouch, into which they gathered meat to feed their young, or serve themselves another time."

The natives ate the flesh of those animals, and greatly prized their skins, of which the state robes worn by the king at his interview with Drake were made.

The admiral named this fair and fertile country New Albion, and erected a monument of his discovery, to which was nailed a brass plate, bearing the name, effigy, and arms of her majesty, and asserting her territorial rights, and the date of possession being taken.

Drake had spent thirty-six days at this place,—a long but necessary sojourn; but the repairs of the ship being completed, on the 23rd July he bore away from Port Drake—the kind-hearted natives deeply bewailing the departure of their new friends. The regret, good-will, and respect were indeed mutual. The Indians entreated the English to remember them; and as a farewell offering or homage, secretly provided what is called a sacrifice. While the ship remained in sight they kept fires burning on the heights. It is delightful at this time to hear of Europeans leaving grateful remembrances of their visits on any coast, and the pleasure is enhanced by being able to claim this honour for our countrymen. It was from some fancied resemblance to the white cliffs of England that Drake bestowed on the coast he had surveyed the name of New Albion.*

Next day a store of seals and birds were caught at

---

* After passing Punta de los Reyes, Captain Beechey awaited the return of day off some white cliffs, which he believed must be those which made Sir Francis Drake bestow on this tract of country the name of New Albion.

some small islands, which are now supposed to be the Farellones of modern charts.

Thus far had Drake boldly explored in search of a passage homeward, either through an undiscovered strait or around the northern extremity of the continent of America; but now this design, so honourable to his enterprise, and even to his sagacity, was for the present abandoned, the winds being adverse, and the season too far advanced to prosecute further so perilous an adventure. Leaving the scene of his discoveries on the western coast of America, which are reckoned to begin immediately to the north of Cape Mendocino and to extend to 48° N., Drake, with the unanimous consent of his company, having formed the design of returning home by India and the Cape of Good Hope, sailed westwards for sixty-eight days without coming in sight of land. On the 13th September he fell in with some islands in 8° N. As soon as the *Golden Hind* appeared, the natives came off in canoes, each containing from four to fourteen men, bringing cocoa-nuts, fish, and fruits. Their canoes were ingeniously formed, and prettily ornamented, hollowed out of a single tree, and so high at the stern and prow as to be nearly semicircular. The islanders were not yet sufficiently enlightened in mercantile affairs to have learned that honesty is the dealers' best policy. Drake, however, instead of imitating the conduct of Magellan, and instantly shooting them for thieving, or burning their houses, endeavoured to bring them to a sense of propriety, merely by refusing to traffic with those who were found dishonest. This excited their displeasure, and a general attack of stones was commenced. A cannon, not shotted, fired over their heads to scare them away, had only this effect for a short time. The general was at last compelled to adopt more severe measures of retaliation, and we are told, in vague terms, that "smart was necessary as well as terror." The natives of those Islands of Thieves, as they were named by the English, had the lobes of their ears cut out into a circle, which hung down on their cheeks. Their teeth were black as jet, from the use of a powder which they constantly employed for the purpose of staining them. This powder they carried about with them in a hollow cane. Another peculiarity observed was the length of their nails, which was above an inch. It has been conjectured, with every mark of probability, that Drake's Islands of Thieves are the islands named De Sequeira, discovered by Diego da Rocha, and the Pelew Islands of our own times. If so, the morals of the inhabitants must have improved greatly in the long interval which elapsed between this first visit of the English and that made by Captain Wilson in the *Duff*. The wind coming fair, on the 3rd October the *Golden Hind* stood westward, and on the 16th of the month made the Philippines in 7° 5' north of the Line. They first fell in with four islands having a thick population, or the appearance of it. These they visited, and afterwards anchored in Mindanao. Sailing hence on the 22nd, they kept a southerly course, and passed between two islands, about six or eight leagues south of Mindanao, supposed to be Sarangan and Candigar.

On the 3rd November the Moluccas were seen, and they steered for Tidore; but in coasting along Motir a boat came off, from which Drake learned that the Portuguese, expelled from Terrenate (or Ternate) by the king of that island, had fixed their headquarters at Tidore. In this boat was the Viceroy of Motir, which island was under the sovereignty of the powerful and warlike King of Ternate. As soon as the viceroy understood that Drake had no reason either to love or trust the Portuguese, he entreated him to change his destination; and the ship accordingly steered for the port of Ternate.

Previous to coming to an anchor before the town, a courteous offer of friendship was made by the general, through a messenger whom he sent on shore, with a velvet cloak as a present to the king, and who was instructed to say that the English came hither only to trade, and to procure refreshments. The Viceroy of Motir had previously disposed the king to give Drake a favourable reception. To the general's message a gracious answer was returned. All that the territories of the King of Ternate afforded was at the disposal of the English; and that prince was ready to lay himself and his whole dominions at the feet of so glorious a princess as the Queen of England. By some of the voyagers this flourish of Oriental hyperbole was most literally interpreted. The English envoy was received with great pomp; and as credentials, or safe-conduct, a signet, we are not told in what form, was transmitted through him to the captain-general. Before the ship came to anchor the king put off to pay it a visit of welcome and ceremony. The royal equipment consisted of three state barges or canoes, filled with the most distinguished persons of his retinue. They wore dresses of white muslin, "white lawn, of cloth of Calicut." Over their heads was a canopy or awning of perfumed mats, supported on a framework of reeds. Their personal attendants, also dressed in white, stood next them; and beyond these were ranks of warriors, armed with dirks and daggers;—these again were encircled by the rowers, of whom there were eighty to each barge, placed in galleries raised above the other seats, three on each side. They rowed, or rather paddled, in cadence to the clashing of cymbals, and altogether made a gallant show. The king, who advanced in the last barge, was saluted with a discharge of all the great guns; and the martial music which Drake employed on occasions of ceremonial struck up. The canoes paddled round and round the ship, the king appearing delighted with the music, and gratified by the signs of wealth and magnificence exhibited by his visitors. He was himself a tall, stout, graceful man, and celebrated as a conqueror and warrior. By policy and force of arms he had not only expelled the Portuguese from this island, but had subdued many others, so that seventy islands now owned his sway. He professed the faith of Mohammed, which was now become the religion of all his dominions. It is worthy of remark that, in the ceremonies and external observances of royalty, the native princes of these Indian islands might have vied with the most polished courts of Europe. Elizabeth, whose board was daily spread with lowly bends and reverences, was not more punctilious in ceremonial and etiquette than the sovereign of Ternate. His courtiers and attendants approached the royal presence with the most profound respect, no one speaking to the king save in a kneeling posture. As soon as the ship came to an anchor the king took leave, promising another visit on the following day.

That same evening a present of fowls, rice, sugar, cloves, and *frigo*, was received, and "a sort of fruit," says the "Famous Voyage," "they call *sago*, which is a meal made out of the tops of trees, melting in the mouth like sugar, but eating like sour curd, but yet when made into cakes will keep so as to be very fit for eating at the end of ten years." It is pleasant to come thus upon the first simple notice of those productions of other climes which have so long contributed to the comfort, variety, or luxury of European communities.

Instead of coming on board next day, the king sent his brother to bear his excuses, and to remain as a hostage for the safe return of the captain-general, who was invited to land. The invitation was not accepted, the English having some doubts of the good faith of the fair-promising sovereign of Ternate. But some of the gentlemen went on shore; their first acquaintance, the Viceroy of Motir, remaining as a hostage as well as the king's brother. On landing they were received with the pomp which had been intended to grace the entrance of Drake into the capital. Another brother of the king and a party of the nobles conducted them to the palace, which stood near the dismantled fort of the expelled Portuguese. There they found an assembly of at least a thousand persons, sixty of them being courtiers or privy councillors, "very grave persons;" and four Turkish envoys in robes of scarlet and turbans, who were then at the court of Ternate concluding a treaty of commerce. The king was guarded by twelve lances. "A glorious canopy, embroidered with gold, was carried over his head." His garb was a robe of cloth of gold hanging loose about his person; his legs were bare, but on his feet he wore slippers of Cordovan leather. Around his neck hung a weighty chain of gold, and fillets of the same metal were wreathed through his hair. On his fingers "were many fair jewels." At the right side of his chair of state stood a page cooling him with a fan, two feet in length and one in breadth, embroidered and adorned with sapphires, and fastened to a staff three feet long, by which it was moved. His voice was low and his aspect benign.

Drake did not afterwards land; and the offers made

of exclusive traffic with the English were, it appears, received by him with indifference.

Having procured a supply of provisions and a considerable quantity of cloves, the *Golden Hind* left the Moluccas on the 9th November, and on the 14th anchored at a small island near the eastern part of Celebes, which they named Crab Island. This place being uninhabited and affording abundance of wood, though no water was found, tents were erected on shore, and fences formed around them; and here they resolved effectually to repair the ship for her homeward voyage. This proved a pleasant sojourn. The island was one continued forest of a kind of trees, large, lofty, and straight in the stem, nor branching out till near the top; the leaves resembling the broom of England. About these trees flickered innumerable bats "as big as hens." There were also multitudes of shining flies, no bigger than the common fly in England, which, skimming up and down in the air between the trees and bushes, made them appear "as if they were burning." There were also great numbers of land-crabs, described as a sort of cray-fish, "which dig holes in the earth like conies, and are so large that one of them will dine four persons, and very good meat."

At a small neighbouring island water was procured, and on the 12th December, having lain at Crab Island about a month, the *Hind* sailed for the west, and soon got entangled among islets and shoals, which induced them to steer for the south to get free of such dangerous ground. At this time occurred the most imminent peril and providential escape that attended this remarkable voyage,—an incident as much resembling a visible interposition of divine aid, where human hope was perished, as any to be found among the almost miraculous records of preservation contained in the relations of maritime adventure.

After being teased for many days, on the 9th January they flattered themselves that the shoals were at last cleared. On that same evening, early in the first watch, while the *Golden Hind*, with all her sails set, was running before a fair wind, she came suddenly upon a shelving rock, and stuck fast. Violent as was the shock, she had sprung no leak, and the boats were immediately lowered to sound, and ascertain if an anchor could be placed in such a situation as would permit the ship to be drawn off into deep water. But the rock in which she was as it were jammed shelved so abruptly that at the distance of only a few yards no bottom could be found. A night of great anxiety was passed; and when the dawn permitted a second search for anchorage-ground, it only ended in more confirmed and bitter disappointment. There seemed no help of man; yet in the midst of their calamity several fortunate, or more properly providential, circumstances intervened. No leak had been sprung; and though the ebb-tide left the ship in only six feet of water, while (so deeply was she treasure-laden) thirteen were required to float her, a strong and steady gale, blowing from the side to which she must have heeled as the tide gradually receded, supported her in this dangerous position. In this dreadful situation, instead of giving themselves up to despair or apathy, Drake and his company behaved with the manliness, coolness, and resolution which have ever in the greatest perils characterized British seamen. The crew were summoned to prayers; and this solemn duty fulfilled, a last united effort was made for the common safety. A quantity of meal, eight of the guns, and three tons of cloves were thrown overboard. This partial lightening produced no visible effect; the ship stuck as fast as before. The simple language of the original narrative is so much more forcible and touching than any modern paraphrase that we at once adopt it. In a single sentence it displays the manly and self-depending character of Drake, and the veneration and implicit confidence with which his crew regarded him. "Of all other days," says one old relation, "on the 9th January, in the yeere 1579 (1580), we ranne upon a rocke, where we stuck fast from eight of the clocke at nighte till four of the clocke in the afternoon of next day, being indeed out of all hope to escape the danger; but our generall, as hee had alwayes shown himself couragious, and of a good confidence in the mercie and protection of God, so now he continued in the same; and lest he should seem to perish wilfully, both hee and wee did our best endevour to save ourselves, which it pleased God so to bless that in the ende wee cleared ourselves most happily of the danger." It was, however, by no effort of their own that they were finally extricated, though nothing that skill and courage could suggest or accomplish was wanting. The wind slackened and fell with the tide, and at the lowest of the ebb veered to the opposite point, when the vessel suddenly heeled to her side. The shock loosened her keel, and at the moment of what appeared inevitable destruction she plunged into the deep water, once more as freely afloat as when first launched on the ocean. The thankfulness of the ship's company may be imagined. This dangerous shoal or reef is not far from the coast of Celebes, in 1° 56′ S.

Their perilous adventure made them afterwards very wary, and it was not till some weeks had elapsed that, cautiously exploring their way, they finally extricated themselves from this entangled coast.

On the 8th February they fell in with the island of Baratane, probably the island now called Booton, a pleasant and fruitful place. It afforded gold, silver, copper, and sulphur. The fruits and other natural productions were ginger, long-pepper, lemons, cocoas, cucumbers, nutmegs, frigo, sago, etc., etc. Ternate excepted, this island afforded better and greater variety of refreshments for the mariner than any land at which our navigators had touched since they had left England. The inhabitants were worthy of the fertile region they inhabited. In form and features they were a handsome people; in disposition and manners, mild and friendly; fair in their dealings, and obliging in their behaviour. The men were naked, save a small turban, and a piece of cloth about their waists; but the women were clothed from the middle to the feet, and had their arms loaded with bracelets, fashioned of bone, horn, and brass. The men universally wore ornaments in their ears. These islanders received the English with kindness and civility, and gladly supplied their wants.

Leaving Baratane, with very favourable impressions of the country and the people, they made sail for Java, which was reached on the 12th of March. Here the navigators remained for twelve days in a course of constant festivity. The island was at this time governed by five independent chiefs or rajahs, who lived in perfect amity, and vied with each other in showing hospitality and courtesy to their English visitors.

The social condition of the Javans at this comparatively early period exhibits a pleasing and attractive picture of semi-barbarous life, if a state of society may be thus termed which appears to realize many of our late Utopian schemes of visionary perfection. The Javans were of good size and well formed, bold and warlike. Their weapons and armour were swords, bucklers, and daggers of their own manufacture,—the blades admirably tempered, the handles highly ornamented. The upper part of their bodies was entirely naked, but from the waist downwards they wore a flowing garment of silk, of some gay and favourite colour. In every village there was a house of assembly or public hall, where these social and cheerful people, whom we may call the French of the Indian islands, met twice a day to partake of a kind of picnic meal, and enjoy the pleasures of conversation. To this common festival every one contributed at his pleasure or convenience, bringing fruits, boiled rice, roast fowls, and sago. On a table raised three feet the feast was spread, and the party gathered round, "every one delighting in the company of another." While the *Hind* lay here, a constant intercourse and interchange of kindnesses and civilities were maintained between the sea and shore—the rajahs coming frequently on board, either singly or together.

But the delights of Java could not long banish the remembrance of England, to which every wish was now directed. Making sail from Java, the first land seen was the Cape of Good Hope, which they passed on the 15th June. The Spaniards had not more studiously magnified the real dangers of Magellan Strait than the Portuguese had exaggerated and misrepresented the storms and perils which surround the Cape; and it required the characteristic intrepidity and consummate skill of Drake to venture, with his single bark, on this doubtful and almost untried navigation. It is, however, probable that he suspected the craft which suggested this attempt to hoodwink and delude all other maritime nations, that Portugal might long retain a monopoly of her important discovery. Certain it is that the ship's company were surprised that close by the Cape,—"the most stately thing and goodliest cape seen in the circumference of the whole earth,"— no violent tempests or awful perils were encountered, and they accordingly shrewdly concluded the report of the "Portugals most false."

Deeming it unsafe or inexpedient to halt here, Drake stood for land of which he had better knowledge; and on the 22nd July arrived at Sierra Leone. Water was obtained, and the refreshment of fruits and oysters, of which we are told "one kind was found on trees, spawning and increasing wonderfully,—the oyster suffering no bud to grow." It was imagined the 26th of September 1580, when, without touching at other land, Captain Drake, after a voyage of two years and ten months, came to an anchor in the harbour of Plymouth, whence he had set out. The day of the week was Monday, though, by the reckoning kept by the voyagers, Sunday, and the 25th the true time; the same loss of a day having befallen them which had puzzled Magellan's crew,—a mystery now clear to the most juvenile student in geography.

The safe return of the expedition, the glory attending so magnificent an enterprise, and the immense mass of wealth brought home, made the arrival of Drake be hailed throughout England as an event of great national importance. Such in fact it was, as his success gave an incalculable impetus to the rapidly-increasing maritime spirit of the country.

The bravery, the exploits, and the wonderful adventures of Drake immediately became the theme of every tongue. Courtiers patronized and poets praised him, and, to complete his celebrity, envious detractors were not wanting, who, with some plausibility, represented that England and Spain, though cherishing the bitterest national antipathy, being still nominally at peace, his enterprises were at best but those of a splendid corsair, and that his spoliation of the subjects of Spain must provoke reprisal on such merchants as had goods and dealings in that country. It was urged that, of all countries, a trading nation like England should carefully avoid offending in a kind which laid her open to speedy punishment, and must frustrate the advancement of her maritime prosperity. On the other hand, the friends and admirers of the navigator contended that he of all men, who had been so deep a sufferer from their perfidy, was entitled to take the punishment of the Spaniards into his own hands; and that his gallant enterprise, while it inspired foreign nations with a high opinion of the maritime talent and power of England, would at home excite the noblest emulation,—an effect which it already had, the island, from the one extreme to the other, being now inflamed with the ardour that his splendid achievements had kindled, and which was soon to be manifested in a series of actions emanating directly from his expedition.

In the meanwhile Drake lost no time in repairing to court. Elizabeth, who with all her faults never favoured the despicable, was more purely the fountain

QUEEN ELIZABETH KNIGHTING DRAKE.
Page 104.

of all favour and honour than any preceding sovereign, and her personal regard more the object of ambition. Drake was graciously received, but not yet openly countenanced. The queen permitted the first fervours of both his admirers and enemies to abate before she openly declared her own sentiments. A show of coldness was also a necessary part of the subtle game she was still playing with Spain.

The complaints of the Spaniards were violent and loud; and the queen deemed it prudent to place the wealth brought home under sequestration till their claims should be investigated, or, more correctly, till the complainers could be either baffled or wearied out in solicitation. It was the policy of Elizabeth to protract the long-impending hostilities between the countries, and among other means the plundered gold was employed. As a foretaste, or a bribe to purchase peace a little longer, several small sums were paid to the agent for Spanish claims; but when tired of the game of diplomacy, which the queen relished as much for the enjoyment of the play as the value of the stakes, she suddenly took the resolution of openly countenancing the daring navigator, whose boldness, discretion, and brilliant success were so happily adapted to gain her favour.

On the 4th of April 1581, the queen went in state to dine on board the *Golden Hind*, now lying at Deptford; and Drake, who naturally loved show and magnificence, spared no pains in furnishing a banquet worthy of his royal guest. After dinner the queen conferred upon him the honour of knighthood,—enhancing the value of the distinction by politely saying "that his actions did him more honour than the title which she conferred." The queen also gave orders that his ship should be preserved as a monument of the glory of the nation and of the illustrious commander. This was done, and when it would no longer hold together a chair was made of one of the planks, and presented as a relic to the University of Oxford. On the day of the queen's visit, in compliment to her majesty's scholarship, a variety of Latin verses, composed by the scholars of Winchester College, were nailed to the mainmast, in which the praises of the ship and of the queen were alternated and intermingled. The *Golden Hind* afterwards became the theme of the muse of Cowley. One translation of a Latin epigram on the ship we select from a multitude of verses, as its quaintness is redeemed by its elegance:—

> " The stars above will make thee known,
> If man were silent here ;
> The Sun himself cannot forget
> His fellow-traveller."

The reputation of Sir Francis Drake had now obtained that court-stamp which, without increasing value, gives currency. Though Elizabeth had so far temporized as to sequestrate for a time the wealth brought home, the Spanish complaints of the English sailing in the South Sea she scornfully dismissed,—

DRAKE'S CHAIR IN THE UNIVERSITY OF OXFORD.

Page 104.

denying "that, by the Bishop of Rome's donation or any other right, the Spaniards were entitled to debar the subjects of other princes from these new countries —the gift of what is another's constituting no valid right; that touching here and there, and naming a river or cape, could not give a proprietary title, nor hinder other nations from trading or colonizing in those parts where the Spaniards had not planted settlements." One objectionable part of Drake's conduct thus obtained royal vindication; and as the war, long impending, was no longer avoidable, his alleged depredations were forgotten even by his envious detractors, and his fame became as universal as it was high. Envy itself had even been forced to acknowledge not merely his maritime skill and genius for command, but the humanity and benevolence that marked his dealings with the Indians, and the generosity with which he uniformly treated his captives of that nation, of all others the most hateful to Englishmen, and in some respects the most injurious to himself.

But the further achievements of the Nelson of the reign of Elizabeth demand a new chapter, the life of Drake from this point being intimately blended with the public history of England.

CHAPTER III.

EXPEDITIONS TO THE WEST INDIES.

HOSTILITIES with Spain, so long protracted by the policy of Elizabeth, were now about to commence in good earnest, and Drake may be said to have struck the first blow. War was not formally declared when he projected an expedition in concert with Sir Philip Sydney,—the two most popular men of their time being to command, the one the land and the other the sea force. On the part of Sir Philip the design was abandoned at the express command of the queen, who required his services in the Netherlands, where he had already been usefully employed for the public cause, and where, in the following year, he met his early and glorious death. Sir Francis Drake's armament consisted of twenty-five sail, of which two vessels were queen's ships. His force amounted to two thousand three hundred seamen and soldiers. Under his command were several officers of experience and high reputation. His lieutenant-general was Christopher Carlile; his vice-admiral, the celebrated navigator Martin Frobisher; and Captain Francis Knollys and other officers of celebrity were among his coadjutors in an enterprise the object of which was to unite public advantage with private emolument.

The fleet stood at once for the coast of Spain, where Drake meditated a bold stroke at the enemy's naval force in passing to his ulterior objects in the West Indies; and this without very rigid preliminary inquiry whether war had been declared or not. His demand to know why an embargo had been laid upon the goods of certain English merchants was answered in terms so pacific that, finding it impossible to fasten a quarrel upon the Spaniards which would justify reprisal, the fleet cruised from St. Sebastian to Vigo, capturing some small tenders. They next stood for the Cape de Verd Islands, where, landing one thousand men in the night, Drake, with a handful of them, surprised and took St. Jago, which the inhabitants hastily abandoned. This was on the 17th November 1585, the anniversary of Elizabeth's accession, which was celebrated by the guns of the castle firing a salute, to which those of the fleet replied. The conquest had proved easy, but the booty was in proportion inconsiderable, consisting chiefly of trifling merchandise, and the tawdry, worthless wares employed in trading with the Indians of the islands and on the shores of the continent of America. If there had been any treasure in the place, it was either carried away or effectually concealed; and the threats of the invaders to burn and slay, unless the terms of ransom which they dictated were complied with, produced no effect. The islanders seemed determined either to weary or to starve out the invaders; and their easy conquest soon became no desirable possession. On the 24th, a village twelve miles in the interior, named St. Domingo, was taken. But the islanders still kept aloof; and, posting placards denouncing the former cowardice and cruelty of the Portuguese and their present pusillanimity, the English prepared to depart. Then, for the first time, a force appeared hanging off and on, as if to annoy their retreat. Burning the town, and every place within reach, the English re-embarked in good order, and stood for the West Indies.

In palliation of what may appear useless severity, it must be stated that, besides refusing the terms of ransom offered them, the Portuguese had perpetrated the most wanton cruelty on an English boy who had straggled, and whose corpse was found by his countrymen torn, disfigured, and dismembered,—as if he had rather fallen into the hands of the most ferocious tribe of cannibals than among a Christian people. The islanders had also, five years before, murdered, under the protection of a truce, the crew of a Bristol vessel commanded by Captain William Hawkins. The vengeance which may afterwards be taken by their countrymen forms a strong protection to a single ship's company or to a weak crew on a distant coast; and if there may not be strict equity, there is at least commendable policy in a commander showing that neither former kindness nor yet treachery to the people of his nation is either unknown or forgotten.

While the fleet lay here, that malignant fever which proves the scourge of soldiers and seamen in these climes broke out with great inveteracy, and carried off between two and three hundred of the men.

They next touched at St. Christopher and Dominica, where they had a friendly interview with some of the aborigines, at which the toys and wares of St. Jago were liberally exchanged for tobacco and cassada.

Attracted by the fame of the "brave city" of St. Domingo, one of the oldest and wealthiest of the Spanish settlements in the West Indies, it was determined to carry it. Drake's common plan of attack was simple and uniform: a party was landed in the night to make the assault from the land side, while the ships co-operated from the water. On New-Year's day the English landed ten miles to the westward of the town, and, forming into two divisions, made the attack at opposite gates; and, to save themselves from the guns of the castle, rushed forward sword in hand, pell-mell, till according to agreement they met in the market-place in the centre of the town, and changed the fight of the Spaniards into precipitate retreat. Here they hastily barricaded themselves, resolved to maintain their post, and confidently expecting an attack. But the Spaniards gave them little trouble. Struck with panic, they next night abandoned the castle to the invaders, and escaped by boats to the other side of the haven. The following day the English strengthened their position, planting the ordnance which they took within their trenches; and, thus secured, they held the place for a month, collecting what plunder was to be found, while they negotiated with the Spaniards for the ransom of the city. The terms were such that the inhabitants were unable to redeem the town; and burning and negotiation went on simultaneously and leisurely. Two hundred seamen, and as many soldiers forming their guard, were employed daily in the work of destruction. But the buildings being lofty piles, substantially constructed of stone, their demolition proved a fatiguing duty to the men; and after much labour, spent with little loss to the enemy and no profit to themselves, the ransom of twenty-five thousand ducats was finally accepted for the safety of what remained of the city. The plunder obtained was very inconsiderable for the size and imagined riches of the place.

A little episode in the history of this enterprise against St. Domingo deserves notice, as it places the energetic character of Drake in a striking point of view. A negro boy, sent with a flag of truce to the leading people while the negotiation for ransom was pending, was met by some Spanish officers, who furiously struck at him, and afterwards pierced him through with a horseman's spear. Dreadfully wounded as he was, the poor boy tried to crawl back to his master; and while relating the cruel treatment he had received, he fell down and expired in the presence of Drake. The insult offered to his flag of truce, and the barbarous treatment of the lad, roused the captain-general to the highest pitch of indignation. He commanded the provost-marshal, with a guard, to carry two unfortunate monks, who had been made prisoners, to the place where his flag was violated, there to be hanged. Another prisoner shared the same fate; and a message was sent to the Spaniards announcing that, until the persons guilty of this breach of the law of nations were given up, two Spanish prisoners should suffer daily. Next day the offenders were sent in; and to make their merited punishment the more ignominious and exemplary, their own countrymen were compelled to become their executioners.

Among other instances of Spanish boasting and vain-glory, recorded by the historians of the voyage, is an account of an escutcheon of the arms of Spain, found in the town-hall of the city, on the lower part of which was a globe, over which was represented a horse rampant, or probably volant, with the legend *Non sufficit orbis*. This vaunt gave great offence at this particular time to the national pride of the English, who told the negotiators that, should their queen be pleased resolutely to prosecute the war, instead of the whole globe not satisfying his ambition, Philip would find some difficulty in keeping that portion of it which he already possessed.

Their next attempt was directed against Carthagena,

which was bravely defended and gallantly carried—Carlile making the attack on the land side, while Drake's fleet presented itself before the town. The governor, Alonzo Bravo, was made prisoner; and after holding the place for six weeks, and destroying many houses, the trifling ransom of eleven thousand ducats was accepted for the preservation of the rest of the town. The Spaniards might not have got off on such easy terms, but that the fearful pest, the deadly bilious fever, which has so often proved fatal to English expeditions in the very same locality, now raged in the fleet, and compelled the commanders to revise their plans and lower their demands. About seven hundred men perished in this expedition of the *calentura* alone, as the disease, since described by Smollett and Glover and others, was then named. Those who struggled through this frightful malady, if we may fully credit the early accounts, were even more to be pitied than those that sunk under the disease. Though they survived, it was with loss of strength, not soon if ever recovered; and many suffered the decay of memory and impaired judgment, so that, when a man began to talk foolishly and incoherently, it became a common phrase in the fleet to say that such an one had been seized with the calenture.

The design of attempting Nombre de Dios and Panama, "there to strike the stroke for treasure," of which they had hitherto been disappointed, was abandoned in a council of war; and, sailing by the coast of

Florida, they burned St. Helena and St. Augustin, two forts and small settlements of the Spaniards, and brought off from Virginia Mr. Lane, the governor, with the remains of an unfortunate colony sent out under the auspices of Sir Walter Raleigh in the former year.

It was July 1586 before the armament returned, bringing two hundred brass and forty iron cannon, and about £60,000 in prize-money, of which £20,000 was divided among the men, and the remainder allotted to the adventurers. Though the private gains resulting from the expedition were trifling, the dismantling of so many fortresses at the beginning of a war was a service to the country of no inconsiderable value. It was but the first of many which our navigator performed in its progress.

The next exploit of Drake was wholly for the public service. The rumour of that formidable armament fitted out by Spain to invade England, and first in fear, though afterwards in jest, named the Invincible Armada, had spread general alarm. In a noble spirit of patriotism, the merchants of London, at their own expense, fitted out twenty-six vessels of different sizes, to be placed under the command of Drake, to annoy the enemy, and, if possible, frustrate or delay the boasted design of invading England. To this armament the queen added four ships of the royal fleet; and with this considerable force Drake bore for Lisbon, and afterwards for the harbour of Cadiz, where he had the good fortune to burn and destroy ten thousand tons burden of shipping, either destined for the threatened invasion or subservient to this purpose. Here he remained for a short time, annoying the enemy's galleys, which he destroyed piecemeal, though his great enterprise had been accomplished in one day and two nights. Drake having thus happily accomplished his public duty, was impelled by gratitude and gallantry to attempt a stroke which might enable him to reward the spirited individuals who had enabled him so essentially to serve their common country. Having private information that the *St. Philip*, a Portuguese carack from the East Indies, was about this time expected at Terceira, he sailed for the Azores. Before he fell in with the prize the fleet became short of provisions; but, by dint of promises and threats, Drake prevailed with his company to bear up against privations, and soon had the felicity of bringing in triumph to England the richest prize that had ever yet been made, and the first-fruits of the numerous captures to which his success soon led the way both among the Dutch and English. The name of the prize was hailed as an omen of future victory to England. Drake is blamed for discovering undue elation at the close of this triumphant expedition. He is said to have become boastful of his own deeds, though the only ground of charge is gaily describing his bold and gallant service as "burning the Spanish king's beard." But surely this may well be forgiven to the hero who, delaying the threatened Armada for a year, laid the foundation of its final discomfiture. Nor were Drake's eminent services to his country limited to warlike operations. In the short interval of leisure which followed this expedition he brought water into the town of Plymouth, of which it was in great want, from springs eight miles distant, and by a course measuring more than twenty miles.

In the following year his distinguished services received the reward to which they were fully entitled, in his appointment of vice-admiral under Lord Charles Howard of Effingham, high-admiral of England.

Drake had hitherto been accustomed to give orders, not to obey them; and his vivacity under command had nearly been productive of serious consequences. Positive information had been received of the sailing of the Invincible Armada, but it was likewise known that the fleet had been dispersed in a violent tempest; and believing that the attempt would be abandoned at this time, orders were despatched to the lord-high-admiral to send four of his best ships back to Chatham, as the frugal government of Elizabeth grudged the expense of keeping them afloat an hour longer than they were positively required. This order had hardly been given when Howard was made aware by the information of Thomas Fleming, the captain of an English pinnace, of the close approach of the fleet; and it soon after passed Plymouth, where he lay taking in supplies after cruising on the Spanish coasts looking out for it. It was four in the afternoon of the 19th July 1588, when the intelligence of Fleming put the lord-high-admiral upon the alert; and by next day at noon his ships were manned, warped out, and in fighting trim. At the same hour the Spanish fleet came in sight; and on the 21st, Howard, with his greatly inferior force, ventured the attack which, by the blessing of Heaven on the valour and skill of the English, was continued from day to day in various quarters, till the proud Armada was swept from the English Channel. On the night of the 21st, Drake, who had been appointed to carry the lantern, forgot this duty, and gave chase to several hulks which were separated from the fleet, and thus so far misled the high-admiral that, following the Spanish lantern under the idea that it was carried by his own vice-admiral, when day dawned he found himself in the midst of the enemy's ships. The high-admiral instantly extricated himself; and Drake amply atoned for this oversight by the distinguished service performed by his squadron in harassing, capturing, and destroying the Spaniards. On the day following this erring night he performed a memorable action. Among the fleet was a large galleon commanded by Don Pedro de Valdez, a man of illustrious family and high official rank, with whom nearly fifty noblemen and gentlemen sailed. His ship had been crippled and separated from the fleet, and Howard, in hot pursuit, had passed it, imagining that it was abandoned. There was on board a crew of four hundred and fifty persons, who, when summoned to surrender in the formidable name of Drake, attempted

DRAKE FIGHTING WITH THE SPANIARDS. *Page 121.*

no resistance. Kissing the hand of his conqueror, Don Pedro said they had resolved to die in battle, had they not experienced the good fortune of falling into the hands of one courteous and gentle, and generous to the vanquished foe; one whom it was doubtful whether his enemies had greater cause to admire and love for his valiant and prosperous exploits, or dread for his great wisdom and good fortune; whom Mars, the god of war, and Neptune, the god of the sea, alike favoured. To merit this high eulogium, Drake behaved with the utmost kindness and politeness to his involuntary guests, who were sent prisoners to England. Two years afterwards he received £3,500 for their ransom. In the ship fifty-five thousand ducats were found, and liberally divided among the crew. The broken, running fight between the fleets was renewed from day to day, and from hour to hour, as the superior sailing of the light English vessels promised advantage, till the Spaniards were driven on that line of conduct which ended in the complete destruction of their mighty armament. In the fight of the 29th, which was desperate on both sides, Drake's ship was pierced with forty shot, two of which passed through his cabin. Of one hundred and thirty-four ships which left the coast of Spain, only fifty-three returned.

In the following year, Drake, as admiral, commanded the fleet sent to restore Don Antonio of Portugal, while Sir John Norris led the land-forces. Differences arose between the commanders about the best mode of prosecuting their joint enterprise. The failure of Norris's scheme gives probability to the assertion that the plan of operations suggested by Drake would, if followed, have been successful. It is at least certain that the expedition miscarried, which had never happened to any single-handed undertaking in which Drake engaged. Don Antonio, taken out to be made a king by the prowess of the English, returned as he went. Before the queen and council Drake fully justified his own share of the affair, and the confidence placed in his ability and skill remained undiminished. This was the first check that the fortunes of Drake had ever received; and it would have been happy for him, it has been said, had he now withdrawn his stake. The principal and fatal error of his succeeding expedition was once more undertaking a joint command.

The war in 1595, though it languished for want of fuel to feed the flame, was not yet giving any prospect of drawing to a conclusion; and in conjunction with Sir John Hawkins, Drake offered his services in an expedition to the West Indies, to be undertaken on a scale of magnificence which must at once crush the Spanish power in that quarter, where the enemy had already been so often and effectually galled by the same commanders. Elizabeth and her ministers received the proposal with every mark of satisfaction. The fleet consisted of six of the queen's ships and twenty-one private vessels, with a crew, in seamen and soldiers, amounting to two thousand five hundred men and boys. They sailed from Plymouth in August, having been detained for some time by the reports of another Armada being about to invade England. This rumour was artfully spread to delay the fleet, of which one object was known to be the destruction of Nombre de Dios and the plunder of Panama. They had hardly put to sea when the demon of discord, which ever attends conjunct expeditions, appeared in their councils. Sir John Hawkins wished at once to accomplish an object recommended by the queen; but time was lost in an attempt, suggested by Sir Thomas Baskerville, to invade or capture the Canaries, and again at Dominica. All these delays were improved by the enemy in the colonies, in preparing for the reception of the English. A few days before sailing, information had been sent to the fleet of a Spanish galleon richly laden, that had been disabled and separated from those ships which annually brought plate and treasure from the Indies to Spain; and the capture of this vessel was recommended to the commanders by the English government as an especial service. The galleon now lay at Porto Rico; but before this time five frigates had been sent by the Spaniards to convoy it away in safety. On the 30th October, Sir John Hawkins made sail from the coast of Dominica, where the ships had been careened, and had taken in water; and on the same evening he sustained the misfortune of having the *Francis*, one of his vessels, captured by the enemy's frigates. This stroke, which appeared fatal to the enterprise, by informing the

Spaniards of his approach and putting them on their guard, gave him inexpressible chagrin. He immediately fell sick, and on the 12th November, when the fleet had got before Porto Rico, died of combined disease and grief. He was succeeded by Sir Thomas Baskerville, who took command in the *Garland*, the queen's ship in which Hawkins had sailed. The English fleet, meditating an instant attack, now lay within reach of the guns of Porto Rico; and while the officers, on the night of Sir John Hawkins's death, were at supper together, a shot penetrated to the great cabin, drove the stool on which Drake sat from under him, killed Sir Nicolas Clifford, and mortally wounded Mr. Brute Browne and some other officers. An attack, this night decided upon, was attempted next day, with the desperate valour which has ever characterized the maritime assaults of the English. But the enemy were fully prepared; the treasure had been carefully conveyed away, and also the women and children. The fortifications had been repaired and placed in good order; and though the hot, impetuous attack of the English inflicted great suffering on the Spaniards, to themselves there remained but a barren victory. After lying two or three days before the place, it was judged expedient to bear off and abandon this enterprise. They stood for the Main, where Rio de la Hacha, La Rancheria, and some other places were taken, and, negotiations for their ransom failing, burned to the ground. The same course was followed with other petty places; but

Drake began seriously to find that, while giving the enemy this trifling annoyance, he was gradually reducing his own force without gaining any substantial advantage. His health was injured by this series of disappointments, and from the first misunderstanding with Hawkins his spirits had been affected. On the morning of the assault on Porto Rico, in taking leave of Mr. Brute Browne, then breathing his last, he exclaimed, "Brute, Brute, how heartily could I lament thy fate, but that I dare not suffer my spirits to sink now."

The Spanish towns, from which everything of value was taken away, were rather abandoned to the occupation than taken by the arms of the English. In this way Santa Martha and Nombre de Dios fell into their hands with scarce a show of resistance. They were both burned. On the 29th December, two days after the capture of Nombre de Dios, Sir Thomas Baskerville, with seven hundred and fifty soldiers, attempted to make his way to Panama through the fatiguing and dangerous passes of the Isthmus of Darien, the Spaniards annoying his whole line of march by a desultory fire of musketry from the woods. At certain passes fortifications had been thrown up to impede their progress; and coming upon these unexpectedly, they were exposed to a sudden fire, by which many fell. About midway the design was abandoned, and the party turned back, still exposed in the retreat to the fire of the Spaniards from the woods. Destitute of provisions, and suffering great privation and fatigue, they returned to the ships depressed and disheartened. This last and most grievous of the train of disappointments that had followed Drake throughout an expedition from which the nation expected so much, and wherein he had embarked much of his fortune and risked his high reputation, threw the admiral into a lingering fever, accompanied by a flux, under which he languished for three weeks. He expired while the fleet lay off Porto Bello. The death of Admiral Drake took place on the 28th January 1596, and in his fifty-first year. His remains were placed in a leaden coffin, and committed to the deep with all the pomp attending naval obsequies. Unsuccessful as his latest enterprises had been, his death was universally lamented by the nation. The tenderness of pity was now mingled with admiration of the genius and valour of this great man, " whose memory will survive as long as the world lasts, which he first surrounded."

Drake is described as low in stature, but extremely well made, with a broad chest and a round, compact head. His complexion was fair and sanguine; his countenance open and cheerful, with large and lively eyes; his beard full, and his hair of a light brown. From the lowest point and rudiments of his art, Drake was a thorough-bred seaman, able in his own person to discharge every duty of a ship, even to attending the sick and dressing the wounded. In repairing and watering his ships, as readily as in what are esteemed

DRAKE'S FUNERAL

Page 126.

higher offices, he at all times bore an active part; and to his zealous superintendence and co-operation in these subordinate duties, much of the facility and celerity of his movements, and of his consequent success, is to be attributed. The sciences connected with navigation, as they were then known, he thoroughly understood, and particularly that of astronomy. Whatever he attempted on his own judgment, without being controlled by the opinions of others, he accomplished with success. He has been charged with ambition; but it is well remarked that no man's ambition ever took a happier direction for his country. His example did more to advance the maritime power and reputation of England than that of all the navigators who preceded him. He indicated or led the way to several new sources of trade, and opened the career of commercial prosperity which his countrymen are still pursuing. Among the many natural gifts of this lowly-born seaman was a ready and graceful eloquence. He was fond of amassing wealth, but in its distribution was liberal and bountiful. Among other deeds of enlightened benevolence was his establishment, in conjunction with Sir John Hawkins, of the CHEST at Chatham for the relief of aged or sick seamen, by the honourable means of their own early providence. Drake sat in two Parliaments,—in the first for a Cornish borough, and in the next for the town of Plymouth in the thirty-fifth of Elizabeth. Though often described as a bachelor, it is ascertained that he married the daughter and sole heiress of Sir George Sydenham, of Coombe Sydenham in Devonshire, who survived him. He left no children, but bequeathed his landed estate, which was considerable, to his nephew Francis Drake, afterwards created a baronet by James the First. Three quarters of the globe had contributed to its acquisition; yet there is certainly no ancient family estate in the south of England of the title-deeds of which the proprietors have less cause to be ashamed than that still held by the heirs of the son of the honest mariner of Tavistock.

CAVENDISH.

CAVENDISH.

CHAPTER I.

VOYAGE ROUND THE WORLD.

THE reign of Elizabeth is by nothing more honourably distinguished than the manliness and dignity which characterized the pursuits of her courtiers, and, through their example, those of the entire body of English gentry. A period illustrious in the national annals owes much of its glory and felicity to this single cause. To the queen herself belongs the praise of having, during her long reign, studiously kept alive the flame of public spirit; and of having striven, by her influence and public acts, to inspire the flower of the youth of her kingdom with that ardent thirst of glory which in so many ways redounded to the national advantage. Distinguished personal merit, whether displayed in the field or at the council-board, was the certain road to the favour of Elizabeth; and though her favourites might have possessed very different degrees of moral worth, all of them were celebrated for ability or patriotism. It was thus, in the age of Elizabeth, nothing unusual for men of the highest rank to devote their private fortunes and personal services to the advancement of the national interests, either by undertaking or promoting voyages of discovery, establishing colonies, opening up new branches of trade, or protecting the state against the aggressions of the Spaniards. At that period it was considered as nothing wonderful that the Earls of Essex and Cumberland, and such men as Raleigh, Dudley, Grenville, Gilbert, and many other persons of family and condition, should, in pursuit of honourable distinction, court fatigue and hardship, from which their degenerate successors in the reigns of the Stuarts would have shrunk in dismay.

Of this class was Thomas Cavendish, the second Englishman that circumnavigated the globe. He was of an ancient and honourable family of Suffolk, the ancestor of which had come into England with the Conqueror. The residence of Cavendish, or Candish, as the name was then written, was at Trimley St. Martin, and his estates lay near Ipswich, at that period a place of considerable trade. From this vicinage to a maritime town he is said to have imbibed an early inclination for the sea.

His father died while Cavendish was still a minor; and coming early into the possession of his patrimony, he is reported to have squandered it " in gallantry, and following the court," and to have been compelled to embrace the nobler pursuits to which his subsequent

THOMAS CAVENDISH. Page 134.

years were devoted to redeem his shattered fortunes. Truth may lie between the contradictory statements of the motives which determined this gentleman to follow the career of Sir Francis Drake, in seeking fortune and reputation on the western shores of America and in the South Sea.

Though the relations of his voyages are ample and complete, the truth is that very little is known of the personal history of Cavendish. In the year 1585, he accompanied Sir Richard Grenville's expedition to Virginia, in a vessel equipped at his own expense. This voyage, undertaken to plant the unfortunate colony which was brought home by Sir Francis Drake in 1586 (see page 115), was both profitless and difficult; but it enabled Cavendish to obtain nautical experience, and in its progress he had seen the Spanish West India settlements, and conversed with some of those who had accompanied Drake into the South Sea. The youthful ambition of Cavendish was thus roused to emulate the glory of so eminent a navigator in this rich and newly-opened field of enterprise.

Grenville's fleet, which sailed for Virginia in April, returned in October, and from the wrecks of his fortune and the remains of his credit, Mr. Cavendish, in six months afterwards, had equipped a small squadron for his projected voyage. While the carpenters were at work he procured every draught, map, chart, and history of former navigations that might be useful to him; and having, through the patronage or recommendation of Lord Hunsdon, procured the queen's commission, he sailed from Plymouth on the 21st July 1586. His light squadron consisted of the *Desire*, a vessel of one hundred and twenty tons burden, in which he sailed himself as admiral and commander of the expedition; the *Content*, of sixty tons; and the *Hugh Gallant*, a light bark of forty tons. A crew of one hundred and twenty-three soldiers, seamen, and officers manned this little fleet, which was provided with every requisite for a long voyage in latitudes with which the navigation of Drake had now made the English somewhat familiar.

If so much interest is still awakened by the maritime undertakings of contemporary navigators, who set out in a familiar track under the guidance of former experience and observation, with the advantage of instruments nearly perfect, and with all appliances and means to boot, how much more must attach to the relation of the adventures of one who, like Cavendish, could have no hope or dependence, save in his own capacity and courage!

The squadron first touched at Sierra Leone, where the conduct of the young commander was not wholly blameless. On a Sunday, part of the ships' companies went on shore, and spent the day in dancing and amusing themselves with the friendly negroes, their secret object being to gain intelligence of a Portuguese vessel that lay in the harbour, and which Cavendish intended to capture. This was found impracticable, and next day the English landed, to the number of seventy, and made an attack on the town, of which they burned one hundred and fifty houses, almost the whole number, and plundered right and left. It was but little that they found. The negroes fled at their landing, but on their retreat shot poisoned arrows at the marauders from the shelter of the woods. This African village is described as neatly built, enclosed by mud walls, and kept, both houses and streets, in the cleanest manner. The yards were paled in, and the town was altogether trim and comfortable, exhibiting signs of civilization, of which at this point the slave-trade subsequently destroyed every trace. A few days afterwards a party of the sailors landed to wash linen; and repeating the visit next day, a number of negroes lying in ambush in the woods nearly surprised and cut them off. A soldier died of a shot from a poisoned arrow; though the case, as described, appears more like mortification of the parts than the effects of poison. Several of the men were wounded, but none mortally save the soldier. On the 3rd of September a party went some miles up the river in a boat, caught a store of fish, and gathered a supply of lemons for the fleet, which sailed on the 6th. No reason is assigned for the unprovoked devastation on this coast, save "the bad dealing of negroes with all Christians."

On the 16th December the squadron made the coast of America, in $47\frac{1}{3}°$ S. The land, stretching west, was seen at the distance of six leagues, and next day the fleet anchored in a harbour in 48° S. This harbour they named Port Desire, in honour of the admiral's ship. Seals were found here of enormous size, which in the fore part of their body resembled lions; their young was found delicate food, equal, in the taste of the seamen, to lamb or mutton. Sea-birds were also found in great plenty, of which the description given seems to apply to the penguin. In this excellent harbour the ships' bottoms were careened. On the 24th December, Christmas eve, a man and boy belonging to the *Content* went on shore to wash their linen, when they were suddenly surrounded and shot at by fifty or more Indians. Cavendish pursued with a small party, but the natives escaped. "They are as wild as ever was a buck," says an old voyager, "as they seldom or never see any Christians." Their footprints were measured, and found to be eighteen inches in length. The squadron left Port Desire on the 28th, and halted at an island three leagues off, to cure and store the penguins that had been taken. On the 30th, standing to sea they passed a rock about fifty miles from the harbour they had left, which resembled the Eddystone Rock near Plymouth. About the first day of the year they saw several capes, to which no names are given, and on the 6th, without further preparation, entered Magellan Strait, which the Spaniards had lately attempted to fortify and colonize. At twilight the squadron anchored near the first Angostura; and in the night lights were observed on the north side of the Strait, which were supposed to be signals. Recognition was made by lights from the ships, and a boat was sent off in the morning, to which three men on the shore made signs by waving a handkerchief. These were part of the survivors of a wretched Spanish colony.

The history of the misfortunes and sufferings of the first settlers in different parts of America would make one of the most melancholy volumes that ever were penned; nor could any portion of it prove more heart-rending than that which should record the miseries of this colony, left by Pedro Sarmiento in the Strait of Magellan. It may be recollected that, on the appearance of Drake on the coast of Peru, this commander was despatched by the viceroy to intercept the daring interloper on his return by the Strait. Sarmiento afterwards bestowed much pains in examining the western shores of Patagonia and the coast of Chili, and the many inlets, labyrinths, and intricate channels of the islands and broken lands of Tierra del Fuego, which, as he conjectured, must communicate with the Strait of Magellan by one or more passages. After a long time had thus been consumed fruitlessly he entered the Strait, and passed through eastward in about a month, minutely examining the coast on both sides. When this discoverer reached Spain, his exaggerated statements, the desire of checking the progress of the English in this quarter, and an apprehension that they were preparing to seize this master-key to the South

Seas (the passage by the Cape of Good Hope being still monopolized by the Portuguese, and that by Cape Horn not yet discovered), induced Philip to listen to the proposals of Sarmiento, an enthusiast in the cause, and to colonize and fortify this important outlet of his American dominions. A powerful armament of twenty-three ships with three thousand five hundred men, destined for different points of South America, was in the first place to establish the new colony. This expedition, undertaken on so magnificent a scale, was from first to last unfortunate. While still on the coast of Spain, from which the fleet sailed on the 25th September 1581, five of the ships were wrecked in a violent gale, and eight hundred men perished. The whole fleet put back, and sailed a second time in December. Misfortunes followed in a thick train. Sickness thinned their numbers; and at Rio Janeiro, where they wintered, many of the intended settlers deserted. Some of the ships became leaky; the bottoms of others were attacked by worms; and a large vessel, containing most of the stores of the colonists of the Strait, sprung a leak at sea, and before assistance could be obtained went down, three hundred and thirty men and twenty of the settlers perishing in her. Three times was Sarmiento driven back to the Brazils before he was able to accomplish his purpose; and it was February 1584 before he at last arrived in the Strait, and was able to land the colonists. Nor did his ill fortune close here. His consort, Riviera, either wilfully abandoned him, or was forced from his anchorage by stress of weather. He stood for Spain, carrying away the greater part of the remaining stores which were to sustain the people through the rigour of the winter of the South, which was now commencing, and until they were able to raise crops and obtain provisions. The foundation of a town was laid, which was named San Felipe, and bastions and wooden edifices were constructed. Another city, named Nombre de Jesus, was commenced. These stations were in favourable points of the Strait, and at the distance of about seventy miles from each other. In the meanwhile the southern winter set in with uncommon severity. In April snow fell incessantly for fifteen days. Sarmiento, who, after establishing the colonists at these two points, intended to go to Chili for provisions, was driven from his anchors in a gale, and forced to seek his own safety in the Brazils, leaving the settlers without a ship. He has been accused of intentionally abandoning this helpless colony, which he was the instrument of establishing, and of which he was also the governor. The accusation appears unjust, as he made many subsequent efforts for its relief, which his ill fortune rendered abortive. The governors at the different settlements at length refused to afford further assistance to a project which had lost the royal favour; and in returning to Spain to solicit aid, Sarmiento was captured by three ships belonging to Sir Walter Raleigh,—luckily, in all probability, for himself, as the indignation of King Philip at the failure of so expensive and powerful an expedition, and at the misrepresentations of this officer, might not have been easily appeased. Of the wretched colonists, about whom neither Old Spain nor her American settlements gave themselves any further trouble, many died of famine and cold during the first winter. The milder weather of the spring and summer allowed a short respite of misery, and afforded the hope of the return of Sarmiento, or some ship with provisions and clothing. But the year wore away, and no vessel appeared, and the colonists at San Felipe, in their despair, contrived to build two boats, in which all who remained alive, fifty men and five women, embarked with the hope of getting out of the Strait. One of their boats was wrecked, and the design was abandoned, as there were no seamen among their number, nor any one capable of conducting the perilous navigation. Their crops all failed; the natives molested them; and out of four hundred men and thirty women landed by Sarmiento, only fifteen men and three women survived when Mr. Cavendish entered the Strait. In San Felipe many lay dead in their houses and in their clothes, the survivors not having strength to bury them; and along the shores, where these miserable beings wandered, trying to pick up a few shell-fish or herbs, they often came upon the body of a deceased companion who had perished of famine, or of the diseases caused by extreme want.

It was, as has been said, part of these forlorn wanderers whom Cavendish saw on the morning after he entered the Strait. A passage to Peru was offered them, but they at first hesitated to trust the English heretics; though afterwards, when willing to accept the generous offer, their resolution came too late, and before they could be mustered, a fair wind offering, Cavendish sailed on, having tantalized these wretched Spaniards with hopes which the safety of his own crew in this precarious navigation, and the success of his expedition, did not permit him to fulfil. The offer had likewise been made in ignorance of their numbers. If Cavendish be blamed for abandoning these wretched victims to their fate, what shall be said of the nation which, having sent out this colony, left it to perish of famine and cold? One Spaniard was brought off, named Tomé Hernandez, who became the historian of the miserable colony of the Strait.

The squadron of Cavendish, after passing both the Angosturas, as the Spaniards named the narrowest points of the Strait, anchored first at the island of Santa Magdalena, where in two hours they killed and salted two pipes full of penguins; and afterwards at San Felipe, the now desolate station of the Spanish colonists, some of whom the English found still lying in their houses, "where they had died like dogs." Here they brought on board six pieces of ordnance which the settlers had buried. This place Cavendish named Port Famine; it was found to be in 53° S. On the 22nd a few natives were seen; but the Spaniard,

Hernandez, cautioned the English against all intercourse, representing them as a treacherous people,—a character which European knives and swords seen in their possession, converted into darts, confirmed; and when they again approached, Cavendish carried his precautions to so extravagant a length as to order a discharge of muskets, by which many of them were killed, and the rest took to flight, certainly not corrected of their bad propensities by this harsh discipline. They were represented as cannibals, who had preyed upon the Spanish colonists, and this excused all wrong.

For the next three weeks the fleet lay in a sheltered port, unable to enter the South Sea from a continuance of strong westerly winds; but on the 24th February, after a favourable though a tedious passage, they finally emerged from the Strait. To the south was a fair high cape with a point of low land adjoining it; on the other side were several islands, with much broken ground around them, at about six leagues off from the mainland. On the 1st of March the stormy Spirit of the Strait, which no fleet ever wholly escaped, overtook Cavendish; and the *Hugh Gallant* was separated from the larger vessels, one of which was found so leaky that the crew were completely exhausted in working the pumps for three days and nights without ceasing. On the 15th the *Hugh Gallant* rejoined her consorts at the Isle of Mocha, on the coast of Chili. They were here taken for Spaniards, and landing on the Main experienced but a rough reception from the

Indians, who bore no good will to the natives of Spain. But a similar mistake sometimes operated to their advantage; and next day, when the captain with a party of seventy men landed on the island of Santa Maria, they were received as Spaniards, with all kindness and humility, by the principal people of the island; and a store of wheat, barley, and potatoes, ready prepared, and presumed by the voyagers to be a tribute to the conquerors, was unscrupulously appropriated. To this the islanders added presents of hogs, dried dog-fish, fowls, and maize, and received in return an entertainment on board the captain's ship. These Indians are represented as being in such subjection that not one of them durst eat a hen or hog of his own rearing, all being sacred to their task-masters, who had, however, made the whole of the islanders Christians. When they came to understand that their visitors were not Spaniards, it was believed that they attempted to invite them to an assault upon their enslavers; but for want of an interpreter their meaning was imperfectly comprehended. The squadron, thus refreshed at the expense of the Spaniards, sailed on the 18th, but overshot Valparaiso, at which place they intended to halt. On the 30th they anchored in the Bay of Quintero, seven leagues to the north of Valparaiso. A herdsman asleep on a hill-side awaking, and perceiving three strange ships in the bay, caught a horse grazing beside him, and fled to spread the alarm. Cavendish, unable to prevent this untoward movement, landed with a party of thirty men, and Hernandez, the Spaniard whom he had brought from the Strait, and who made strong protestations of fidelity. Three armed horsemen appeared, as if come to reconnoitre. With these Hernandez conferred, and reported that they agreed to furnish as much provision as the English required. A second time the interpreter was despatched to a conference; but on this occasion, forgetting all his vows of fidelity to his benefactors, he leaped up behind one of his countrymen, and they set off at a round gallop, leaving Cavendish to execrate Spanish bad faith. The English filled some of their water-casks, and attempted in vain to obtain a shot at the wild cattle, which were seen grazing in great herds. Next day a party of from fifty to sixty marched into the interior in the hope of discovering some Spanish settlement. They did not see one human being, native or European, though they travelled till arrested by the mountains. The country was fruitful and well watered with rivulets, and abounded in herds of cattle and horses, and with hares, rabbits, and many kinds of wild-fowl. They also saw numerous wild dogs. The party did not sleep on shore. The boats were sent next day for water, which was found a quarter of a mile from the beach. While the seamen were employed in filling the casks, they were suddenly surprised by a party of two hundred horsemen, who came pouncing down upon them from the heights, and cut off twelve of the party, some of whom were killed, and the rest made prisoners. The remainder were rescued by the soldiers, who ran from the rocks to support their unsuspecting comrades, and killed twenty-four of the Spaniards. Notwithstanding this serious misadventure, Cavendish, keeping strict watch and ward, remained here till the watering was completed. Of the nine prisoners snatched off in this affray, it was afterwards learned that six were executed at Santiago as pirates, though they sailed with the queen's commission, and though the nation to which they belonged was at open war with Spain.

The discipline which the Spaniards had taught the natives was again found of use to our navigators, who, after leaving Quintero, came on the 15th to Morro Moreno, or the Brown Mountain, where the Indians, on their landing, met them with loads of wood and water, which they had carried on their backs down the rocks. These slaves of the Spaniards were found to be a very degraded race, almost at the lowest point in the scale of civilization. Their dwellings consisted of a few sticks placed across two stakes stuck in the ground, on which a few boughs were laid. Skins spread on the floor gave a higher idea of comfort. Their food consisted of raw, putrid fish; yet their fishing-canoes were constructed with considerable ingenuity. They were made of skins "like bladders." Each boat consisted of two of these skins, which were inflated by means of quills, and sewed or laced together with gut, so as to be perfectly water-tight. In these they fished, paying large tribute of their spoils to their conquerors. When any one died, his bows and arrows, canoe, and all his personal property, were buried along with him, as the English verified by opening a grave.

On the 23rd a vessel, with a cargo of Spanish wine, was captured near Arica, and also a small bark, the crew of which escaped in their boat. This vessel was permanently added to the squadron, and named the *George*. Another large ship, captured in the road of Arica, proved but a worthless prize, the cargo having been previously taken away, and the ship deserted by the crew. A design of landing and storming the town was abandoned, as, before the squadron could be mustered, the Spaniards were apprised of their danger, and prepared to stand on the defensive. A third vessel was taken close by the town; and the English squadron and the batteries even exchanged a few harmless shots; after which Cavendish, in hopes of relieving some of the English prisoners made at Quintero, sent in a flag of truce inviting the Spaniards to redeem their vessels; but proposals of this nature were, by order of the viceroy at Lima, in all cases rejected.

On the 25th, while the squadron still rode before the town, a vessel from the southward was perceived coming into the port. Cavendish sent out his pinnace to seize this bark; while the towns-people endeavoured from the shore to make the crew sensible of their danger. They understood the signals, and rowed in among the rocks, while a party of horsemen advanced from the town to protect the crew and passengers.

Among these were several monks, who had a very narrow escape. The deserted vessel, when searched, afforded nothing of value; and burning their prizes, early on the 26th they bore away northward from Arica. Next day they captured a small vessel which had been despatched from Santiago with intelligence to the viceroy that an English squadron—probably Drake himself— was upon the coast. Great severity was used to make the crew reveal the nature of their despatches, which were thrown overboard while the English gave chase. They had solemnly sworn not to tell their errand; but their fidelity was barely proof against the torture to which Cavendish thought it necessary to subject them to extort their secret. An old Fleming whom he threatened to hang, and actually caused to be hoisted up, stood the test, and chose rather to die than to perjure himself by betraying his trust. At last one of the Spaniards confessed; and burning the vessel, Cavendish carried the crew along with him as the safest way to prevent tale-telling. In this vessel was found a Greek pilot well acquainted with the coast of Chili.

On the 3rd May they landed at a small Spanish town, where they obtained a supply of bread, wine, figs, and fowls. This cruise was continued for a fortnight, and several prizes were made, from which needful supplies were obtained, but none that afforded the species of wealth which the captors valued. On the 20th they landed at Payta, to the amount of seventy men, took the town, drove out the inhabitants, and

continued the pursuit till they came to the place
whither the towns-people had conveyed their most
valuable goods. Here they found twenty-five pounds
of silver, with other costly commodities. Cavendish,
however, expecting an attack, had the prudence not to
allow his men to encumber themselves with much spoil
on their return to the ships. The town, which was
regularly built and very clean, consisted of two hundred
houses. It was burned to the ground, with goods to
the value of five or six thousand pounds. A ship in
the harbour was also burned; and the fleet held a course
northward, and anchored at the island of Puna in a
good harbour. A Spanish sloop of two hundred and
fifty tons burden, which they found here, was sunk.
They landed forthwith at the dwelling of the cacique,
who was found living in a style of elegance and even
magnificence rarely seen among the native chiefs. His
house stood near the town, by the water's edge, and
contained many handsome apartments, with verandas
commanding fine prospects seaward and landward.
The chief had married a beautiful Spanish woman, who
was regarded as the queen of the island. She never
set her foot upon the ground, holding it "too low a
thing for her," but was carried abroad on men's shoulders
in a sort of palanquin, with a canopy to shelter her
from the sun and wind, and attended by native ladies
and the principal men of the island. The cacique and
his lady fled on the first approach of the English,
carrying with them one hundred thousand crowns,

which, from the information of a captive scout, were ascertained to have been in their possession. Induced by the information of the Indian captive, Cavendish landed on the Main with an armed party, intending to surprise the fugitives; but they once more fled, leaving the meat roasting at their fires, and their treasures could not be discovered. In a small neighbouring island the cacique had previously for safety deposited his most valuable furniture and goods, consisting of hangings of Cordovan leather, richly painted and gilded, with the tackling of ships, nails, spikes, etc., of which the English took a large supply. At Puna sail-cloth of sea-grass was manufactured for the use of the ships in the South Sea. The island was about the size of the Isle of Wight, and contained several towns; the principal one, near which was the cacique's palace, consisted of two hundred houses, with a large church. This the English burned down, carrying away the bells.

The Indian chief of Puna had been baptized previous to his marriage; and the Indians were all obliged to attend Mass. Adjoining the dwelling of the cacique was a fine garden laid out in the European style, with a fountain. In it were cotton-plants, fig-trees, pomegranates, and many varieties of herbs and fruits. An orchard, with lemons, oranges, etc., ornamented the other side of this pleasant dwelling, the under part of which consisted of a large hall, in which goods of all kinds were promiscuously stored. Cattle and poultry were seen in great abundance, with pigeons, turkeys, and ducks of unusual size. Though the general, both from personal observation and report, was aware that a force was to be sent against him from Guayaquil, he hauled up his ship to have her bottom cleaned, keeping vigilant watch in the chief's house, where the English had established their headquarters.

The ship was again afloat, and the squadron about to sail, when, by one of those mischances which prove the danger of indulging for a single moment in false security, the English suffered a severe loss. On the 2nd of June, before weighing anchor, a party were permitted to straggle about the town to amuse themselves and forage for provisions. Thus scattered, they were suddenly assailed in detached groups by a hundred armed Spaniards; and of the twenty thus dispersed, seven were killed, three made prisoners, and two drowned, while eight escaped. Forty-six Spaniards and Indians fell in this skirmish. Cavendish immediately landed with an armed band, drove the Spanish soldiers from the town, and burned it completely down, together with four ships then building. He also destroyed the gardens and orchards. Persisting in maintaining his ground, Cavendish next day laid up the other ship to be careened, and did not sail till the 5th, when they went to Rio Dolce, where they watered. Here they sunk the *Hugh Gallant*, all the hands being now required for the other vessels. They also sent on shore their Indian prisoners, and without touching at any other land, held a northerly course for nearly a month. On the 9th July they captured a new ship of one hundred and twenty tons, which, first taking away her ropes and sails, they immediately burned. In this vessel was a Frenchman, Michael Sancius, who gave information of the Manilla ship then expected from the Philippines. This was a prize worth looking after; and they were so far fortunate as to intercept a small bark sent to give her warning. On the 27th, by daybreak, they entered the harbour of Guatulco, and burned the town, the church, and custom-house, in which was found a quantity of dye-stuffs and cocoas. Some trifling adventures marked the following day, in which they by mistake oversailed Acapulco. Landing at Puerto de Navidad, they burned two ships, each of two hundred tons, then on the stocks, and made prisoner a mulatto, who carried letters of advice of their progress along the coast of New Galicia. In this manner they proceeded northward, often landing small detachments, and spreading alarm along the shores. On the 8th they came into the bay of Chaccalla (supposed Compostella), described as being eighteen leagues from Cape de los Corrientes, and to a harbour presumed to be that known in modern geography as San Blas. Next morning an officer with forty men, and Michael Sancius as their conductor, marched two leagues into the interior, by "a most villainous and desert path through the woods and wilderness," and came to a place where they found three Spanish families, a carpenter of the same nation, a Portuguese, and a few Indians. Their ordinary mode of proceeding on such occasions is told in few words: "We bound them all, and made them to come to the seaside with us." The general, however, set the women free; and on their bringing to the ships a supply of pine-apples, lemons, and oranges, allowed their husbands to depart, as there was nothing to be obtained from them. The carpenter and the Portuguese were kept, and next day the fleet sailed. On the 12th September they reached the Isle of St. Andrew, where they laid in a store of wood, and of dried and salted wild-fowl. Seals were also found, and iguanas—a species "of serpent, with four feet and a long sharp tail, strange to them who have not seen them," but which, nevertheless, made very palatable food to the keen appetites of seamen. In their frequent exigencies these hardy voyagers never scrupled to act upon the opinion of the old Symeron chief in the Isthmus of Darien. When Drake, with the natural disgust of an Englishman, showed some tokens of aversion to otter's flesh, the Indian is reported to have thus addressed him: "Are you a warrior and in want, and yet doubt if that be food which hath blood in it?"

On the 24th September they put into the Bay of Mazatlan, and at an island a league to the northward careened the ships, new-built the pinnace, and by digging deep in the sands found water, of which they stood much in need, as without this seasonable supply they must have been compelled to turn back, and thus might have missed their prey.

The squadron sailed from this island on the night of the 9th of October for the Cape of St. Lucas, which was made on the 14th. Here they lay in wait for the anticipated prize, cruising about the headland, without going far off, till the 4th of November, on the morning of which day the trumpeter from the mast-head descried a sail bearing in for the cape. Chase was immediately given, and continued for some hours, when the English came up with the *Santa Anna*, gave her a broadside, poured in a volley of musketry, and prepared to board. The attempt was bravely repelled by the Spaniards, who courageously repulsed the assailants, with the loss of two men killed and five wounded. The most formidable weapons of the Spaniards were stones, which, from behind their protecting barricades, they hurled upon the boarders. "But we new-trimmed our sails," says the early relation, "and fitted every man his furniture, and gave them a fresh encounter with our great ordnance, and also with our small-shot, raking them through and through, to the killing and wounding of many of their men. Their captain still, like a valiant man, with his company, stood very stoutly into his close-fights, not yielding as yet. Our general, encouraging his men afresh with the whole voice of trumpets, gave them the other encounter with our great ordnance and all our small-shot, to the great discouragement of our enemies, raking them through in divers places, killing and wounding many of their men. They being thus discouraged and spoiled, and their ship being in hazard of sinking by reason of the great shot which were made, whereof some were under water, within five or six hours' fight, sent out a flag of truce, and parleyed for mercy, desiring our general to save their lives and to take their goods, and that they would presently yield. Our general, of his goodness, promised them mercy, and called them to strike their sails, and to hoist out their boat and come on board; which news they were full glad to hear of, and presently struck their sails, hoisted out their boat, and one of their chief merchants came on board unto our general, and, falling down upon his knees, offered to have kissed our general's feet, and craved mercy. Our general graciously pardoned both him and the rest, upon promise of their true dealing with him and his company concerning such riches as were in the ship; and sent for their captain and pilot, who, at their coming, used the like duty and reverence as the former did. The general, out of his great mercy and humanity. promised their lives and good usage."

The *Santa Anna* was a prize worth the trouble bestowed in securing her. She was of seven hundred tons burden, and the property of the King of Spain. Besides a rich cargo of silks, satins, damasks, wine, preserved fruits, musk, etc., there were on board one hundred and twenty-two thousand pesos in gold. The provision made for the passengers was also of the best kind, and afforded luxuries to the English ships' companies to which they had hitherto been strangers.

Cavendish carried his prize into a bay within Cape St. Lucas, named by the Spaniards Aguada Segura, or the Safe Watering-place, where he landed the crew and passengers to the number of one hundred and ninety persons, among whom were some females.

The captain-general deemed it impolitic to allow these persons to proceed direct to New Spain; and the place on which he landed them afforded water, wood, fish, fowl, and abundance of hares and rabbits. He presented them with part of the ship's stores, with wine, and with the sails of their dismantled vessel to construct tents for their shelter. He also gave the seamen weapons for their defence against the natives, and planks, of which they might build a bark to convey the whole party to the settlements.

Among the passengers by the *Santa Anna* were two lads, natives of Japan, who could both read and write their own language; and three boys from Manilla. These, with a Portuguese who had been in Canton, the Philippines, and the islands of Japan, Cavendish carried with him, and also a Spanish pilot.

The division of the spoils occasioned great discontent, particularly among the crew of the vice-admiral's ship, who imagined that Cavendish favoured the company of the *Desire*. But the dissatisfaction was apparently suppressed; and by the 17th November, "the Queen's-day," all business being completed, a few hours were devoted by the loyal English to gaiety and festivity; and a discharge of the great guns and a display of fire-works proclaimed to these lonely shores the glory of Elizabeth of England. As the completion of their rejoicing, the *Santa Anna*, with all of her goods that could not be stowed into the English ships, was set on fire, and left burning; and, firing a parting salute to the deserted Spaniards, the *Desire* and the *Content* bore away for England, which before they could again arrive at, so much of the circumference of the globe must be traversed. Before coming to St. Lucas, the *George*, the Spanish prize, had been abandoned; and now, in coming out of the bay, the *Content* lagged astern, and was never again seen by her consort.

The *Desire* thus left alone, as the *Golden Hind* had been before her, holding her solitary course across the Pacific, on the 3rd January 1588 came in sight of Guahan, one of the Ladrones. For forty-five days the English had enjoyed fair winds, and had sailed a distance roughly estimated at between seventeen and eighteen hundred leagues. When within five or six miles of Guahan, fifty or more canoes full of people came off to meet the ship, bringing the commodities with which they were now in the habit of supplying the Spaniards,—namely, fish, potatoes, plantains, and cocoas, which were exchanged for pieces of iron. This traffic was plied so eagerly that it became troublesome, and Cavendish, who was never distinguished for patience or forbearance, with five of his men, fired to drive the natives back from the ship. They dived so nimbly to evade the shot that it could not be ascertained what execution was done. The people here were of tawny complexion, corpulent, and of taller stature than ordinary-sized Englishmen. Their hair was long, but some wore it tied up in one or two knots on the crown of the head. The construction of their canoes greatly excited the admiration of the English seamen, formed as they were without any "edge-tool." These canoes were from six to seven yards in length, but very narrow, and moulded in the same way at prow and stern. They had square and triangular sails of cloth made of bulrushes, and were ornamented with head-figures carved in wood, "like unto images of the devil." The natives appeared in the canoes entirely naked, and were dexterous divers and excellent swimmers.

On the 14th January the *Desire* made Cape Spirito Santo, the first point of the Philippines which was seen; and on the same night entered the strait now named the Strait of San Bernardino. Next morning they came to anchor in a fine bay and safe harbour in the island then named Capul. Though the Spanish settlement at Manilla was still comparatively recent, it had risen and flourished so rapidly that it was already become a place of great wealth and commercial importance. Besides the annual fleet to New Spain, it possessed a very considerable trade with China and the Indian islands in the most valuable commodities. The people with whom Manilla enjoyed this trade, and particularly a people they name the Sanguelos, are described by the voyagers as "of great genius and invention in handicrafts and sciences; every one so expert, perfect, and skilful in his faculty, as few or no Christians are able to go beyond them in that they take in hand. For drawing and embroidery upon satin, silk, or lawn, either beast, fowl, fish, or worm; for liveliness and perfectness, both in silk, silver, gold, and pearl, they excel."

As soon as the *Desire* came to anchor off Capul, one of the chiefs, of whom there were seven in the island, came on board, presuming the ship to be Spanish. His people brought a supply of potatoes, which they called camotaes, and green cocoas. The rate of exchange, or the prices, would now be thought high. A yard of linen was given for four cocoas, and the same quantity for about a quart of potatoes. These roots were thought good either boiled or roasted, and were much relished by the crew. The cacique was "carved" (tattooed) in various streaks and devices. He was requested to remain on board, and a message of invitation being sent to the other chiefs, they also repaired to the ship, bringing hogs and hens to exchange. The rate, which was uniform, was, for a hog eight ryals of plate, and for a fowl one. This trade went on all day, and the ship, after her long run, was well supplied with refreshments. On the same night a fortunate discovery was made by the Portuguese taken out of the *Santa Anna* on account of his knowledge of the Philippines and of China. The

Spanish pilot had, it appeared, prepared a letter, which he hoped secretly to convey to the governor at Manilla, informing him of the English ship, which it would not be difficult to surprise and overpower. If this vessel was allowed to escape with impunity, he pointed out that the settlement might next year be taken by those who had now the audacity, with so small a force, to approach its vicinity. He described in what manner the English ship might be taken where she now rode. This crime, or act of patriotism, was clearly brought home to the pilot, who was next morning hanged for doing his duty to his native country and sovereign.

Cavendish remained here nine days for the refreshment of the ship's company, and to obtain a store of provisions. Some singular customs are ascribed to the natives of Capul. They practised circumcision. By an opinion not rare "of the heathen" in those days, nor yet altogether exploded among persons better instructed than the early navigators, the islanders are alleged to have "wholly worshipped the devil, and oftentimes to have conference with him, who appeareth unto them in a most ugly, monstrous shape." On the 23rd January the captain-general caused the seven chiefs of this island, "and of a hundred islands more," to appear before him and pay him tribute in hogs, poultry, cocoas, and potatoes; at which ceremony he informed them of his country, spread the banner of England from his mast-head, and sounded the drums and trumpets. Due homage and submission were made to the representative of England and the enemy of Spain; and this being all that was required, the value of the tribute was paid back to the natives in money. The Indians, at parting, promised to assist the English in conquering the Spaniards at any future time, and, to amuse their new friends, showed feats of swift rowing round the ship. The general fired off a piece of ordnance as a farewell, and the new tributaries went away contented and pleased. The "hundred islands more" look like a flourish of the narrator, thickly as islands are clustered together at this place.

Next day they ran along the coast of Manilla, and on the 28th chased a frigate, which escaped into some inlet. Chase was given by the boat in those places which were so shallow that the ship could not approach. The crew was afterwards shot at by a party of Spanish soldiers from the shore; and a frigate was manned by them and sent in pursuit, which chased the English boat till within reach of the guns of the *Desire*. The boat's crew had previously made a Spaniard prisoner, whom they found in a canoe from which the natives escaped; and next day Cavendish sent a message by him to the captain of the Spanish party, who at different stations kept watch along the coast, desiring that officer to provide a good store of gold, as he intended to visit him at Manilla in a few years, and, if his boat had been larger, would have visited him then.

About the middle of February Cavendish passed

near the Moluccas, but did not touch at these islands. Fever now visited the ship's company, which had hitherto been very healthy; but only two of the men died, and one of these had long been sick, so that his death could not be attributed to the climate and the excessive heat which occasioned the illness of the others. On the 1st of March the *Desire* passed through the strait at the west end of Java Minor, and on the 5th anchored in a bay at the west end of Java Major. A negro found in the *Santa Anna* was able to converse with some natives who were here found fishing. Through this interpreter, who spoke the Morisco or Arabic language, they were informed that provisions might be obtained; and in a few days afterwards two or three canoes arrived laden with fowls, eggs, fresh fish, oranges, and limes. That the ship might be more conveniently victualled, they stood in nearer the town, and were visited by the king's secretary, who brought the general a present, including, among other things, " wine as strong as aqua vitæ, and as clear as rockwater." This distinguished official, who promised that the ship should be supplied in four days, was treated with all the magnificence that Cavendish could command. The wines and preserves of the Spanish prize were produced for his entertainment, and the English musicians exerted their skill. The secretary, who remained on board all night, saw the watch set and the guns fired off, and was informed that the ship's company were Englishmen, natives of a country which already traded with China, and that they were come hither for discovery and traffic. The Portuguese had already established a factory on the island, where they traded in cloves, pepper, sugar, slaves, and other merchandise of the East. Two of these Portuguese merchants afterwards visited the ship, eager to obtain news of their country and of Don Antonio their prince. They were informed that he was then in England, honourably entertained by the queen; and were delighted to hear of the havoc Cavendish had made among the Spanish shipping in the South Sea, as he told them that he was "warring upon them (the Spaniards) under the King of Portugal." The Europeans who met on this distant coast were mutually delighted with their short intercourse. Cavendish banqueted the Portuguese merchants, and entertained them with music as well as with political intelligence; and to him they described the riches of Java, and the most remarkable customs observed by the natives. The reigning king or rajah was named Bolamboam, and was reported to be one hundred and fifty years of age. He was held in great veneration by his subjects, none of whom durst trade with any nation without his license under pain of death. The old king had a hundred wives, and his son fifty. In Bolamboam the old voyagers give a perfect picture of an absolute prince. The Javans paid him unlimited obedience. Whatever he commanded, be the undertaking ever so dangerous or desperate, no one durst shrink from executing it; and their heads were the forfeit of their failure. They were "the bravest race in the south-east parts of the globe, never fearing death." The men were naked, and dark in colour; but the women were partly clothed, and in complexion much fairer. When the king died his body was burned, and the ashes were preserved. Five days afterwards his queen, or principal wife, threw a ball from her with which she was provided, and wherever it ran thither all the wives repaired. Each turned her face eastward, and, with a dagger as sharp as a razor, stabbed herself to the heart, and, bathed in her own blood, fell upon her face, and thus died. "This thing," we are assured, "is as true as it may seem to any hearer to be strange." The Portuguese factors, before parting with Cavendish, proposed that their acknowledged king, Don Antonio, should come out and here found an empire, which should comprehend the Moluccas, Ceylon, China, and the Philippines. They were assured that all the natives of these countries would declare for him. A kind reception was also promised to the English at their return; and Cavendish, having fully satisfied them for the supplies furnished to his ship, fired a parting salute of three guns, and on the 16th March sailed for the Cape of Good Hope.

The rest of this month and the month of April were spent "in traversing that mighty and vast sea between the island of Java and the main of Africa, observing the heavens, the Crosiers or South Pole, the other stars, and the fowls, which are marks unto seamen; fair weather, foul weather, approaching of lands or islands, the winds, tempests, the rains and thunders, with the alteration of the tides and currents." On the 10th of May a storm arose, and they were afterwards becalmed; and, in the thick hazy weather of the calm, mistook Cape False for the Cape of Good Hope, which they passed on the 16th, having run one thousand eight hundred and fifty leagues in nine weeks.

On the 8th June the island of St. Helena was seen, and on the 9th they anchored in the harbour. The description of this station, so important to navigators, would apply with perfect accuracy even at this day, so far as regards external appearance or the natural productions of that delicious resting-place, of which at that time the Portuguese still enjoyed sole possession. They had now held this island for upwards of eighty years; and, though it had never been regularly colonized, they had done much to store it with everything necessary to the refreshment of seamen on a long voyage. Already it abounded in all sorts of herbs, and in delicious fruits. Partridges, pheasants, turkeys, goats, and wild hogs, were also obtained in abundance.

At St. Helena Cavendish remained till the 20th, cleaning the ship, and obtaining refreshments, when the *Desire* once more got under way for England. About the end of August they passed the Azores, and on the 3rd September met a Flemish hulk from Lisbon, which informed them of the defeat of the Spanish Armada, to their "great rejoicing." In the Channel they were overtaken by the same terrible tempest that made such havoc among the Spanish ships which were driven round the coast of Ireland and to the north of Scotland; but were so fortunate as to complete the third circumnavigation of the globe at Plymouth on the 9th September, 1588,—two years and fifty days from the time they had left the same harbour, and in a considerably shorter time than either Magellan or Drake had made the same voyage.

Very copious nautical notes and remarks on this voyage were published by Mr. Thomas Fuller of Ipswich, the sailing-master of the *Desire*. They must have been of great value at the time, but have been superseded by more modern charts, in forming which, though the observations may not be more accurate, the navigators have had the advantage of more perfect instruments. The only geographical discovery made by Cavendish in this navigation was Port Desire, on the Patagonian coast, the landmarks of which Fuller has accurately described, though it has frequently been made the subject of dispute among modern voyagers.

The fame of the exploits of Cavendish, and of the great wealth which he had brought home, "enough to buy a fair earldom," almost rivalled the accounts of Drake's wonderful voyage. Among other rumours it was said that when he entered the harbour of Plymouth his sails were all of silk. In the tempest which overtook them in the Channel the sails were lost; and it is probable that Cavendish might have been compelled to employ some of his rich Indian damasks in the homely office of rigging his vessel; though it is conjectured, with more feasibility, that his new suit of sails was canvas fabricated of the silk-grass used in the South Seas, which, being very lustrous, might easily be mistaken for silk.

The earliest leisure of Cavendish was employed in writing to his patron, Lord Hunsdon, giving an account of his prosperous expedition. Whatever blame may in a more enlightened age be imputed to this navigator, for the wanton outrages committed on the Spanish settlements and on the subjects of Spain, he appears to have thought himself entitled to credit for their performance. Instead, therefore, of trying to conceal these deeds, in setting forth his services for her majesty, he makes them his boast; and doubtless they were highly esteemed. No better recapitulation of the events of this celebrated voyage can be found than that contained in his letter to Lord Hunsdon, an extract of which may form an appropriate conclusion to this chapter. "It hath pleased Almighty God," says the writer, "to suffer me to circumpass the whole globe of the world, entering in at the Strait of Magellan, and returning by the Cape de Buena Esperança; in which voyage I have either discovered or brought certain intelligence of all the rich places of the world which were ever discovered by any Christian. I navigated along the coast of Chili, Peru, and New Spain, where I made great spoils. I burned and sunk nineteen sails of ships small and great. All the villages and towns that ever I landed at I burned and spoiled. And had I not been discovered upon the coast, I had taken great quantity of treasure. The matter of most profit unto me was a great ship of the king's, which I took at California; which ship came from the Philippines, being one of the richest of merchandise that ever passed those seas......From the Cape of California, being the uttermost part of all New Spain, I navigated to the islands of the Philippines, hard upon the coast of China, of which country I have brought such intelligence as hath not been heard of in these parts; the stateliness and riches of which I fear to make report of, lest I should not be credited......I found out by the way homeward the island of Santa Helena, where the Portuguese used to relieve themselves; and from that island God hath suffered me to return into England. All which services, with myself, I humbly prostrate at her majesty's feet, desiring the Almighty long to continue her reign among us; for at this day she is the most famous and victorious princess that liveth in the world."

CHAPTER II.

SECOND VOYAGE TO THE SOUTH SEA.

THE second and final expedition of Cavendish to the South Sea was as remarkable for ill fortune as his first voyage had been distinguished by uninterrupted prosperity. This fortunate voyage, however, which gave such strong confirmation to the hopes excited by the adventure of Drake, encouraged many to a similar attempt, and during the two years following his return several expeditions were fitted out from England, though none of them proved successful.

In three years after his return, Cavendish having, according to some accounts, spent the greater part of the riches he had acquired in the South Sea, planned an expedition for China by Magellan Strait, and upon an extensive scale. It is asserted, with as much probability, that his wealth was laid out in equipping the new squadron, with which he put to sea on the 26th August 1591. It consisted of "three tall ships" and two barks. As admiral of the fleet Cavendish sailed in the *Leicester* galleon; and his old ship, the *Desire*, was commanded by the celebrated pilot, navigator, and fortunate discoverer, Captain John Davis. The *Roebuck*, commanded by Mr. Cook, the *Black Pinnace*, and a small bark named the *Dainty*, which belonged to Mr. Adrian Gilbert, a gentleman of Devonshire, who had been among the promoters of the discovery of the North-west Passage, completed the fleet. The two Japanese youths, captured in the Acapulco ship on the former voyage, accompanied Cavendish in this.

Under the equinoctial line they were becalmed for twenty-seven days, burning beneath a hot sun, and exposed to the deadly night-vapours, which threw many of the men into the scurvy. Their first capture was a Portuguese vessel, on the 2nd December, off the coast of Brazil. It was laden with sugar, small-wares, and slaves.

On the 5th they pillaged Placenzia, a small Portuguese settlement; and on the 16th surprised the town of Santos, where the inhabitants were at Mass when the party landed. Though Cavendish, both from principle and from natural disposition, never lost an opportunity of spoiling the enemy, the object of this attack was to obtain provisions; but this design, from the negligence of the captain of the *Roebuck*, was completely frustrated. The Indians carried everything away; and next day the prisoners in the church were either set free or contrived to escape, four old men being retained as hostages till the supplies came in. They never appeared; and the consequence of mismanagement and delay was, that in lying five weeks before this place the provisions were wasted which should have sustained them in passing the Strait, and the voyage was delayed, by this and other causes, till they found themselves, in the beginning of the southern winter, distant from the Strait, and short of stores.

On the 22nd January they left Santos, burned St. Vincent on the 23rd, and next day bore for the Strait of Magellan; Port Desire, which Cavendish had discovered on his former voyage, being appointed as a rendezvous in case of separation. On the 7th February the fleet was overtaken by a violent gale, and next day they were separated. Davis, in the *Desire*, made for the appointed harbour, and on the way fell in with the *Roebuck*, which had suffered dreadfully. On the 6th of March these two ships reached Port Desire together, and in ten days afterwards were joined by the *Black Pinnace*. The *Dainty*, the volunteer bark, returned to England, having stored herself with sugar at Santos while the other ships lay idle: her captain was in the meanwhile on board the *Roebuck*, and was left without anything save the clothes which he wore.

In the gale, which scarcely abated from the 7th of February to the middle of March, Cavendish suffered severely, and his officers and men had shown a disposition to mutiny; so that, on rejoining the other ships on the 18th, he left the *Leicester* galleon in displeasure, and remained in the *Desire* with Captain

Davis. Cavendish did not at this time complain more bitterly of the gentlemen of his own ship than he afterwards violently accused Davis of having betrayed and abandoned him. His subsequent misfortunes affected his temper, and, it may be presumed, perverted his sense of justice. Though his company had not recovered from the excessive fatigue and exhaustion caused by the late continued tempest, the galleon sailed with the fleet on the 20th, and after enduring fresh storms all the ships made the Strait on the 8th April, and on the 14th passed in. In two days they had beat inward only ten leagues.

An account is given in Purchas's Pilgrims of this most disastrous voyage, drawn up at sea by Cavendish in his last illness. It is addressed to Sir Tristram Gorges, whom the unfortunate navigator appointed his executor, and is one of the most affecting narratives that ever was written,—the confession, wrung in bitterness of heart, from a high-spirited, proud, and headstrong man, who having set his all upon a cast, and finding himself undone, endured the deeper mortification of believing he had been the dupe of those he implicitly trusted. Though we cannot admit the force of many of his allegations, nor the justice of his unmeasured invective, it is impossible to withhold sympathy from his extreme distress. " We had been almost four months," says this melancholy relation, "between the coast of Brazil and the Strait, being in distance not above six hundred leagues, which is commonly run in twenty or thirty days; but such was the adverseness of our fortune, that in coming thither we spent the summer, and found the Strait, in the beginning of a most extreme winter, not durable for Christians......After the month of May was come in, nothing but such flights of snow, and extremity of frosts, as in all my life I never saw any to be compared with them. This extremity caused the weak men (in my ship only) to decay; for in seven or eight days in this extremity, there died forty men and sickened seventy, so that there were not fifteen men able to stand upon the hatches." Another relation of the voyage, written by Mr. John Jane, a friend of Captain Davis, even deepens this picture of distress. The squadron, beating for above a week against the wind into the Strait, and in all that time advancing only fifty leagues, now lay in a sheltered cove on the south side of the passage, and nearly opposite Cape Froward, where they remained till the 15th May, a period of extreme suffering. "In this time," says Jane, "we endured extreme storms with perpetual snow, where many of our men died of cursed famine and miserable cold, not having wherewith to cover their bodies, nor to fill their belly, but living by mussels, water, and weeds of the sea, with a small relief from the ship's stores of meal sometimes." Nor was this the worst. "All the sick men in the galleon were most uncharitably put on shore into the woods, in the snow, wind, and cold, when men of good health could scarcely endure it, where they ended their lives in the highest degree of misery." Though Cavendish was still on board the *Desire*, it is impossible to free him of the blame of this inhuman abandonment of the sick. A consultation was now held, at which Davis, who had had great experience of the severities of the seasons in his north-west voyages, declared for pushing forward, as the weather must speedily improve; while Cavendish preferred the attempt of reaching China by doubling the Cape of Good Hope. For this voyage, however, the other commanders thought there were neither provisions nor equipments. At length, on a petition by the whole company being presented to Cavendish, he agreed to return to the coast of Brazil for supplies, and, thus furnished, again to attempt the Strait.

On the 15th May they accordingly sailed eastward, and on the midnight of the 20th, Davis in the *Desire*, and the *Black Pinnace*, were separated from the galleon, to which Cavendish had now returned. They never met again, and Cavendish, to the last moment of his unhappy life, accused Davis of having wilfully abandoned him. This treacherous desertion, if such it was, —and by the friends of Davis it is strenuously denied, —took place in the latitude of Port Desire, for which harbour Davis stood in, and also the *Black Pinnace*, expecting, as they at least pretended, to find the general. Here they took in water, and obtained at ebb-tide mussels, and with hooks made of pins caught smelts, and thus spared their slender stock of provisions.

An effort made by Davis to go in search of the captain-general in the pinnace was overruled, it is alleged, by the ship's company, who would not permit its departure. They are even charged with open mutiny, and two ringleaders are named.

To clear himself of all suspicion, Davis, on the 2nd June, drew up a relation of the voyage, of the separation, and of the state of the two ships lying here, which all the men subscribed. It certainly goes far to exonerate him. They remained in Port Desire till the 6th of August, keeping watch on the hills for the galleon and the *Roebuck;* one part of the company foraging for provisions of any kind that could be obtained, while others made nails, bolts, and ropes from an old cable, and thus supplied their wants in the best manner they could devise. There are, however, surmises that all this labour was undertaken that Davis might be able to accomplish his great object of passing the Strait, whatever became of the general, and whatever might have been his wishes or orders. After this refitting was accomplished, it was accordingly resolved to await the coming of Cavendish in the Strait, for which, having at Penguin Isle salted twenty hogsheads of seals, they sailed on the night of the 7th August, "the poorest wretches that ever were created."

Several times they obtained a sight of the South Sea, but were driven back into the Strait. While tossed about, they were on the 14th driven in "among certain islands never before discovered by any known relation, lying fifty leagues or better off the shore, east and northerly from the Strait." These were the Falkland Islands, of which Captain Davis certainly has the honour of being the original discoverer, as he had already been of the Strait which still goes by his name, and of other ports in the North Seas. This discovery was shortly afterwards claimed by Sir Richard Hawkins, who gave these islands the name of Hawkins's Maiden Land, "for that it was discovered in the reign of Queen Elizabeth, my sovereign lady, and a maiden queen." The discovery of these islands has been claimed by the navigators of other countries, and a variety of names have been imposed upon them. Burney christens them anew, " Davis's Southern Islands,"—a distinction to which that celebrated navigator is fully entitled, though it will not be easy to change a name so established as that of the Falkland Islands. On the 2nd October they got into the South Sea once more, and in the same night encountered a severe gale, which continued with unabated violence for many days. On the 4th the pinnace was lost: on the 5th the fore-sail was split and all torn; "and the mizzen was brought to the fore-mast to make our ship work, the storm continuing beyond all description in fury, with hail, snow, rain, and wind, such and so mighty as that in nature it could not possibly be more; the sea such and so lofty, with continual breach, that many times we were doubtful whether our ship did sink or swim." The relation proceeds thus with earnest pathetic simplicity:—" The 10th of October, being, by the account of our captain and master, very near the shore, the weather dark, the storm furious, and most of our men having given over to travail, we yielded ourselves to death without further hope of succour. Our captain (Davis) sitting in the gallery very pensive, I came and brought him some *Rosa Solis* to comfort him; for he was so cold he was scarce able to move a joint. After he had drunk, and was comforted in heart, he began for the case of his conscience to make a large repetition of his forepassed time, and with many grievous sighs he concluded in these words:— 'Oh most glorious God, with whose power the mightiest things among men are matters of no moment, I most humbly beseech thee, that the intolerable burden of my sins may through the blood of Jesus Christ be taken from me; and end our days with speed, or show us some merciful sign of thy love and our preservation.' Having thus ended, he desired me not to make known to the company his intolerable grief and anguish of mind, because they should not thereby be dismayed; and so, suddenly before I went from him, the sun shined clear; so that he and the master both observed the true elevation of the Pole, whereby they knew by what course to recover the Strait." The narrative goes on to relate a wonderful instance of preservation in doubling a cape at the mouth of the Strait on the 11th of October.

They at last put back into the Strait in a most pitiable condition, the men "with their sinews stiff, their flesh dead," and in a state too horrible to be described. They found shelter and rest in a cove for a few days, but famine urged them on, and the weather, after a short interval of calm, became as stormy as before. "The storm growing outrageous, our men could scarcely stand by their labour; and the Strait being full of turning reaches, we were constrained, by the discretion of the captain and master in their accounts, to guide the ship in the hell-dark night when we could not see any shore." In this extremity they got back to Port Desire, and obtained wood and water; and in Penguin Island found abundance of birds. One day, while most of the men were absent on their several duties, a multitude of the natives showed themselves, throwing dust upon their heads, "leaping and running like brute beasts, having vizards on their faces like dogs' faces, or else their faces are dogs' faces indeed. We greatly feared lest they should set the ship on fire, for they would suddenly make fire, whereat we much marvelled. They came to windward of our ship, and set the bushes on fire, so that we were in a very stinking smoke; but as soon as they came within reach of our shot we shot at them, and striking one of them in the thigh they all presently fled, and we never saw them more." At this place a party of nine men were killed by the Indians, or were presumed to be so, as they went on shore, and were never again heard of.

The relation points out that "these were the mutineers, and this the place at which they had formerly devised mischief" against Davis and his officers. Here they made salt by pouring salt water in the hollows of the rocks, which in six days was granulated from evaporation by the heat of the sun. They found abundance of food in eggs, penguins, seals, and young gulls; and with train-oil fried scurvy-grass with eggs, "which (herb) took away all kinds of swellings, whereof many had died, and restored us to perfect health of body, so that we were in as good case as when we left England." —"Thus God did feed us as it were with manna from heaven."

On the 22nd December they sailed for Brazil with a stock of fourteen thousand dried penguins, of which they had an ample allowance, though their other provision was scantily dealt out. In the beginning of February, in attempting by violence to obtain some provisions at the Isle of Placenzia, on the coast of Brazil, thirteen of the men were killed by the Indians and Portuguese; and of an original company of seventy only twenty-seven were now left in the *Desire*. They were again the sport of baffling winds; the water ran short; and in the warm latitudes the penguins, their sole dependence for food, began to corrupt, "and ugly loathsome worms of an inch long were bred in them." The account of this plague is painfully striking. "This worm did so mightily increase, and devour our victuals, that there was in reason no hope how we should avoid famine, but be devoured of the wicked creatures. There was nothing that they did not devour, iron only excepted—our clothes, hats, boots, shirts, and stockings. And for the ship, they did eat the timbers; so that we greatly feared they would undo us by eating through the ship's side. Great was the care and diligence of our captain, master, and company to consume these vermin; but the more we laboured to kill them, the more they increased upon us, so that at last we could not sleep for them, for they would eat our flesh like mosquitoes." The men now fell into strange and horrible diseases, and some became raging mad. A supply of water was, however, obtained from the heavy rains which fell; and this was the only solace of this most miserable voyage. Eleven died between the coast of Brazil and Bear Haven in Ireland; and of the sixteen that survived only five were able to work the ship. If the design of Davis had been treacherously to abandon Mr. Cavendish, he was subjected to speedy and severe retribution.

To this unfortunate commander we must now return; and brief space may suffice to relate a series of calamities which might weary the attention and exhaust the sympathies of even the most compassionate reader. The conjecture which Cavendish formed of the proceedings of Davis and the captain of the *Black Pinnace* was perfectly correct. He states in his letter that he believed they would return to Port Desire—a safe place of anchorage for ships of small burden, though not such as he could safely approach—and there refresh themselves, lay in a store of seals and birds, and seize a favourable season to pass the Strait. And they did so. In speaking of Davis, and of his conduct, Cavendish exclaims: "And now to come to that villain, that hath been the death of me and the decay of this whole action—I mean Davis—whose only treachery in running from me hath been utter ruin of all, if any good return by him, as ever you love me, make such friends, as he, least of all others, may reap least gain. I assure myself you will be careful in all friendship of my last requests. My debts which be owing be not much; but I (most unfortunate villain!) was matched with the most abject-minded and mutinous company that ever was carried out of England by any man living."—"The short of all is this—Davis's only intent was utterly to overthrow me, which he hath well performed."

After the *Desire* and the *Black Pinnace* separated from the fleet, the *Leicester* galleon and *Roebuck* shaped their course for Brazil, keeping sight of each other. In 36° S. they encountered a dreadful storm, and were parted. For some time the galleon lay at anchor in the Bay of St. Vincent; and while here a party, almost in open defiance of the orders of Cavendish, landed to forage for provisions, and plunder the houses of the Portuguese farmers on the coast. They were wholly cut off, to the number of twenty-four men and an officer; and the only boat which Cavendish had now left was thus lost.

The *Roebuck*, about this time, returned without masts or sails, and "in the most miserable case ever ship was in." The captain-general felt the want of the boats and pinnace doubly severe, from being unable in the larger ships to enter the harbours, which were often barred, to be revenged on the "base dogs" who had killed his men. At some risk he made an attempt to go up the river before the town, that he might have the gratification of razing it; but was compelled by his company to desist from an attempt which "was both desperate and most dangerous." With some difficulty they got back into deep water, and with the boat of the *Roebuck*, and a crazy boat seized from the Portuguese, a party landed which destroyed a few of the farm-houses and got some provisions. It was now the intention of Cavendish to break up the *Roebuck*, and with the *Leicester* galleon, as Davis never appeared, return to the Strait alone. But of this purpose he did not venture to inform his company, lest they might have broken out into open mutiny. So great was their horror of returning, "that all of the better sort," he says, "had taken an oath upon the Bible to die rather than go back." St. Helena was therefore the point now talked of; and in the meanwhile an attempt was made to seize three Portuguese ships in the harbour of Spirito Santo. The plan of attack was unsuccessful. Of eighty armed men who left the ship on this ill-starred expedition, about thirty-eight were killed and forty wounded. Among the killed was Captain Morgan, an officer whom Cavendish highly esteemed, who in this expedition was taunted into the commission of acts of foolhardy daring by the insulting speeches of those whom he led; a weakness which, despite of their better judgment, has often proved fatal to brave men, as well as to the rash persons themselves whose ignorance and vanity tempt them to become the critics and censors of enterprises of which they cannot comprehend the danger. Inability to endure the imputation of cowardice is indeed one of the most lamentable infirmities of noble minds. On the present occasion some of the seamen swore "that they never thought other than that Morgan was a coward that durst not land upon a bauble ditch;" upon which, wilfully running upon what he saw to be certain destruction, he declared that he would land happen what would, and though against the counsel of his commander, who remained in the ship. The consequences have been told.

One circumstance strongly moved the generous indignation of Cavendish. A party with the great boat called to another, which were attempting to storm a fort, to come and help them to hasten off, as they were exposed to a galling fire. The numbers that rushed into the boat ran her aground, and ten men were obliged to leave her, who, to save themselves from the Indian arrows which flew thick, again ran in under the fort, and poured in a volley of musketry. Meanwhile the boat was got afloat, "and one that was master of the *Roebuck* (the most cowardly villain that ever was born of a woman), caused them in the boat to row away, and so left those brave men a spoil for the Portugals. Yet they waded up to their necks in the water to them; but those merciless villains in the boat would have no pity on them. Their excuse was, that the boat was so full of water, that had they come in she would have sunk with them all in her. Thus vilely were those poor men lost."

By the fatal adventure which he has thus narrated, Cavendish, already in want of every necessary, was left with hardly as many efficient men as could raise the anchor. To add to his already accumulated misfortunes, the *Roebuck* forsook him, the company of that ship being resolved to return home; and though the wounded lay in his vessel, they carried off the two surgeons and a great part of the common stores. In these distressing circumstances he got to the small uninhabited island of St. Sebastian, where he mended the old boats, and obtained a seasonable supply of water, of which they were in great want. Again Cavendish spoke of returning to the Strait, and used all the arts of persuasion with his company; but in vain. He showed them that they could "relieve themselves by salting seals and birds, etc.; and further, should they get through the Strait (which they might easily perform, considering they had the chiefest part of the summer before them), they could not but make a most rich voyage; and that we should be the most infamous in the world, being within six hundred leagues of the place where we so much desired—to return home again so far being most infamous and beggarly. These persuasions," continues Cavendish, "took no place with them; but most boldly they all affirmed that they had sworn they would never again go to the Strait; neither by no means would they. And one of the chiefest of this faction most proudly and stubbornly uttered these words to my face, in presence of all the rest; which I seeing, and finding mine own faction to be so weak (for there were not any favoured my side but my poor cousin Locke, and the master of the ship), I took this bold companion by the bosom, and with mine own hands put a rope about his neck, meaning resolutely to strangle him, for weapon about me I had none. His companions seeing one of their chief champions in this case, and perceiving me go roundly to work with him, they all came to the master and desired him to speak, affirming they would all be ready to take any course I thought good of; so I, hearing this, stayed myself, and let the fellow go."

Having now boldly avowed his intention of returning to the Strait, Cavendish landed on the island with a party of his soldiers and the carpenters, to new-build the boat, while the sailors on board mended and patched up the rigging and tackle of the ship. But he still suspected his men of treachery, and of the intention of deserting, and was in constant anxiety to get them once more on board, that the ship might depart for the

Strait. Before this could be accomplished, Cavendish, whom fortune never wearied of persecuting, sustained another severe mischance. The wounded men were on shore on the island, which lay about a mile from the mainland, from whence the Portuguese watched all the proceedings of the ship's company during the building of the boat. Before all the wood and water were got in, and while some soldiers and seamen were still on the island, an Irishman, "a noble villain," contrived to go over to the continent upon a raft, and betray his defenceless comrades to the Portuguese. This was done in the night-time; and besides those employed on the island and the sick, there chanced to be several men ashore, who frequently stole away from the ship at night to enjoy the freedom of the land. All were indiscriminately butchered. One of the few remaining sails which lay here was also seized, and in their distressed circumstances proved another serious loss. "Thus," says the luckless adventurer, "I was forced to depart, Fortune never ceasing to lay her greatest adversities upon me. And now I am grown so weak that I am scarce able to hold the pen in my hand; wherefore I must leave you to inquire of the rest of our most unhappy proceedings. But know this, that for the Strait I could by no means get my company to give their consent to go. In truth, I desired nothing more than to attempt that course, rather desiring to die in going forward than basely in returning back again; but God would not suffer me to die so happy a man."

These " unhappy proceedings " to which he refers may, so far as they are known, be very briefly noticed. An attempt was made to reach the island of St. Helena, for which the company had reluctantly consented to steer only on Cavendish solemnly declaring that to England he would never go, and that, if they refused to take such courses as he intended, the "ship and all should sink in the seas together." This for a time made them more tractable; but having beat to the 20° S. they refused to proceed further, choosing rather to die where they were "than be starved in searching for an island which could never be found again." They were, however, once more induced to proceed southward, and in dreadful weather beat back to 28° S., and stood for St. Helena, which was most unhappily missed, owing to contrary winds and the unskilfulness of the sailing-master. One more effort this unfortunate commander made to induce his mutinous crew to regain the island, alarming them with the scarcity of provisions; but they unanimously replied, "that they would be perished to death rather than not make for England."

It is believed that Cavendish did not long survive the events recorded above; and it is certain that he died before the ship reached England. His letter, from which we have quoted, was not closed when the galleon reached 8° N. From its commencement —and it must have been written at many different sittings—Cavendish had considered himself a dying man. It opens with great tenderness :—" Most loving friend, there is nothing in this world that makes a truer trial of friendship than at death to show mindfulness of love and friendship, which now you shall make a perfect experience of; desiring you to hold my love as dear dying poor as if I had been most infinitely rich. The success of this most unfortunate action, the bitter torments whereof lie so heavy upon me, as with much pain am I able to write these few lines, much less to make discourse to you of all the adverse haps that have befallen me in this voyage, the least whereof is my death." He adverts to the illness of "a most true friend, whom to name my heart bleeds," who, like himself, became the victim of the complicated distresses of this voyage. After the crowning misfortune of missing St. Helena, he says :—" And now to tell you of my greatest grief, which was the sickness of my dear kinsman John Locke, who by this time was grown in great weakness, by reason whereof he desired rather quietness and contentedness in our course than such continual disquietness as never ceased me. And now by this, what with grief for him and the continual trouble I endured among such hell-hounds, my spirits were clean spent, wishing myself upon any desert place in the world, there to die, rather than thus basely return home again. Which course, I swear to you, I had put in execution, had I found an island which the cardes (charts) make to be in 8° S. of the line. I swear to you I sought it with all diligence, meaning there to have ended my most unfortunate life. But God suffered not such happiness to light upon me, for I could by no means find it; so, as I was forced to go towards England, and having got eight degrees by the north of the Line, I lost my most dearest cousin. And now consider whether a heart made of flesh be able to endure so many misfortunes, all falling upon me without intermission. And I thank my God, that in ending me he hath pleased to rid me of all further troubles and mishaps." The rest of the letter refers to his private concerns, and especially to the discharge of his debts and the arrangement of his affairs for this purpose—an act of friendship which he expected from the kindness of the gentleman he addressed. It then takes an affecting farewell of life and of the friend for whom he cherished so warm an affection.

In his two voyages Cavendish experienced the greatest extremes of fortune, his first adventure being even more brilliant and successful than the last (chiefly through the bad discipline and evil dispositions of his company) was disastrous and unhappy. Cavendish was still very young when he died. No naval commander ever more certainly sunk under the disease to which so many brave men have fallen victims—a broken heart. In many things his conduct discovered the rashness and impetuosity of youth, and the want of that temper and self-command which are among the first qualities of a naval chief. The reproach of cruelty, or at least of culpable indifference to the claims of humanity, which, from transactions in both voyages, and especially in the first, must rest upon his memory, ought in justice to be shared with the age in which he lived, and the state of moral feeling among the class to which he belonged by birth. By the aristocracy, "the vulgar," "the common sort," were still regarded as creatures of a different and inferior species; while among seamen the destruction of Spaniards and "Portugals" was regarded as a positive virtue. By all classes, negroes, Indians, and Gentiles were held in no more esteem than brute animals—human life as existing in beings so abject being regarded as of no value whatever. But if Cavendish was tinged with the faults of his class, he partook largely of its virtues —high spirit, courage, and intrepidity. Those who might be led to judge of some points of his conduct with strictness, will be disposed to lenity by the recollection of his sufferings. As an English navigator his name is imperishable. On the authority of the accurate and veracious Stowe, we may in conclusion state that Thomas Cavendish "was of a delicate wit and personage."

DAMPIER.

DAMPIER.

CHAPTER I.

THE BUCCANEERS OF AMERICA.

CAPTAIN WILLIAM DAMPIER, the remarkable person whose eventful life forms the subject of the remaining portion of this volume, was so long and so intimately associated with the buccaneers of America, that an account of this extraordinary brotherhood forms an almost indispensable introduction to the adventures and discoveries of this eminent navigator.

The buccaneers owed their origin to the monopolizing spirit and selfish and jealous policy with which Spain administered the affairs of her West India colonies. Early in the sixteenth century, both English and French ships, bound on trafficking adventures, had found their way to these settlements; but it was not till after the enterprises of Drake, Raleigh, and Cumberland that they became frequent. The jealousy of Spain had been alarmed by their first appearance; and the adoption of that system of offensive interference with the vessels of every nation that ventured near the tropic, soon gave rise to the well-known maxim of the buccaneers—" No peace beyond the Line."

Though the name—

"Linked to one virtue and a thousand crimes"—

by which the freebooters came to be distinguished, is of much later date than the era of Drake and his daring follower John Oxnam, there is no great violation of historical truth in ascribing to them the character which it signified, of indiscriminate plunderers of the Spaniards by sea and land, and in peace as well as in war.

To the gradual rise of the extraordinary association, of which Drake and Oxnam were only the precursors, many causes contributed. The diminished population and decayed manufactures of Old Spain could no longer supply her wealthy and rapidly-increasing settlements with those commodities which the West Indies and South America still continue to receive from the workshops and looms of France, England, and the Low Countries; nor could the strictness and severity of the Spanish laws for regulating trade prevent the settlers on many parts of the coast and the islands from cheaply supplying themselves with luxuries and necessaries brought direct from these countries. Thus the contraband trade, eagerly followed by the ships of England, France, and Holland, and encouraged by the colonists, increased in defiance of prohibitions and of *guarda costas*, as the ships

WILLIAM DAMPIER. *Page 197.*

armed to protect the exclusive commerce of Spain were named, and became a thriving seminary for the growth of maritime freebooters, self-defence leading the contraband traders to retaliation, injustice to reprisal, and spoliation to actual piracy.

Another collateral branch of the buccaneering system sprung up at the same time in a different quarter. No portion of the New World had suffered more from the injustice and enormous cruelty of the Spaniards than the fine islands of Cuba and Hispaniola. About the beginning of the sixteenth century, the mines and plantations of these islands had been abandoned for the more productive new settlements and richer mines of Mexico; and the desolated and depopulated tracts, from which the aboriginal inhabitants had been extirpated, were soon overrun by immense herds of cattle, which, originally introduced by the Spaniards, had multiplied so rapidly that it was become a profitable employment to hunt them for the hides and tallow alone. While the *matadores*, or Spanish hunters, pursued this avocation, a more peaceful description of settlers began to form plantations around them, and to both classes the stolen visits of the French and English traders became every year more welcome. From trafficking on the coast, and occasionally foraging for provisions for their vessels on these uninhabited shores, the smugglers from time to time adopted the hunter's life, and ranged at will, though regarded by the Spanish government and settlers as interlopers.

The first predatory hunters of Cuba and Hispaniola, if men following the chase in a desert may be so harshly termed, were natives of France. From the customs connected with their vocation in the woods arose the formidable name of *Buccaneer*, by which the association came to be distinguished, whether pirates or forayers, on shore or in the wilderness. The term was adopted from the Carib Indians, who called the flesh which they prepared *boucan*, and gave the hut, where it was slowly dried and smoked on wooden hurdles or barbecues, the same appellation. To the title by which the desperadoes of England were known the French preferred the name of *Flibustier*, said to be a corruption of the English word "freebooter." The Dutch named the natives of their country employed in this lawless mode of life *Sea-rovers*. *Brethren of the Coast* was another general denomination for this fraternity of pirates and outlaws; till all distinctions were finally lost in the title of Buccaneers of America. But the same feeling which induced men of respectable family to lay aside their real names on entering this association, led others of them to sweeten their imaginations with a term less intimately allied with every species of crime and excess; and Dampier, among others, always spoke of the individual members of the brotherhood as "privateers," while their vocation of piracy was named "privateering."

The depredations of this fortuitous assemblage of bold and dissolute men had been carried on in time of

INDIANS BUCCANING A TAPIR.

Page 202.

peace as hunters, smugglers, and pirates, and in time of war as privateers holding commissions from their respective countries, for a long series of years before they attempted to form any regular settlement. During this time they had acted as the rude pioneers of the European states to which they respectively belonged, clearing the way for the industrious and peaceful settlers of France and England, both of which countries secretly cherished, while they ostentatiously disclaimed, the buccaneers. From the era of the discovery of Columbus, both of these nations had cast longing eyes upon the West India Islands, and if not under the auspices, yet by the assistance of their bold though lawless offspring the buccaneers, settlements were at last effected. At the beginning of the seventeenth century, a point on which to rest their levers was all that was required; and by a previous treaty of joint occupation and partition, the French and English, in 1625, on the same day, landed at opposite points of the island of St. Christopher, and took possession. The rights of the Caribs, whom the Spaniards had neither been able to enslave nor wholly to extirpate, do not appear to have obtained a moment's consideration from the statesmen of either France or England. Though the Spaniards had no settlement upon this island themselves, their policy and interests did not quietly permit the natives of two active and industrious nations to obtain a permanent footing at a point whence they might quickly extend their territory; and instead of patiently waiting the result of misunderstanding between the colonists, which would more effectually have fought their battle, in 1629 they expelled the intruders by force of arms, after a residence of above three years. The settlers only waited the departure of the Spanish armament to return to their old possessions, though some of them, thus cruelly expelled from their newformed homes, and rendered desperate by poverty and hatred of the Spaniards, had meanwhile augmented the bands of the freebooters, and to the reckless bravery of these lawless vagabonds brought their own knowledge and experience, and the habits of social life.

It was thus that step by step the narrow policy and oppression of the Spaniards raised up those predatory hordes, haunting the ocean and the coasts, which, from infringing their absurd commercial laws, or shooting a wild bullock in the forests, came at last continually to infest their trade, and to destroy and pillage their richest settlements.

As a convenient mart for their trade, which had been prodigiously increased by the settlement of St. Christopher and other causes, the hunters of Hispaniola and Cuba seized the island of Tortuga by surprising the small Spanish garrison which defended it, and here built magazines for their hides, tallow, and *boucan* or dried meat, established their headquarters, and opened a place of retreat for all buccaneers. In the course of a few years European adventurers of every nation save Spain flocked to Tortuga; and

French and English settlements were rapidly planted, almost at random, on different islands, the new colonists being the natural allies and also the best customers of the buccaneers, whom they on the other hand supplied with powder, shot, rum, tobacco, hatchets, and everything necessary to their wild and irregular mode of life. As these new colonies rose into consequence, they were severally claimed by the mother-country of the settlers, who, whether French or English, were not unfrequently turned out to make way for new proprietors who had been able iniquitously to obtain or purchase, from the venal government at home, the lands cleared and improved by the industry of the original adventurers. Many of the French settlers, indignant at the unmerited injustice of their distant government, who had left them unprotected in the first instance and pillaged them in the last, retired to other deserts, or joined the ranks of their friends the buccaneers.

The buccaneer settlement of Tortuga, situated at the very threshold of Hispaniola, was on every account obnoxious to the Spaniards, who took the first opportunity of destroying it. This was effected while the boldest of the population were absent in the chase, which they often followed for months and even years together on the western shores of Hispaniola, without once visiting the scene of comparative civilization which they had created on the smaller island. Of the more peaceful of the settlers of Tortuga, who had already formed plantations, and begun with success to cultivate tobacco, which turned out of excellent quality, many were massacred; those who fled to the woods and afterwards surrendered themselves were hanged; while only a few escaped to their brethren in the forests of Hispaniola. Thus every new occurrence tended to inflame the mutual hatred which had so long subsisted between the Spaniards and all other Europeans, and to propagate outrage. Tortuga was soon abandoned by the Spaniards, who took so much pains to destroy the nest that they flattered themselves the hornets would not again congregate. In this they were deceived. The buccaneers returned almost immediately, and became more formidable than ever, giving Spain a practical lesson on the impolicy of converting those who were in the fair way of becoming peaceful and industrious neighbours into active enemies, regularly banded and organized, and cordially united against a common foe.

Above three hundred of the hunters returned to Tortuga after it had been thus desolated and abandoned by the Spaniards; and their ranks were speedily recruited by constant levies of the young, the brave, and the enterprising of different European countries.

From about this time cruising upon the Spaniards became more and more frequent, and as the diminished number of cattle made the chase a less profitable occupation, piratical excursions increased, and became more bold and alarming. The Brethren of the Coast had now been long known as a distinct association, and their laws, manners, and customs had become the subject of speculation and curiosity. Though their peculiarities have been egregiously magnified by the natural love of the marvellous, from which even philosophic historians are not altogether exempt, many of their customs were sufficiently remarkable to deserve notice. Like the laws and customs of other communities, the "statutes of the buccaneers" originated in the necessities and exigencies of their condition. Property, so far as regarded the means of sustenance, whether obtained in the chase or by pillage, was in common among this hardy brotherhood; and as they had no domestic ties, neither wife nor child, brother nor sister being known among the buccaneers, the want of family relations was supplied by strict comradeship, one partner occasionally attending to household duties while the other was engaged in the chase. It has been said that the surviving partner in this firm, whether seaman or hunter, became the general heir; and this was probably often the case, though not a fixed law, as the buccaneers frequently bequeathed property to their relatives in France or England. Their chief virtue was courage, which, urged by desperation, was often carried to an extreme unparalleled among other warlike associations. The fear of the gallows, which has frequently converted the thief into a murderer, made the buccaneer a hero and a savage. Hardihood, the habit and the power of extreme endurance, might also, if exerted in a better cause, be reckoned among the virtues of the buccaneers, had not their long seasons of entire privation been always followed by scenes of the most brutal excess. Their grand principle, the one thing needful to their existence, was fidelity; and so far, at least, as regarded the Spaniards, the maxim of "Honour among thieves" was never more scrupulously observed than among them. As their associations were voluntary, their engagements never extended beyond the cruise or enterprise on hand, though they were frequently renewed. The ablest, the most brave, active, fortunate, and intriguing of their number, was elected their commander; but all the fighting-men appear to have assisted at councils. The same power which chose their leader could displace him, which was frequently done, either from caprice or expediency. They sometimes settled personal quarrels by duel; but offences against the fraternity were visited by different punishments, as in extreme cases death, abandonment on a desert island, or simply banishment from the society. There appears to have been no obstacle to voluntarily quitting the brotherhood as often as inclination dictated such a step. Many of the peculiar habits of the buccaneers are so fully detailed in the adventures of Dampier, that it is unnecessary to expatiate upon them in this place. In the division of their booty, one main concern of all banditti, they appear, as soon as buccaneering became a system, to have followed nearly the same laws which regulate privateers; the owners' shares being of course included in those of the company, who were themselves the owners. A party being agreed upon a cruise, the day and place for embarkation were fixed, and every man repaired on board the ship with a specified quantity of powder and shot. The next concern was to procure provisions, which consisted mostly of pork. Many of the Spaniards raised large herds of swine for the supply of the planters, and from their yards abundance was procured with no trouble save that in which the ferocious buccaneers delighted—robbery often accompanied by murder. Turtle slightly salted was another article of the food which they stored; and for beeves and wild hogs they trusted to their fire-arms. Bread they seldom tasted, and at sea never thought about, though in later periods they sometimes procured supplies of cassada, maize, and potatoes. Of this food every man ate generally twice a day, or at his own pleasure, and without limitation, there being in this respect no distinction between the commander and the meanest seaman. The vessel fairly victualled, a final council was held, which determined the destination of the cruise and the plan of operations; and articles were generally drawn up and subscribed, which regulated the division of the spoils. The carpenter, the sail-maker, the surgeon, and the commander, were in the first place paid out of the common stock. Wounds were next considered—the value of the right arm, the most useful member of the buccaneer's body, being reckoned equal to six slaves, or six hundred pieces of eight. It is worthy of notice that the eye and finger of the buccaneer had the same value, which was one slave, or a hundred pieces of eight. The remainder was equally shared, save that the captain, besides his specific agreement, had five shares, and his mate two. Boys received a half-share. The first maxim in the code of the buccaneer, dictated by necessity, was "no prey, no pay." An oath was sometimes taken, to prevent desertion before the cruise was ended, and against concealment of booty.

In their cruises the freebooters often put into remote harbours to careen or refit their ships, to obtain fruits and fish, to lie in wait for the Spanish traders, and to plunder either natives or Spaniards. The former they sometimes carried away, selling the men as slaves, while the women were compelled to labour among those of the buccaneers who followed the chase. The dress of these ruffians assorted well with their brutal and ferocious character. It has been described as a fixed costume, though there is little doubt that the same necessity which dictates to the savage his clothing of skins, prescribed to the buccaneer his filthy and terrific garb. This consisted of a shirt dipped in the blood of the cattle hunted and killed; trowsers prepared in the same rude manner; buskins without stockings, a cap with a small front, and a leathern girdle, into which were stuck knives, sabres, and pistols. The bloody garments, though attributed to design, were probably among the hunters the effect of chance and slovenliness. Such was the complete equipment of the buccaneer.

Among some few of the French buccaneers, who had been driven to adopt an outlaw's life by the severity and injustice of the colonial government and other causes, there sometimes existed sentiments of honour, and even a perverted sense of religion. Prayers were occasionally put up for the success of a piratical expedition, and thanks given for victory. We hear of one buccaneer commander who shot a seaman for behaving indecently during the performance of Mass, but never once of the chalices and images belonging to any church being spared, whether the plunderers were French Catholics or English heretics. One rare instance is mentioned, where a buccaneer carried his notions of honour to so overstrained a height as to punish breach of faith with a Spaniard, and to repress symptoms of treachery to the common foe with the most prompt severity. Under a humane commander these lawless bands were occasionally less brutal and remorseless; though, taking them as a whole, more unfavourable specimens of humanity could not be selected. In the buccaneer were united the cruelty and ferocity of the savage with the circumvention and rapacity which are among the worst consequences of an imperfect civilization. The buccaneers, however, have their admirers. They are said to have been open and unsuspecting among themselves, liberal in their dealings, and guided in their private intercourse by a frank and strictly honourable spirit. The French fondly name them "*nos braves;*" the English boast of their unparalleled exploits; and writers of fiction grace the character with many brilliant traits of generosity and delicacy of feeling. We confess that there appears little in their actual history to vindicate the elevated character given by those who from bravoes and lawless ruffians would fashion heroes of romance, and convert the buccaneers of America into a new order of chivalry; yet there is a wild and vivid interest about their roving adventures, independently of the powerful curiosity naturally felt to learn how men placed in circumstances so different from the ordinary modes and usages of social life in civilized communities thought and acted. They afford another lesson. All forms of privation and endurance, with which the vicissitudes of maritime adventure bring us acquainted, sink into insignificance when compared with the hardships voluntarily and heroically sustained by the buccaneers from the love of a life of boundless license and rapacity for Spanish gold. Base as were their governing motives, and ruthless as was their trade, it is impossible not to admire their manly hardihood and unconquerable perseverance.

The buccaneers had not long regained Tortuga, when it was betrayed by certain Frenchmen of their number into the hands of the French governor of the West Indies, who took possession of the island for the crown of France, and expelled the English buccaneers, who had domineered over their associates. From that time the English pirates began to frequent the islands which were now reckoned to belong to their own nation.

These they enriched by the lavish expenditure of their spoils. In 1655, the buccaneers lent powerful aid to their countrymen in the conquest of Jamaica, which thenceforth became their principal haunt when not cruising upon the enemy. There, in a few weeks or nights, they disgorged the plunder or gains of months and years in a course of riotous excess and the most dissolute profligacy.

In a few years after the capture of Jamaica, the French freebooters had increased amazingly on the western shores of Hispaniola. The first remarkable exploits of the buccaneers at sea were chiefly performed by these Frenchmen. Ships were their primary want; but from small Indian canoes, in which they at first embarked, the naval power of the pirates soon rose to large fleets. Among their first brilliant exploits, which led the way to many others, was the capture of a richly-laden galleon, vice-admiral of the yearly Spanish fleet. This was achieved by Pierre Legrand, a native of Dieppe, who by one bold stroke gained fame and fortune. With a boat carrying four small pieces, which proved of no use to him, and twenty resolute followers, Pierre surprised this ship. For days and weeks he and his comrades had lain in wait for a prey, burning under a tropical sun. They were almost exhausted by suffering and disappointment, when the galleon was descried separated from the fleet. The manner in which the capture was made offers a fair specimen of buccaneering daring and strategy. The boat in which the men lay concealed had been seen by the galleon all day, and one of the company had warned the captain of his suspicion of a nest of pirates lurking in the distant speck. The Spaniard haughtily and carelessly replied, "And what then? shall I be afraid of so pitiful a thing? No, though she were as good a ship as my own." He probably thought no more of the circumstance till, seated at cards with his friends in the same evening, he saw the buccaneers rush into his cabin, having already overpowered the crew. Nor had the task proved difficult.

Pierre and his company had kept aloof till dusk, when they made for the galleon with all the force of oars. The game was for death—ignominious and cruel death; slavery in the mines—or victory and fortune: they must make good their attempt to board the galleon or perish. To render their courage desperate, Pierre ordered the surgeon to bore holes in the side of the boat, that no other footing might be left to his men than the decks of the Spaniard. This was directly performed, while each man, armed with a sword and pistols, silently climbed the sides of the ship. While one party rushed into the great cabin, and presented their pistols to the officers who sat at cards, another seized the gun-room, cutting down whoever stood in their way. As the Spaniards had been completely surprised, little opposition was offered. The ship surrendered, and was carried into France by Pierre, who, by a rare instance of good sense and moderation, from the time of obtaining this prize gave up the vocation of a buccaneer, in which, if fortunes were sometimes quickly acquired, they were as often rapidly lost or certainly squandered. Legrand appears to have exercised no unnecessary cruelty, and all of the Spanish seamen not required in navigating the vessel were sent on shore.

The enterprise by which Pierre Legrand had in one night gained fame and fortune was a signal for half the hunters and planters of Tortuga to rush to the sea. In their small canoes they cruised about, lying in wait for the barks in which the Spaniards conveyed to Havannah, and other adjacent ports, hides, tobacco, and the produce of the boucan. These cargoes, together with the boats, were sold at Tortuga, and with the proceeds the freebooters were enabled to procure and equip larger vessels. Campeachy and even the shores of New Spain were now within their extended range of cruising, and their expeditions became daily more distant and bold. The Spaniards now found it necessary to arm ships to protect the coast-trade, as well as the galleons and *flota*. The Indian fleet and the treasure-ships were always the especial mark of the pirates, who found no species of goods so convenient either for transport or division as pieces of eight, though their friends and correspondents in the islands did all in their power to relieve them of the embarrassment of heavier cargoes. The merchants of Jamaica and Tortuga might at this time have not inaptly been termed the brokers of the buccaneers.

Among other brilliant acts, Pierre François, another Frenchman, with a handful of men in a boat, surprised and captured the vice-admiral of the pearl fleet; and was no sooner possessed of this ship than he raised his ambitious thoughts to the capture of the ship of war which formed the convoy. In this bold project he was disappointed, and his prize retaken; but not before he had stipulated for honourable conditions to himself and his company, and that they should be safely set on shore. About this time another noted buccaneer, Bartholomew Portugues, cruising from Jamaica with a boat carrying four small pieces and a crew of thirty men, captured a large ship of twenty great guns, with a crew of seventy men. This prize also was retaken in a few days by three Spanish ships, and the pirate carried into Campeachy; whence, however, he contrived to escape, burning for vengeance upon the Spaniards for the severity with which he had been treated. The ingenuity of the Portuguese in evading the jail and the gallows, and his hair-breadth escapes and stratagems to extricate himself from the consequences of his crimes, may vie with those of any hero in the Newgate calendar.

The Spanish coasting-vessels, taught by experience, now ventured cautiously to sea, and the number of buccaneers at the same time increasing, land-expeditions were first undertaken, and villages, towns, and cities pillaged, sacked, and held to ransom. The first land-pirate was named Lewis Scot, who stormed and plundered Campeachy, and obtained a large sum for its ransom. Mansvelt, and John Davies, a renowned buccaneer born in Jamaica, next followed this new career with success. In these attempts Mansvelt conceived the design of forming an independent buccaneer establishment, holding neither of France, England, nor Holland, which should form a place of safe retreat to the freebooters of every nation. His success will be seen in the course of the narrative.

In the annals of the sea-rovers no names are to be found more terrible than those of Lolonnois and Montbar, natives of France, and distinguished among the fraternity by pre-eminence in crime. The former was rather a monster in human form than a merely cruel man; the latter appears to have had a taint of constitutional madness, which, however, took a most diabolical character. The *nom de guerre* of Lolonnois was borrowed from the native place of this fiend, which was near the Sands of Olone. Little, however, is known about the ancestry of the pirate, who afterwards became so celebrated for the variety and vicissitudes of his life, for desperate courage, and for insatiable cruelty. He had either been kidnapped when young, or had left France under a form of engagement, then in common use in several countries of Europe, by which the adventurer agreed to serve for a certain number of years in the colonies. This practice, which was termed indenting, was indeed common till a very recent period, and was liable to great abuses. From this servitude Lolonnois escaped, and entered with the buccaneers. His address and courage soon rendered him conspicuous, and in a few years he was the owner of two canoes, and commanded twenty-two freebooters. With this small force he captured a Spanish frigate off the coast of Cuba. This buccaneer commander, of whom almost incredible atrocities are related, is said to have frequently thrown overboard the crews of the ships which he took. He is said to have struck off the heads of eighty prisoners with his own hand, refreshing himself by sucking the blood of the victims as it trickled down his sabre. It is even related that, in transports of frantic cruelty, he has been known to tear out and devour the hearts of those who fell by his hand, and to pluck out the tongues of others. To this monster cruelty was an affair of calculation as well as of delight, and he reckoned the terror inspired by his name among the best means of success.

With the fruits of rapine Lolonnois extended his range of depredation, and at last joined forces with another notorious brother of the order, Michael de Basco. With a force of eight ships and six hundred and fifty men they stormed and plundered the towns of Gibraltar and Maracaibo; the former place being burned on ransom not being paid, and the latter pillaged though terms of safety had been agreed upon. We shall not dwell upon the atrocities which distinguish this expedition, the most lucrative that had yet been undertaken, as many ships were captured during the cruise, besides the plunder and ransom obtained in the towns. In this affair many of the French hunters had joined; and the booty divided among the whole band, at the island to which they retired for this purpose, amounted to four hundred thousand pieces of eight in money, plate, merchandise, household furniture, and clothes, —for nothing escaped the ravages of the buccaneers. The name of François Lolonnois, already so formidable on the Spanish Main and the islands, now became a word of deeper horror to the miserable settlers, who lived in continual dread of a descent.

After the plunder had been obtained and divided, the next stage of a regular buccaneering voyage was to some friendly island, Tortuga or Jamaica, where a market might be obtained for the divided spoils, and an opportunity given for the indulgence of the unbridled and gross licentiousness in which the pirates squandered their gains. This was either in gaming, to which the buccaneers were strongly addicted, in the most brutal debauchery, or in those freaks of profligate extravagance which more or less characterize all uneducated seamen after long voyages. "Some of them," says their brother and historian, Exquemelin, "will spend three thousand pieces of eight in one night, not leaving themselves, peradventure, a shirt to wear on their backs in the morning." He tells of one who would place a pipe of wine in the streets of Jamaica, and, offering his pistols at their breast, force all who passed to drink with him. "At other times he would do the same with barrels of ale and beer; and very often with both his hands he would throw these liquors about the streets, and wet the clothes of such as passed by, without regarding whether he spoiled their apparel or not, were they men or women." Of Roche Braziliano, a pirate somewhat less cruel than many of the fraternity, and of great courage and capacity in the affairs of his command, the chronicler states, " Howbeit in his domestic and private affairs he had no good behaviour nor government over himself; for in these he would oftentimes show himself either brutish or foolish. Many times, being in drink, he would run up and down the streets, beating or wounding whom he met,—no person daring to oppose him or make any resistance." Such was the buccaneer in his moments of relaxation and social enjoyment, and such the delights, which in a few weeks left the companions of Lolonnois penniless, and eager for the new expedition in which that detestable monster met a death worthy of his enormous crimes.

The reputation which Lolonnois had gained by his last expedition made many new adventurers eager to swell his armament. Cruising along the coast of Cuba, and wherever he went making rapid descents on Indian villages or Spanish settlements, he at last experienced reverses, and on proposing to go to Guatemala many of the leading buccaneers left him upon projects of their own. Finally, after a train of disasters, Lolonnois fell into the hands of certain of the Indians of the Darien, a fierce and cruel tribe, who were not unacquainted with the atrocities of the buccaneers. By them he was torn alive limb from limb,—his body consumed, and the ashes scattered abroad, "to the intent," says his historian, "that no trace nor memory might remain of such an infamous creature." Many of his companions shared the same fate.

The character of Montbar, the other French buccaneer formerly mentioned, is more romantic, if not more humane. He appears to have been one of those unhappy though detestable beings, to whom the soil of France occasionally gives birth, who are created with a raging thirst for blood, and with whom cruelty is a passion and appetite. Montbar was a gentleman of Languedoc, who, from reading in his youth of the horrible cruelties practised by the Spaniards upon the Mexicans and Caribs, imbibed a hatred of the whole Spanish nation which possessed him like a frenzy. It is, however, somewhat strange that the impulse which led this singular person to join the ranks of the buccaneers urged him to the commission of worse cruelties than those which he reprobated. His comrades were often merciless from the lust of gold; but Spanish blood was the sole passion of Montbar. It is related by Raynal that while at college, in acting the part of a Frenchman who quarrels with a Spaniard, he assaulted the youth who personated an individual of that hated nation with such fury that he had well-nigh strangled him. His imagination was perpetually haunted by the shapes of multitudes of persons butchered by monsters from Spain, who called upon him to revenge them. While on his passage outward to league himself with the Brethren of the Coast, the inveterate enemies of Spain, the vessel in which he sailed fell in with a Spanish ship and captured it. No sooner had the Frenchmen boarded the vessel, than Montbar, with his sabre drawn, twice rushed along the deck, cutting his frantic way through the ranks of Spaniards, whom he swept down. While his comrades divided the booty acquired by his prowess, Montbar gloated over the mangled limbs of the detested people against whom he had vowed everlasting and deadly hate. From this and similar actions he acquired the name of the *Exterminator*.

The buccaneers of America had now become so numerous and powerful, and had been so successful in their depredations upon the richest and best fortified places, both on the Main and the Spanish islands, that several settlements were compelled to submit to the degradation of purchasing their forbearance by paying them contributions, equivalent in principle to the *black-mail* formerly levied by banditti in Scotland. This, however, merely increased their gains, and partially changed the scene of havoc. Their predatory excursions were immediately carried further into the interior, and stretched more extensively along the coasts of the continent. It was about this time that the popular buccaneer commander named Mansvelt formed the design before alluded to, of establishing a buccaneer independent empire,—a project which was afterwards entertained by his lieutenant, the famous or infamous Morgan, and reluctantly abandoned by such of the fraternity as were endowed with more foresight or greater ambition than their associates. The intended seat of an empire, which might easily have been extended on all sides, was the island of Santa Katalina, now known by the name of Old Providence Island. For this point Mansvelt sailed from Jamaica in 1664, stormed the fort, and garrisoned the place with his own men; but the English governor of Jamaica, who thought the buccaneers more profitable as customers than desirable as independent allies, looked coldly upon the project of a settlement so far beyond his control. He forbade recruiting in Jamaica in furtherance of this project, and Mansvelt died suddenly before it could otherwise be effected. He was succeeded by the most renowned of the English buccaneers, Captain Sir Henry Morgan. The new buccaneer generalissimo, though equally brave and daring with his predecessor, was of a more sordid and brutal character, selfish and cunning, and without any spark of the reckless generosity which sometimes graced the freebooter and contrasted with his crimes. He was a native of Wales, and the son of a respectable yeoman. Early inclination led him to the sea; and embarking for Barbadoes, by a fate common to all unprotected adventurers, he was sold for a term of years. After effecting his escape, or emancipation, Morgan joined the buccaneers, and in a short time saved a little money, with which, in concert with a few comrades, he equipped a bark, of which he was chosen commander. The adventurers made a fortunate cruise in the Bay of Campeachy; after which Morgan joined Mansvelt in the assault on Santa Katalina or Providence, and by a lucky stroke, at the death of Mansvelt, succeeded, as has been noticed, to the chief command. Notwithstanding the efforts of Morgan to retain Old Providence, as the governor of Jamaica still refused to allow recruits to go from that island, and the merchants of Virginia and New England declined sending him supplies, it fell once more into the hands of the Spaniards, and the buccaneers were driven to seek a new place of refuge. The *Cayos*, or islets near the south coast of Cuba, had for some time been their haunting-place. At these *Keys*, as they were corruptly termed by the English, they mustered from all quarters as often as a joint expedition was contemplated; and here they watered, refitted, held their councils in safety, and waited till their fleet had been victualled either by pillage or purchase.

To the Keys on the south of Cuba, the rendezvous appointed by Morgan, about twelve sail in ships and boats had now repaired, with above seven hundred fighting-men, French and English. The disposal of this armament and force was the cause of difference of opinion, some wishing to attack Havannah, while others, deeming this enterprise too formidable for their numbers, declared for Puerto del Principe in Cuba, which was accordingly taken and plundered, after a desperate assault and brave resistance. The buccaneers, as soon as they became masters, shut up the principal inhabitants in the churches, as the easiest way of disposing of them while they pillaged the city. Many of these unfortunate persons died of hunger; others were put to the torture to compel them to discover concealed treasures, which probably had no existence save in the rapacious desires and extravagant fancies of the brutal and ignorant buccaneers. The booty obtained, or wrung from the inhabitants, was, however, considerable. Five hundred bullocks formed part of the ransom, which the insolent freebooters compelled the Spaniards to kill and salt for them. A characteristic quarrel between a French and an English buccaneer, which took place at this time, crippled the strength of Morgan, from whom, in consequence of this difference, many of his Gallican followers withdrew. The occasion of this national quarrel was an English buccaneer snatching the marrow-bones which the Frenchman had carefully prepared for his own repast. A challenge was the consequence; and the Frenchman was unfairly or treacherously stabbed by his opponent. His countrymen embraced his cause, and Morgan put the murderer in chains, and afterwards had him hung in Jamaica for this breach of the laws of honour and of brotherhood.

In the meanwhile the pillage of Puerto del Principe being divided, the French buccaneers, indignant at the murder of their countryman, left Morgan in spite of his entreaties, and the English were obliged to pursue their fortunes alone.

The enterprises of Morgan, who was at once ambitious and greedy, display capacity, coolness, and daring. His next attempt combined all these qualities in a remarkable degree. With nine ships and boats, and four hundred and sixty of his countrymen, he resolved to assault Porto Bello; but did not venture to disclose so bold a design, till it was no longer advisable to conceal it. To those who then objected that their force was inadequate to the attack, Morgan boldly replied, "that though their numbers were small, their hearts were good; and the fewer the warriors the larger the shares of plunder." This last was an irresistible argument; and this strongly-fortified city was carried by a handful of resolute men, who never scrupled at cruelty needful to the accomplishment of their object, and often revelled in the wantonness of unnecessary crime. The first fort or castle was deliberately blown up by fire being set to the powder magazine, after many miserable prisoners, whose mangled limbs soon darkened the air, had been huddled into one room. Resistance was still attempted by the Spaniards, which greatly exasperated the besiegers, as it was into the forts which held out that the wealthy inhabitants had retired with their treasure and valuables. One strong fort it was necessary to carry without delay; and broad scaling-ladders being constructed, Morgan compelled his prisoners to fix them to the walls. Many of those employed in this office were friars and nuns, dragged for this purpose from the cloisters. These it was thought their countrymen would spare; while under their protection the buccaneers might advance without being exposed to the fire of the castle. In these trying circumstances, forgetting the claims of country, and the sacred character of the innocent persons exposed to suffering so unmerited, the Spanish governor consulted only his official duty; and while the unhappy prisoners of the buccaneers implored his mercy, he continued to fire upon all who approached the walls, whether pirates or the late peaceful inhabitants of the cloisters, his stern answer being that he would never surrender alive. Many of the friars and nuns were killed before the scaling-ladders could be fixed; but that done, the buccaneers, carrying with them fire-balls and pots full of gunpowder, boldly mounted the walls, poured in their combustibles, and speedily effected an entrance. All the Spaniards demanded quarter except the governor, who died fighting, in presence of his wife and daughter, declaring that he chose rather to die as a brave soldier than be hanged like a coward. The next act in the horrid drama of buccaneering conquest followed rapidly,—pillage, cruelty, brutal license,— the freebooters giving themselves up to so mad a course of riot and debauchery that fifty resolute men might have cut them off and regained the town, had the panic-struck Spaniards been able to form any rational plan of action or to muster a force. During these fifteen days of demoniac revel, interrupted only by torturing the prisoners to make them give up treasures which they did not possess, many of the buccaneers died from the consequences of their own brutal excesses, and Morgan deemed it expedient to draw off his force. Information had by this time reached the governor of Panama; and though aid was distant from the miserable inhabitants of Porto Bello, it might still come. Morgan, therefore, carried off a good many of the guns, spiked the rest, fully supplied his ships with every necessary store, and having already plundered all that was possible, insolently demanded an exorbitant ransom for the preservation of the city and for his prisoners, and prepared to depart from the coast. These terms he even sent to the governor of Panama, who was approaching the place, and whose force the buccaneers intercepted in a narrow pass, and compelled to retreat. The inhabitants collected among themselves a hundred thousand pieces of eight, which Morgan graciously accepted, and retired to his ships.

The astonishment of the governor of Panama at so small a force carrying the town and the forts, and holding them so long, induced him, it is said, to send a message to the buccaneer leader, requesting a specimen of the arms which he used. Morgan received the messenger with civility, gave him a pistol and a few bullets, and ordered him to bid the president to accept of so slender a pattern of the weapons with which he had taken Porto Bello, and to keep it for a twelvemonth, at the end of which time he (Morgan) proposed to come to Panama to fetch it away. The governor returned the loan with a gold ring, and requested Morgan not to give himself the trouble of travelling so far, certifying to him that he would not fare so well as he had done at Porto Bello.

On this subject Morgan formed and afterwards acted upon his own opinions. In the meanwhile, the spoils were divided at the Keys of Cuba. The booty amounted to two hundred and fifty thousand pieces of eight, besides goods of all kinds, including silks, linen, cloth, and many things that found a ready market in Jamaica, for which buccaneers' paradise the fleet next sailed, to fit themselves for a fresh expedition by a month's carousing, and the prodigal expenditure of the fruits of their toils and crimes.

This brilliant exploit, in which so few men, and these armed only with pistols and sabres, had taken a large fortified city, raised the character of Morgan as a commander higher than ever; and his invitation to the Brethren of the Coast to meet him at the Isla de la Vaca, or Cow Island, which was appointed as a rendezvous preparatory to another cruise, was so eagerly accepted that he found himself at the head of a considerable force. A large French buccaneering vessel, which refused to join in this expedition, he obtained by fraud. Inviting the commander and several of the best men to dine with him, under some frivolous pretext he made them prisoners. But Morgan did not reap much advantage from this act of treachery. While the men whom he had placed in the ship were carousing, celebrating the commencement of another cruise, it suddenly blew up, and three hundred and fifty Englishmen and the French prisoners perished together. This accident, so disastrous to Morgan, was imputed to the revengeful spirit of the Frenchmen confined in the hold. The true character of the sordid buccaneer was never more strongly displayed than in the way in which Morgan tried to make the best for himself of this mischance. When eight days of mourning had elapsed, he made the dead bodies be fished up, stripped of clothes, linen, and of the gold rings which buccaneers often wore, and then be thrown back into the sea to feed the sharks.

Morgan had now a fleet of fifteen ships, some of which he owed to the kindness of the governor of Jamaica, who connived at, or took a share in, such adventures. His force consisted of one thousand fighting-men. Several of his vessels were armed, and his own carried fourteen guns. With these, which, however, through discontent, diminished a full half on the way, he shaped his course for the devoted cities of Gibraltar and Maracaibo, formerly visited by Lolonnois, which were once more taken and plundered. At the former place the cruelties of Morgan exceeded, if that were possible, the enormities of the French pirate. Such of the inhabitants as fled to the woods and were retaken were tortured with fiend-like ingenuity to make them discover their wealth. It would be painful and revolting to dwell upon the black record of the atrocities perpetrated here.

So much time had been consumed at Gibraltar that Morgan, when about to withdraw, found himself in a snare, from which it required all his talent and presence of mind to extricate the buccaneer fleet. Coolness and readiness were, however, the familiar qualities of men whose lives were a series of perils and escapes, and whose natural element was danger; and they never were more admirably displayed than by Morgan and his men at this time.

In the interval spent by the buccaneers in pillage and debauchery at Gibraltar, the Spaniards had repaired the fort which protected the passage of the lake or lagoon of Maracaibo, and stationed three men-of-war at the entrance, whose vigilance it was conceived impossible the pirates could escape. These vessels carried one twenty, another thirty, and the third forty guns. Putting a bold face upon his embarrassing situation, Morgan, with the audacity natural to him, and which was one of his instruments of success, sent a message to the Spanish admiral, demanding a ransom as the only condition on which the city could be preserved. To this insolent vaunt the Spaniard replied, that though the buccaneer commander had taken the castle from a set of cowards, it was now in a good state of defence; and that he not only intended to dispute the egress from the lagoon, but to pursue the pirates everywhere. If, however, they chose to give up the prisoners and the slaves they had taken, they would be permitted to pass forth unmolested.

This reply was as usual submitted to a council of buccaneers, and at this assembly one of their number suggested the stratagem by which Morgan destroyed the Spanish men-of-war. One of the buccaneer vessels was prepared as a fire-ship, and at the same time was made to wear the appearance of a vessel ready for action. Logs were placed in rows on the deck, on which clothes, hats, and montero caps were placed; and these decoy-figures were also armed with swords and muskets. When this was done, the plate, jewels, female prisoners, and whatever was of most value to the buccaneers, were placed in their large boats, each of which carried twelve armed men. These boats were to follow the fire-ship, which led the van; an oath was exacted from each buccaneer of resistance to the last, and the refusal of quarter from the Spaniards; and ample rewards were promised for valour and firmness.

Next evening the fleet sailed, and about dusk came up with the Spanish ships riding at anchor in the middle of the lagoon. The buccaneer vessels also anchored, resolved to await here the effect of their stratagem, and either to fight, escape, or perish. No attack was offered that night, and they lay in quiet till dawn, when the anchors were weighed, and they steered directly towards the Spanish ships, which advanced as if to meet them. The fire-ship, still in advance, with all her decoys of armed men as before, came up with the largest of the Spanish vessels and grappled to her; then the deception was first discovered, but too late for escape. The conflagration commenced. The Spanish ship caught fire in tackling and timbers, and the fore part of her hull soon went down. The second Spanish vessel escaped under the guns of the castle, and was sunk by her own company as a fate preferable to falling a prey to the buccaneers. The third vessel was taken. The crew of the burning ship endeavoured to escape to the shore, and all chose rather to perish in the sea than accept of the quarter offered by the pirates. The triumphant buccaneers, without losing a moment, gave chase, and immediately landed, resolving forthwith to attempt the castle; but as they were ill-armed for such an assault, and the place was well-fortified and manned, they desisted from the attempt, and returned to their ships, having lost in that day's work thirty men killed and many more wounded.

Though the Spanish ships were destroyed, the castle still remained to be passed; and the Spaniards had laboured all night in completing its defences. Morgan again had recourse to stratagem. All day long, in sight of the garrison, he affected to be sending boats filled with men to a point of the shore concealed from view of the castle by trees. These men returned on board lying flat in the boats, where, in going back, only the rowers were visible. They mounted their ships at a side on which the Spaniards could not perceive their return. This manœuvre was repeated, till the Spaniards believed that from the number of men landed an attack upon the castle was meditated. This seemed the more probable, as Morgan, who had now hoisted his flag in their captured war-ship, again sent a message demanding a ransom for Maracaibo as the condition of his departure. To meet the presumed movement of the buccaneers, the guns of the castle were changed from a position which commanded the lagoon, and pointed to landward. As soon as he was aware of this arrangement, Morgan raised his anchors by moonlight, and favoured by the ebb-tide, the wind also being favourable, pressed past the castle—the mortified Spaniards trying in vain to hasten back with their pieces to bear upon him. He gave them a parting volley from his great guns, so lately their own, and bore away for Jamaica, exulting in good fortune, enhanced likewise by what he learned of the misadventures of those who had forsaken him in the early part of the cruise.

Money and credit were, as usual, quickly outrun in the taverns of Port Royal by the dissolute companions of Morgan, and another expedition was concerted, which was to exceed all the former achievements of the sea-rovers. And no time was to be lost, as a pending treaty between Great Britain and Spain threatened for ever to put an end to what their admiring countrymen termed the "unparalleled exploits of the buccaneers." Letters were despatched by the commander to every noted buccaneer, and the south side of the island of Tortuga was named as the rendezvous. Early in October 1670 Morgan found himself surrounded by pirates, hunters, cultivators, English, French, and Dutch, who, from land and sea, the plantation and the wilderness, had flocked to the standard of him who was to lead them to fortune and victory. The first duty was to victual the fleet, and this was done by pillaging the hog-yards, and with the boucan sent in by hunters who either joined in the expedition or traded with the pirates. The buccaneer fleet, consisting of thirty-seven vessels fully provisioned, next sailed for Cape Tiburon, on the west coast of Hispaniola,—the fighting-men amounting to two thousand. At the general council now held three places of attack were deliberated upon, —Vera Cruz, Carthagena, and Panama. The last and most difficult was that which was chosen, recommended by the extravagant notions entertained in Europe and the West Indies of its amazing wealth, and of the great riches of Peru.

Morgan had never renounced the idea, which originated with Mansvelt, of a buccaneer settlement on the conveniently-situated island of Providence. Once more it was captured on his way, the Spanish governor making a farce of resistance. From this point Morgan detached a force of four hundred men to attack the castle of Chagre, the possession of which he judged necessary to the success of his future operations against Panama. It was eventually carried by the accident of fire communicating with the powder-magazine, which blew up part of the defences.

While the Spaniards were occupied in suppressing the conflagration, the buccaneers laboured hard to increase the confusion, by setting fire to the palisades in several places. At last they effected a breach, in defiance of the liquid combustibles which the Spaniards poured down among them, and which occasioned considerable loss of their numbers. But the attack and resistance were still continued throughout the whole night, the buccaneers directing an incessant fire towards the breaches, which the Spanish governor pertinaciously defended.

By noon the next day the buccaneers had gained a breach, which was defended by the governor himself and twenty-five soldiers. The Spanish soldiers fought with desperate valour, despair lending them supernatural courage. But nothing could resist the impetuosity of the pirates: they burst their way through every obstacle, and the unfortunate Spaniards who survived, preferring death to the dishonour of either falling into the hands of these infuriated ruffians, or of begging quarter, precipitated themselves into the sea. The governor had retired into the *corps du garde*, before which he planted two pieces of cannon, and bravely maintained the hopeless and unequal conflict till he fell by a musket-shot which entered the brain. Of the garrison of three hundred and fourteen men only thirty remained alive, and of these few twenty were wounded. Not a single officer escaped.

From the survivors of the siege the buccaneer party learned that the governor of Panama was already apprised of their design against that place; that all along the course of the Chagre ambuscades were laid, and that a force of three thousand six hundred men awaited their arrival. But this did not deter Morgan, who pressed forward for Chagre the instant that he received intelligence of the capture of the castle, carrying with him all the provisions that could be obtained in Santa Katalina, to which island he intended to return after the capture of Panama.

The English colours flying upon the castle of Chagre was a joyful sight to the main body of the buccaneers upon their arrival. Morgan was admitted within the fort by the triumphant advanced troop with all the honours of conquest. Before his arrival, the wounded, the widows of the soldiers killed in the siege, and the other women of the place, had been shut up in the church, and subjected to the most brutal treatment. To their fate Morgan was entirely callous; but he lost no time in setting the prisoners to work in repairing the defences and forming new palisades. He also seized all the craft in the river, many of which carried from two to four small pieces.

These arrangements concluded, Morgan left a garrison of five hundred men in his castle of Chagre, and in the ships one hundred and fifty; while at the head of one thousand two hundred buccaneers, he, on the 18th January 1671, commenced his inland voyage to Panama, indifferent about or determined to brave the Spanish ambuscades. His artillery was carried by five large boats, and thirty-two canoes were filled with part of the men. Anxious to push forward, Morgan committed one capital blunder in carrying almost no provisions, calculating upon a shorter period being consumed on the march than it actually required, and on foraging upon the Spaniards. Even on the first day their provisions failed; and on the second they were compelled to leave the canoes, the lowness of the river, and the fallen trees lying across it, making this mode of travelling tedious and nearly impracticable. Their progress was now continued by land and water alternately, and was attended with great inconvenience, the extremity of famine being of the number of their hardships. Their best hopes were now placed in falling in with the threatened ambuscades, as there they might find a store of provisions. So extremely were they pinched with hunger, that the leathern bags found at a deserted Spanish station formed a delicious meal. About this delicacy they even quarrelled, and, it is said, openly regretted that no Spaniards were found, as, failing provisions, they had resolved to have roasted or boiled a few of the enemy to satisfy their ravenous appetites.

Throughout the whole track to Panama, the Spaniards had taken care not to leave the smallest quantity of provisions, and any other soldiers than the buccaneers must have perished long before even a distant view was obtained of the city; but their powers of endurance, from their hardy modes of life, were become almost superhuman. At nightfall, when they reached their halting-place, "happy was he who had reserved since morn any small piece of leather whereof to make his supper, drinking after it a good draught of water for his greatest comfort." Their mode of preparing this tough meal deserves to be noticed. The skins were first sliced, then alternately dipped in water and beat between two stones to render them tender; lastly, the remaining hair was scraped off, and the morsel broiled, cut into small bits, and deliberately chewed, with frequent mouthfuls of water to eke out and lengthen the repast.

On the fifth day, at another deserted ambuscade, a little maize was found, and also some wheat, wine, and plantains. This, scanty as it was, proved a seasonable supply to those who drooped, and it was thriftily dealt out among them. Next day a barn full of maize was discovered, which, beating down the door, the famished buccaneers rushed upon and devoured without any preparation. Yet all this hardship could not turn them aside from the scent of prey, though symptoms of discontent became visible in their ranks. At a village called Cruz, perceiving from a distance a great smoke, they joyfully promised themselves rest and refreshments; but on reaching it found no inhabitant, and every house either burned down or in flames, so determined were the Spaniards to oppose the onward march of the terrible beings, presented to their imaginations under every shape of horror. The only animals remaining, the dogs and cats of the village, fell an immediate sacrifice to the wolfish hunger of the buccaneers.

Morgan had now some difficulty in preserving discipline, and in keeping his companions or followers from falling into the hands of the Spaniards or Indians when straggling about in search of anything they could devour. In this way one man was lost.

They were now within eight leagues of Panama, and the nearer they approached, the more anxious and vigilant was Morgan in looking out for the threatened ambuscades of the enemy, who, he naturally conjectured, might have retired to consolidate his forces. On the eighth day, they were surprised by a shower of Indian arrows poured upon them from some unseen quarter, and advancing into the woods, maintained a sharp, short contest with a party of Indians, many of whom fell, offering a brave though vain resistance. Ten of the freebooters were killed in this skirmish. The buccaneers, who had already three Indian guides, runaways found in Santa Katalina, endeavoured at this place to make some prisoners for the purpose of procuring intelligence; but the Indians were too swift of foot.

After another twenty-four hours of suffering, under which only freebooters or Indians could have borne up, on the morning of the ninth day of the march, from a high mountain, the majestic South Sea was joyfully descried, with ships and boats sailing upon its bosom, and peacefully setting out from the concealed port of Panama. Herds of cattle, horses, and asses, feeding in the valley below the eminence on which they stood, formed a sight not less welcome. They rushed to the feast, and, cutting up the animals, devoured their flesh half-raw, "more resembling cannibals than Europeans at this banquet, the blood many times running down from their beards unto the middle of their bodies."

This savage meal being ended the journey was resumed, Morgan still endeavouring to gain information by taking prisoners, as on his whole line of march he had obtained speech of neither Spaniard nor Indian.

In the same evening the steeple of Panama was beheld at a distance; and, forgetting all their sufferings, the buccaneers gave way to the most rapturous exultation, tossing their caps into the air, leaping, shouting, beating their drums, and sounding their trumpets at the sight of so glorious a plunder, and as if victory were already consummated. They encamped for the night near the city, intending to make the assault early in the morning. The same night, a party of fifty Spanish horsemen came out as if to reconnoitre, advanced within musket-shot of the pirates, scornfully challenged "the dogs" to come on, and then retired, leaving six or eight of their number to watch the enemy's motions. Upon this the great guns of the town began to play on the camp, but were too distant or ill-directed to do any execution; and instead of betraying alarm, the buccaneers, having placed sentinels around their camp, made another voracious meal preparatory to the next day's business, threw themselves upon the grass, and, lulled by the Spanish artillery, slept soundly till the dawn.

The camp was astir betimes, and the men being mustered and arrayed, with drums and trumpets sounding they advanced towards the city; but instead of taking the ordinary route, which the Spaniards were prepared to defend, by the advice of one of the Indian guides they struck through a wood, by a tangled and difficult path, in which, however, immediate obstruction could not be apprehended. Before the Spaniards could counteract this unexpected movement, the buccaneers had advanced some way. The governor of Panama, who led the forces, commanded two hundred cavalry and four regiments of infantry; and a number of Indian auxiliaries conducted an immense herd of wild bulls, to be driven among the ranks of the buccaneers, and which were expected to throw them into disorder. This extraordinary arm of war was viewed by the hunters of Hispaniola and Campeachy with indifference; but they were somewhat alarmed at the regular and imposing array of the troops drawn up to receive them. It was, however, too late to retreat. They divided into three detachments, two hundred dexterous marksmen leading the advance. They now stood on the top of a little eminence, whence the whole Spanish force, the city, and the champaign country around, were distinctly seen. As they moved downward, the Spanish cavalry, shouting "Viva el Rey," immediately advanced to meet them; but the ground happened to be soft and marshy, which greatly obstructed the manœuvres of the horsemen. The advance of the buccaneers, all picked marksmen, knelt and received them with a volley, and the conflict instantly became close and hot. The buccaneers, throwing themselves between the Spanish horse and foot, succeeded in separating them, and the wild bulls, taking fright from the tumult and the noise of the guns, ran away, or were shot by the buccaneers before they could effect any mischief.

After a contest of two hours the Spanish cavalry gave way. Many were killed, and the rest fled; which the foot-soldiers perceiving, fired their last charge, threw down their muskets, and followed the example of the cavaliers. Some of them took refuge in the adjoining thickets; and though the buccaneers did not continue the pursuit, they took a savage pleasure in shooting without mercy all who accidentally fell into their hands. In this way several priests and friars who were made prisoners were pistolled by the orders of Morgan. A Spanish officer who was made prisoner gave the buccaneers minute intelligence of the force of the enemy and the plan of defence, which enabled them to approach the town from the safest point; but the advance was still attended with difficulty.

After the rout which had taken place in the open field, and the slaughter which followed, the buccaneers rested for a little space, and during this pause solemnly plighted their honour, by oaths to each other, never to yield while a single man remained alive. This done, carrying their prisoners with them, they advanced upon the great guns planted in the streets, and the hasty defences thrown up to repel them. In this renewed assault the buccaneers suffered severely before they could make good those close quarters in which they ever maintained a decided superiority in fighting. Still they resolutely advanced to the final grapple, the Spaniards keeping up an incessant fire. The town was gained after a desperate conflict of three hours, maintained in its open streets.

In this assault the buccaneers neither gave nor accepted quarter, and the carnage on both sides was great. Six hundred Spaniards fell on that day: nor was the number of the buccaneers who perished much less; but to those who survived a double share of plunder was at all times ample consolation for the loss of companions whose services were no longer required in its acquisition. The city was no sooner gained than Morgan, who saw the temper of the inhabitants in the obstinate nature of the resistance they had offered, and who well knew the besetting sins of his followers, prudently prohibited them from tasting wine; and, aware that such an order would be very little regarded were it enforced by nothing save a simple command, he affirmed that he had received private intelligence that all the wine had been poisoned. They were therefore enjoined not to touch it under the dread of poisoning and the penalties of discipline. Neither of these motives was sufficient to enforce rigid abstinence among the buccaneers, though they operated till indulgence became more safe.

As soon as possession of the city was gained guards were placed; and, at the same time, fires broke out simultaneously in different quarters, which were attributed by the Spaniards to the pirates, and by them to the inhabitants. Both assisted in endeavouring to extinguish the dreadful conflagration, which raged with fury; but the houses, being built of cedar, caught the flames like tinder, and were consumed in a very short time. The inhabitants had previously removed or concealed the most valuable part of their goods and furniture.

The city of Panama consisted of about twelve thousand houses, many of them large and magnificent. It contained also eight monasteries and two churches, all richly furnished. The concealment of the church-plate drew upon the ecclesiastics the peculiar vengeance of the heretical buccaneers, who, however, spared no one. The conflagration which they could not arrest they seemed at last to take a savage delight in spreading. A slave-factory belonging to the Genoese was burned to the ground, together with many warehouses stored with meal. Many of the miserable Africans, whom the Genoese brought for sale to Peru, perished in the flames, which raged or smouldered for nearly four weeks.

For some time the buccaneers, afraid of being surprised and overpowered by the Spaniards, who still reckoned ten for one of their numbers, encamped without the town. Morgan had also weakened his force by sending a hundred and fifty men back to Chagre with news of his victory. Yet by this handful of men the panic-struck Spaniards were held in check and subjection, while the buccaneers either raged like demons through the burning town, or prowled among the ruins and ashes in search of plate and other valuable articles.

The property which the Spaniards had concealed in deep wells and cisterns was nearly all discovered, and the most active of the buccaneers were sent out to the woods and heights to search for and drive back the miserable inhabitants, who had fled from the city with their effects. In two days they brought in about two hundred of the fugitives as prisoners. Of those unhappy persons many were females, who found the merciless buccaneers no better than their fears had painted them.

In plundering the land Morgan had not neglected the sea. By sea many of the principal inhabitants had escaped; and a boat was immediately sent in pursuit, which brought in three prizes, though a galleon, in which were embarked all the plate and jewels belonging to the King of Spain and the wealth of the principal nunnery of the town, escaped, from the buccaneers indulging in a brutal revel in their own bark till it was too late to follow and capture the ship. The pursuit was afterwards continued for four days,—at the end of which the buccaneers returned to Panama with another prize, worth twenty thousand pieces of eight in goods, from Payta.

Meanwhile, on the opposite coast, the ships' companies left at Chagre were exercising their vocation, and had captured one large Spanish vessel, which, unaware of the hands into which the castle had fallen, ran in under it for protection.

While the buccaneers were thus employed at sea, and at Panama and Chagre, parties continued to scour the surrounding country, taking in turn the congenial duty of foraying and bringing in booty and prisoners, on whom they exercised the most atrocious cruelties, unscrupulously employing the rack, and sparing neither age, sex, nor condition. Religious persons were the subjects of the most refined barbarity, as they were believed to direct and influence the rest of the inhabitants, both in their first resistance and in the subsequent concealment of property. During the perpetration of these outrages, Morgan fell in love with a beautiful Spanish woman, his prisoner, and the wife of one of the principal merchants. She rejected his infamous addresses with firmness and spirit; and the buccaneer commander, alike a ruffian in his love and hate, used her with severity that disgusted even those of his own gang who had not thrown aside every feeling of manhood, and he was fain to charge his fair prisoner with treachery, to excuse the baseness of the treatment she received by his orders. This alleged treachery consisted in corresponding with her countrymen, and endeavouring to effect her escape.

In the meanwhile a plan had entered the minds of a party of the buccaneers, which did not suit the views nor meet the approbation of their leader. They had resolved to seize a ship in the port, cruise upon the South Sea on their own account till satiated with booty, and then either establish themselves on some island or return to Europe by the East Indies. Captain Morgan could neither spare equipments nor men for this project, of which he received private information. He immediately ordered the mainmast of the ship to be cut down and burned, together with every other vessel in the port, thus effectually preventing desertion on this side of America. The arms, ammunition, and stores, secretly collected for this bold cruise on the South Sea, were applied to other purposes.

Nothing more was to be wrung from Panama, which, after a destructive sojourn of four weeks, Morgan resolved to leave. Beasts of burden were therefore collected from all quarters to convey the spoils to the opposite coast. The cannon were spiked, and scouts sent out to learn what measures had been taken by the governor of Panama to intercept the return to Chagre. The Spaniards were too much depressed to have made any preparation either to annoy or cut off the retreat of their inveterate enemies; and on the 24th February the buccaneers, apprehensive of no opposition, left the ruins of Panama with a hundred and seventy-five mules laden with their spoils, and above six hundred prisoners, including women, children, and slaves. The misery of these wretched captives, driven on in the midst of the armed buccaneers, exceeds description. They believed that they were all to be carried to Jamaica, England, or some equally wild, distant, and savage country, to be sold for slaves; and the cruel craft of Morgan heightened these fears, the more readily to extort the ransom he demanded for the freedom of his unhappy prisoners. In vain the women threw themselves at his feet, supplicating for the mercy of being allowed to remain amidst the ruins of their former homes, or in the woods in huts with their husbands and children. His answer was, "that he came not there to listen to cries and lamentations, but to get money, which unless he obtained, he would assuredly carry them all where they would little like to go." Three days were granted in which they might avail themselves of the conditions of ransom. Several were happy enough to be able to redeem themselves, or were rescued by the contributions sent in; and with the remaining captives the pirates pushed onward, making new prisoners and gathering fresh spoils on their way.

The conduct of Morgan at this time disproves many of the extravagant notions propagated about the high honour of the buccaneers in their dealings with each other. Halting at a convenient place for his purpose, in the midst of the wilderness, and about half-way to Chagre, he drew up his comrades, and insisted that, besides taking an oath declaring that all plunder had been surrendered to the common stock, each man should be searched, he himself submitting in the first place to the degrading scrutiny, though it was suspected that the leading motive of the whole manœuvre was the desire of concealing his own peculation and fraudulent dealing with his associates. The French buccaneers who accompanied the expedition were indignant at treatment so much at variance with the maxims and usages of the gentlemen rovers; but being the weaker party, they were compelled to submit.

The buccaneers and their prisoners performed the remainder of the journey by water, and when arrived at Chagre, Morgan, who knew not how to dispose of his unredeemed prisoners, shipped them all off for Porto

Bello, making them the bearers of his demand of ransom from the governor of that city for the castle of Chagre. To this insolent message the governor of Porto Bello replied that Morgan might make of the castle what he pleased,—not a ducat should be given for its ransom.

There was thus no immediate prospect of any more plunder in this quarter, and nothing remained to be done but to divide the spoils already acquired. The individual shares fell so far short of the expectations of the buccaneers that they openly grumbled, and accused their chief of the worst crime of which in their eyes he could be guilty,—secreting the richest of the jewels for himself. Two hundred pieces of eight each man was thought a very small return for the plunder of so wealthy a city, and a very trifling reward for the toil and danger that had been undergone in assaulting it. Matters were assuming so serious an aspect among the fraternity, that Morgan, who knew the temper of his friends, deemed it advisable to steal away with what he had obtained. He immediately made the walls of Chagre be destroyed, carried the guns on board his own ship, and, followed by one or two vessels commanded by persons in his confidence, sailed for Jamaica, leaving his enraged associates in want of every necessary. Those who followed him were all Englishmen, who, as the French buccaneers fully believed, connived at the frauds and shared in the gains of Morgan. They would instantly have pursued him to sea, and the Spaniards might have enjoyed the satisfaction of seeing the buccaneer fleet divided and fighting against itself, had they, with a force so much weaker, dared to venture so unequal an encounter. The vessels deserted by Morgan separated here, and the companies sought their fortunes in different quarters, none of them much the richer for the misery and devastation they had carried to Panama.

Morgan, on arriving at Jamaica laden with plunder, and exulting in his late exploit, endeavoured once more to levy recruits for the independent state he still longed to establish at Santa Katalina, and of which he himself, already admiral and generalissimo of the buccaneers, was to be the prince or governor. But circumstances were still unfavourable. Lord John Vaughan, the newly-appointed governor of Jamaica, had orders strictly to enforce the treaty with Spain formed in the previous year, but to proclaim pardon and indemnity, and offer a grant of lands to such of the buccaneers as chose to become peaceful cultivators. Future depredations on the trade or settlements of Spain were forbidden by the royal proclamation, and under severe penalties. But it was not a proclamation, however strongly worded, that could at once tame down the lawless buccaneer into a planter, or confine to thirty-seven acres of ground him who had for years freely roamed through sea and land, with his sword reaping his harvest wherever men of greater industry had sown it. To adopting the habits of peaceful life many of the English buccaneers preferred joining the flibustiers at Tortuga, or becoming logwood-cutters in the Bay of Campeachy; and, luckily for the remainder, in the next year a war broke out between Great Britain and Holland, which enabled some of them to follow their old vocation as privateers, —buccaneers and flibustiers alike exercising their industry for a short time against the Dutch, instead of their old enemies the Spaniards.

Before quitting this part of the subject, it may be proper to notice the conclusion of the adventures of the notorious Morgan. In the years which elapsed between the plunder of Panama and 1680, he had sufficient address and interest, or, more probably, skill in the appliance of his ill-gotten wealth, to obtain from Charles II. the honour of knighthood, and afterwards to be appointed deputy-governor of Jamaica. Though it was believed that he still secretly shared in the plundering adventures of the buccaneers, Morgan treated many of his old comrades with very great severity. Several of them were hanged under his administration, and others he delivered up to the Spaniards at Carthagena, as was believed, for the price of blood; nor does the character of Morgan make this suspicion improbable. The strict justice and severity exercised by the deputy-governor on his old friends and countrymen did not, however, dispose the Spaniards to unlimited confidence in Morgan; and suspecting him of secretly favouring the buccaneers, who had once more increased, they were able, after the accession of James II., to get him removed from his office and committed for a time to prison in England.

The same unwise restrictions, and troublesome interference with the cultivation and commerce of the colonies, which had encouraged the system of buccaneering in its commencement, fostered it once more, though France, instead of Spain, was become the agent in this mistaken policy. The regulations adopted by the government of France for the West India trade, and the partial and oppressive administration of colonial affairs, tended more than any other circumstance to recruit the ranks of the freebooters,—men, disturbed in their peaceful industry by vexatious and annoying prohibitions and monopolies, readily placing themselves beyond the law, which was more their torment than protection. Thus, though the freebooters were at length crushed by the express prohibitions of their several countries, they were incited by causes more powerful, originating in the same source.

In 1683, the buccaneers, led by three noted chiefs, Van Horn, Grammont, and Laurent de Graff, by a stratagem took the city of Vera Cruz in the Gulf of Mexico. Many of the English buccaneers were engaged in this expedition, though none of them held high command. This was reckoned the most brilliant exploit that had yet been achieved by the flibustiers. Their mode of attack was similar to that which had been practised by Drake a century before. In the darkness of night a sufficient force was landed, which marched three leagues over-land, and before dawn surprised and captured the city. The inhabitants were shut up in the churches, the usual prison of the buccaneers, at the door of each of which barrels of gunpowder were placed, and sentinels beside them, holding a lighted match, ready to produce an explosion at a moment's notice, or on the slightest symptom of revolt. The city was thus pillaged without molestation from the inhabitants; and the famished prisoners in the churches were afterwards glad to purchase their freedom on any terms their conquerors chose to dictate. Ten millions of livres were demanded as a ransom; and the half of it had been raised and paid in, when the appearance of a body of troops, and a fleet of seventeen ships, caused the freebooters to make a precipitate but well-ordered retreat, carrying off one thousand five hundred slaves. Loaded with their booty and prisoners, they boldly sailed through the fleet sent to attack them, which did not venture to fire a single gun. They might probably have roused the Spaniards from their fear or lethargy by an assault, had they not been more careful to preserve the plunder they had obtained than desirous of a barren naval victory over ships carrying no cargoes.

Fortunately for the freedom and repose of the Spanish colonists, no buccaneer corps ever agreed or acted in harmony for any length of time. Their lawless unions fell to pieces even more rapidly than they were formed; and those of the French and English seldom adhered even to the conclusion of a joint expedition. On the present occasion they separated in wrath, the Frenchmen employing the pretext of the quarrel they artfully fomented to withhold the Englishmen's share of the pillage. The later cruises of the buccaneers were in few respects distinguished by the honour and integrity among themselves which were said to have marked their first exploits. The French flibustier now sought but a shallow excuse to plunder the English buccaneer, who, on the other side, lost no opportunity of retaliation.

The tardy though now earnest efforts of France and Britain to crush the Brethren of the Coast, the increasing military and maritime strength of the Spanish colonists, and above all a field too narrow and exhausted for the numerous labourers, together with wild and magnificent ideas of the wealth of Peru, were so many powerful motives urging the buccaneers, whether French or English, upon enterprises in a new and wider region. Among them an estimate was formed of the riches of the western shores from the single circumstance that, in a few years after the visit of Morgan, a new city of Panama had arisen, which in splendour and wealth eclipsed the desolated town. The Peruvian coast and the South Sea, in all their riches and extent, presented a field which neither the long arm of France nor the powerful hand of England could reach; and of the opposition to be feared from the indolent and effeminate inhabitants, the expedition of Morgan had afforded a very satisfactory specimen. In the new design of crossing the continent, and searching for untried regions of conquest and spoliation, the buccaneers were rather urged by personal motives of rapacity, and the desire of escaping from the colonial officials of the West India Islands—who latterly either shared their booty or treated them with great severity, and not unfrequently did both—than influenced by any enlightened or comprehensive plan of operations. The wealth of this new region, and the ease with which it might be acquired, were primary reasons; personal security was merely secondary; and beyond these motives this chaotic banditti never once looked— all their ideas of conquest being limited to the plunder of a city or a ship, to plate, silks, and pieces of eight; nor were their enjoyments and pleasures of a more liberal or elevated kind. We may therefore, without much regret, here close this general sketch of the buccaneers. All that is interesting in their subsequent career, from the plundering of Vera Cruz in the Bay of Mexico to their decay and suppression, is closely interwoven with the personal adventures of Dampier, on which we are now to enter. And in the narrative of this remarkable navigator, instead of monotonous details of fraud, rapacity, and cruelty, on which it has been painful to linger, the reader is gratified with the researches and discoveries of natural science, and with pictures of life and manners, curious, novel, and attractive, which have never yet, among the multitude of succeeding European navigators, fallen under the notice of a more acute and accurate observer, or obtained a delineator more faithful and lively, and occasionally more glowing and poetical, than the extraordinary man whose history we are now to follow, commencing with his early wanderings among the buccaneers.

CHAPTER II.

ADVENTURES AMONG THE WOOD-CUTTERS AND BUCCANEERS.

To Captain Dampier himself the world is indebted for the only record of his early history which can be considered authentic. He was born about 1652, at East Coker, near Yeovil, a considerable market-town in Somersetshire. His father was probably a farmer; and we learn incidentally that his mother, when a widow, along with whatever other property she might possess, held the lease of a small farm at East Coker from Colonel Hellier, the lord of the manor. The small farms in this parish were held for lives, and varied in rent from £20 to £50. By a singular but probably a then common arrangement, each occupier had a patch of land of every different kind of soil, lying apart or scattered throughout the parish, as black-loam, clayey, and sandy ground, which varied in rent from forty, thirty, and twenty shillings an acre, down to ten groats for the poorest. On these scattered patches every yeoman raised wheat, oats, barley, beans, rye, hemp, and flax, for the consumption of his own family. The statistics of East Coker afford a curious picture of English agriculture, and of that race of primitive cultivators who have long since disappeared, and will ever be regretted.

Before the death of his parents, which happened while he was very young, Dampier had begun to receive the elements of a classical education; but on this event taking place his studies were suspended, and he was sent to acquire writing and arithmetic, to qualify him for some humbler employment than might have been originally designed; and in a short time after the death of his mother he was placed with a shipmaster belonging to Weymouth. Slender as his advantages of early education appear to have been, he profited so largely by them as to afford one more proof that the best part of a man's learning is that which he acquires by himself.

William Dampier's first voyage was to France, his next to Newfoundland, in which he suffered so severely from the climate that he almost resolved against returning to sea; but this determination was commuted into a resolution not to try the same ungenial quarter. Dampier, now about eighteen, was already animated by the restless activity, the curiosity, love of vicissitude, adventure, and peril, which form the strong and marking characteristics of the youth who is born a seaman. "The offer," he says, "of a *long* voyage and a *warm* one soon carried me to sea again." He entered as a foremastman on board the *Martha* East Indiaman, which sailed direct from London to Bantam; from whence, after a stay of two months, he returned within little more than the year. From his early childhood Dampier had been a keen observer. On his former voyages he had gained some nautical experience, which he enlarged during the present, diligently studying the practical part of his profession, though he had not yet commenced a journal, the keeping of which came to be the solace of his roaming, unconnected life, and the means of great mental improvement.

The summer after his return from India Dampier spent with his brother in Somersetshire, whose house, in early life, seems to have been his home while on shore. His next service was on board the *Royal Prince*, in which he enlisted, England being then at war with Holland. He was in two engagements; but of a third fought by the ship, in which the commander, Sir Edward Sprague, was killed, he was not a witness, having previously fallen into bad health. From the ship he was sent to Harwich Hospital, and finally to his brother's, where he slowly recovered.

With returning health the love of the sea recurred; but Dampier meanwhile accepted the offer of Colonel Hellier, and went to Jamaica as under-manager of a plantation belonging to that gentleman, forming a special agreement with the captain to protect himself from the frauds of the kidnappers. The ship went "merrily along," steering for Barbadoes, which was the first of the islands that Dampier beheld. He was at this time twenty-two years of age, active, intelligent, and full of an instinctive curiosity, already under the guidance of a strong, clear, and prompt understanding.

St. Lucia was next seen, and afterwards Tobago and St. Vincent. He whose glance was ever quick and sure for every natural production of a new country, was not likely to neglect its people. The condition of the Carib Indians, the aborigines of the islands, forcibly arrested the attention of the young voyager; and he relates a contemporary incident in a manner which betrays rather than states the soundness and, when the era is considered, the liberality of his opinions and the correctness of his moral feelings, while it places the Indian character in a favourable and also in a fair light, as contrasted with the European of the colonies.

In passing St. Lucia, the captain of the vessel seeing a smoke on the shore, the usual token of inhabitation, sent off a boat to purchase those fruits with which the Indians often supplied English vessels sailing by. Three Indians came to the ship's side in a canoe laden with sugar-canes, and also with plantains, pine-apples, and other tropical fruits. They seemed much agitated, and often repeated the name of "Captain Warner." It proved that this Captain Warner was the son of Governor Warner of Antigua, by an Indian woman. He had been bred in his father's family as an English youth, but had acquired the language of his mother's tribe. As he grew up, finding himself ill-treated and despised, he fled to St. Lucia, and living among his

Carib kinsmen, adopted their manners, and became one of their chiefs, roving with them from island to island, making inroads upon the planters, not sparing even Antigua. To avenge these injuries the legitimate son of the governor went out at the head of a party to encounter the Indians, and accidentally met with his Carib brother. The young man affected great joy at the meeting, and invited his half-blood elder brother with his warriors to a feast, at which, on a preconcerted signal, the chief and all the Indians were treacherously slaughtered. It was said that the murdered Warner had been the friend of the English, and that pride alone instigated the young Creole to this perfidious butchery. "Such perfidious doings as these," says Dampier, "are great hinderances to our gaining an interest with the Indians, besides the baseness of them."

As a planter Dampier was "clearly out of his element;" and after spending some time in this uncongenial occupation, he engaged with different traders belonging to Port Royal, who coasted round Jamaica, carrying goods from the plantations to that port. In these coasting voyages he became thoroughly acquainted with all the harbours and bays of the island, and with the land and sea winds and currents. Availing himself of every opportunity and means of acquiring knowledge, Dampier appears through life to have become wearied of every scene the moment he had exhausted the information it afforded, and to have longed for change as soon as he had overmastered its difficulties. His next voyage, undertaken in August 1675, was to the island of Trist, in the Bay of Campeachy, for a cargo of logwood. In these later voyages he acted in the capacity of a common sailor in a small vessel; but he now kept a regular journal, and was no common observer. On this voyage to Campeachy, his nautical remarks, and observations on the appearances and bearings of the coasts, the headlands, bays, and islands, are ample and exact—distinguished by the clearness and perspicuity which are visible in all his subsequent relations. They anchored at One-Bush-Key, an islet about a mile from the shore, and so named from having a single stunted tree.

The life of the logwood-cutters of the Bay of Campeachy, free and unrestrained, had many charms for the young adventurer; and their jovial manners and frank hospitality, with the lucrative nature of the occupation of these merry foresters, made him resolve to return and join their ranks as soon as his present engagement terminated.

Logwood-cutting had now in many instances taken the place of hunting wild cattle, which were become scarce. Some adventurers pursued both vocations, and others were wood-cutters alone. A third class occasionally added the variety and profit of a privateering cruise to their quieter employments.

The logwood-cutters in the Bay of Campeachy at this time amounted to about two hundred and fifty men, mostly natives of England, though there were also Scotchmen and Irishmen among their number. By Spain they were considered interlopers, and the trade contraband; but this did not much disturb their consciences. Their general practice was to make up a cargo in joint-stock companies, the partnership lasting till the contract for the number of tons agreed on was completed.

The traders who bought the dye-wood carried the wood-cutters rum, sugar, tobacco, and other things necessary to them. The trade was usually opened by a solemn drinking-match on board the ships, where healths were pledged, and salvoes fired in honour of each pledge, with all the customary demonstrations of buccaneer banqueting. The trader who was the most liberal of his rum-punch on such festive occasions might assure himself of the best bargain of logwood—the cutters priding themselves upon cheating those they thought niggardly of their liquor and good cheer.

While taking in the cargo Dampier was often on shore, and frequently visited the cabins of the wood-men, who hospitably entertained him with the rough substantial fare which abounded among them—pork and pease; or beef, for which they hunted in the savannas; with dough-boys, a kind of thick unleavened cake, which, when on shore, the buccaneers and hunters often kneaded for themselves. They were equally profuse of their liquor while the supply lasted.

The returning voyage of Dampier to Jamaica was

singularly disastrous, and between Trist and Port-Royal the passage occupied thirteen weeks. Of the adventures and perils of this voyage he has left a very lively account. A passenger who returned with them to Jamaica—a prisoner who had escaped from the Spaniards—from his experience of this coast, was the means of saving them from being captured by a Spanish vessel, which gave chase to their bark. Though the crew had both fished and hunted at several places before they reached Jamaica, they were during most part of the passage greatly pinched for provisions; and on coming to anchor after so many hardships, they sent ashore for a supply, made a feast, and were just compounding a flowing bowl of punch, when the captain of a New England trader came on board to visit them, and was invited to share in the carouse. What follows is an amusing trait of the nautical manners of the place and time:—"Mr. Hooker being drank to by Captain Rawlins, who pledged Captain Hudswell, and having the bowl in his hands, said that he was under an oath to drink but three draughts of strong liquor in one day, and putting the bowl to his head turned it off at one draught, and so making himself drunk, disappointed our expectations till we made another bowl. I think it might contain six quarts."

As soon as he was discharged, Dampier returned to the Bay of Campeachy to try his fortunes among the logwood-cutters. Preparatory to this voyage he had provided himself with hatchets, knives, axes, saws, wedges, the sleeping-pavilion necessary for defence against the insects in this climate, and a gun, with a supply of powder and shot. A power of attorney, lodged with a merchant who acted as factor for the logwood-cutters, completed his arrangements.

The logwood-forest, in which the men laboured who were joined by Dampier, was on the west lagoon of Trist Island, in the Bay of Campeachy.

The first wood-cutters were men who had adopted this occupation when buccaneering was overdone from the number of competitors, and become dangerous from prohibitory edicts. They originally settled near the forests of the dye-wood at Cape Catoch. When these were exhausted, they had removed to the Isle of Trist, —the first intimation to the Spaniards of their arrival on a new point being the strokes of their axes on the trees, or the report of their guns in the woods and savannas. These wood-cutters were divided into parties of from three to ten or twelve. The company which consented to receive Dampier as a helper, ignorant as he still was of their employment, consisted of six individuals, who had a cargo of logwood of a hundred tons already felled and chipped, and ready to be brought to the creek, whence it was to be shipped for New England. His wages were to be the price of a ton of wood per month.

The wood-cutters had constructed their cabins close by the sides of the creeks of the east and west lagoons of Trist, for the enjoyment of the refreshing sea-breezes, and to be as near the dye-wood groves as was found convenient. As the nearest trees gradually fell beneath their axes, they frequently, instead of abandoning a favourite habitation, repaired to the scene of their daily labours in their canoes. To each company belonged a canoe, pirogue or large boat, which was necessary in conveying their lading to the traders, and also in the chase; for they hunted cattle by water as well as land, for this purpose driving them into narrow creeks. Their cabins were of fragile construction, but thickly thatched with palm-leaves, to shelter the inmates from the violent rains of the wet season. Above the floor a wooden frame was raised three or four feet, and this barbecue, with the pavilion or mosquito-curtains stretched and supported over it, formed the sleeping-place of the wood-cutters; another, equal in height, covered with earth, formed the domestic hearth; and a third served as seats.

The first adventurers who frequented the Bay, after the existence and the value of the dye-wood in this tract had been accidentally discovered by an English ship, were actual buccaneers, "who, though they could work well enough, yet thought it a dry business to toil at cutting wood." They were, moreover, good marksmen, and took great delight in hunting, though piracy was still their favourite pursuit. Besides plundering on the seas, they often sallied out among the nearest Indian villages, which they pillaged without remorse, carrying off the Indian women to serve in bearing wood and other drudgery, while their husbands were sold to the logwood-merchants who visited the Bay, and resold at Jamaica. To these ruffians the cabins of the ships, which came to minister to their pleasures and necessities, were now what the taverns of Port-Royal, from which they were banished, had been. In these vessels they would gather at a grand drinking-match, and spend £30 or £40 at a sitting, carousing and firing off guns for three or four days successively. Whatever might have been the prevailing character of the wood-cutters at the time of Dampier's visit, the small company to which he was attached appear to have been of a more respectable description than ordinary. Two or three of them were natives of Scotland, who, if not actuated by higher motives, were restrained from falling into the extravagance and riot of their companions by the desire of accumulating money sufficient to enable them to enter upon a better way of life.

The logwood groves were near the sea—this wood growing and thriving best in low wet ground, and among timber of lower growth. The trees were from two to six feet in circumference. They resembled the white thorn of England save in size. The heart of the trunk, which is red, is alone used as a dye-stuff, the spongy outer part being chipped away. It is a heavy wood, and burns well; and for this reason the hunters, wood-cutters, and buccaneers always, when it could be obtained, preferred it for hardening the steel of their fire-arms. Bloodwood, another dye-stuff much esteemed, was found in the Gulf of Nicaragua, and sold at double the price of the logwood—the latter selling at £15 per ton, when the bloodwood cost £30.

Through five days, the logwood-cutters, while the industrious fit was upon them, plied their labours in the groves, and on Saturday hunted in the savannas as a recreation, and also to store their larders for the ensuing week. When a bullock was shot, it was cut up where it lay, divided into quarters, and the large bones taken out, when each man thrust his head through a portion, and trudged home. If his load became too weighty, part was cut off and flung to the beasts and birds of prey which ever prowled and hovered near the hunter. But this mode of lightening their burdens was rarely resorted to from necessity. The wood-cutters were sturdy, robust fellows, accustomed to carry loads of wood of from three to four hundredweight, though their burdens, like everything else, were regulated by their own pleasure and discretion. During the rainy season, when the logwood-grounds were flooded, they would step from their high bed-frames into two feet of water, and remain thus all day—improving this cool season as that most favourable to a good day's work. If there were more than four about the killing of a bullock, while two or three dressed the meat the others went in search of more game—a carcass being the ordinary weekly allowance of four persons.

In this part of the Bay of Campeachy, the dry season commences in September and continues till April or May, when the wet weather sets in with fierce tornadoes, and continues thus till June, from which period rain falls almost incessantly till the end of August. By this time the rivers have risen, and the savannas and all the low grounds are overflowed; and in this state they remain, the savannas appearing like inland lakes, till December and January, when the water begins visibly to drain off, and by the middle of February leaves the land dry. About the beginning of April the pools in the savannas are dried up, and the whole country is so parched that, but for a bountiful provision of Nature, the human beings and the birds and beasts, so lately surrounded with water, must perish of thirst.

During the fervid consuming heats of this season, the wood-cutters betook themselves to the forests in search of the wild pine, which afforded them a hearty and refreshing draught. This interesting plant is minutely described by Dampier, in that clear and succinct manner which characterizes all his notices of natural productions. "The wild pine," he says, "is a plant so called because it somewhat resembles the bush that bears the pine; they are commonly supported, or grow from some bunch, knot, or excrescence of the tree, where they take root and grow upright. The root is short and thick, from whence the leaves rise up in folds one within another, spreading off at the top. They are of a good thick substance, and about ten or twelve inches long. The outside leaves are so compact as to contain the rain-water as it falls. They will hold a pint and a half, or a quart; and this water refreshes the leaves and nourishes the root. When we find these pines we stick our knives into the leaves just above the root, and that lets out the water, which we catch in our hats, as I have done many times to my great relief." Dampier's account of all the natural productions of this country is equally curious. The animals, besides those termed domestic, were the squash, the warce, and peccary, a species of wild-hog, the opossum, tiger-cat, monkeys, ant-bears, armadilloes, porcupines, land-turtle, and the sloth, besides lizards, snakes, and iguanas of many varieties.

The general features of the country in this part of the Bay are, the land near the sea, and the lagoons, always wet and "mangrovy." A little way back from the shore the soil is a strong yellow clay, with a thin surface of black mould. Here logwood-trees and low-growing timber of many kinds thrive. As it recedes further from the sea, the land rises, and trees of taller growth are met with, till the forests terminate in large savannas covered with long grass. These flats or natural meadows are generally three miles wide, and often much more. The soil of the savannas is black, deep, and rich, and the grass luxuriant in growth, but of a coarse kind. As an easy mode of husbandry which suited them well, the cattle-hunters at the close of the dry season set fire to the grass of the savannas, which, immediately after the setting in of the rains, were covered by a new and delicate herbage. These plains are bounded by high ridges and declivities of the richest land, covered with stately trees; and these alternate ridges and flats, fine woodlands and grassy plains, stretch from ten to twenty miles into the interior, which was as far as Dampier's knowledge extended.

In the woods, monkeys abound, ranging in bands of from twenty to thirty, leaping from tree to tree, incessantly chattering with frightful noise, making antic gestures, and throwing sticks and other missiles at the passers-by. When first alone in the woods Dampier felt afraid to shoot at them. They accompanied him on his ramble, leaping from branch to branch, swinging overhead with threatening gestures, as if about to leap upon him, and only took leave at the wood-cutters' huts. Though they were easily shot, it was difficult to take them, as after being wounded they pertinaciously clung to the high branches by their tails or claws while life remained. "I have pitied," says our navigator, "the poor creature, to see it look on and handle the wounded limb, and turn it about from side to side." The sloths feed on leaves, and are very destructive to trees, never forsaking one on which they have pitched till it is stripped as bare as winter. A sloth requires eight or nine minutes to move one of its feet three inches forward, and it can neither be provoked nor frightened to move faster. Of some of the species of snakes,

Dampier relates that they lurk in trees, "and are so mighty in strength as to hold a bullock fast by one of his horns," if it comes so near the tree as to allow the snake to twist itself about the horn and a limb of the tree at the same time. The buccaneers sometimes ate them, though Dampier makes no favourable report of this kind of food. An anecdote, which he relates of a snake in the Bay, gives a rational account of what is termed *fascination* in birds. The green-snake, which is from four to five feet long and no thicker than a man's thumb, lurked among green leaves, from which it could hardly be distinguished, and preyed upon small birds. Dampier was one day about to take hold of a bird, which, to his astonishment, though it fluttered and cried, did not attempt to fly away. He discovered that about the upper part of the poor bird a green-snake had twisted itself. Spiders of prodigious size were seen here, some almost as big as a man's hand, with long small legs like the spiders of Europe:— "They have two teeth, or rather horns, an inch and a half in length, and of a proportionable bigness, which are black as jet, smooth as glass, and their small end sharp as a thorn." These the buccaneers and wood-cutters used as tooth-picks, as they were said to cure toothache. They also used them to pick their tobacco-pipes. The country abounded in ants of different species, some of which had a sting "sharp as a spark of fire." They build their habitations between the limbs of great trees; and some of the hillocks were "as large as a hogshead."

In this manner the ants provide against the consequences of the rainy season, when their hillocks, if on the ground, must be overflowed. One species marched in troops, always in haste, as if in search of something, but steadily following their leaders wherever they went. Sometimes a band of these ants would march through the cabins of the wood-cutters, over their beds, or into their chests,—wherever the foremost went the rest all following. The logwood-cutters let them pass on, though some hours might be spent in the march.

Frequently as the humming-bird has been described since it was seen by Dampier, his account of this, the most delicate and lovely of the feathered tribes, is as fresh and beautiful as when the young seaman, charmed with its loveliness, first entered a description of it into his rude journal:—" The humming-bird is a pretty little feathered creature, no bigger than a great overgrown wasp; with a black bill no bigger than a small needle, and with legs and feet in proportion to his body. This creature does not wave its wings like other birds when it flies, but keeps them in a continued quick motion, like bees or other insects; and like them makes a continued humming noise as it flies. It is very quick in motion, and haunts about flowers and fruit like a bee gathering honey; making many addresses to its delightful objects, by visiting them on all sides, and yet still keeps in motion, sometimes on one side, sometimes on the other, as often rebounding a foot or two back on a sudden, and as quickly returns again, keeping thus about one flower five or six minutes or more."

The wood-cutters and hunters, in their out-door and silvan life, became familiar with all the living creatures of these prolific regions, and gave them English names significant of their habits. They adopted the superstition of the Spaniards against killing the carrion-crows, which were found so useful in clearing the country of the putrid carcasses of animals. Trains of these birds gathered from all quarters about the hunters, and regularly followed them into the savannas for their own share of the prey. A bird which they named the Subtle Jack was about as big as the pigeons of the Bay. It suspended its nest from the boughs of lofty trees, choosing such as, up to a considerable height, were without limbs. The branches selected were those that spread widest; and of these the very extremity was chosen. The nests hung down two or three feet from the twigs to which they were fastened, and looked like "cabbage-nets stuffed with hay." The thread by which it is suspended, like the nest itself, is made of long grass ingeniously twisted and interwoven, small at the twig, but thickening as it approaches the nest. On trees that grow singly and apart the birds build all round; but where the trees stand in proximity to others, the Subtle Jack chooses only those that border upon a savanna, pool, or creek; and of these, the limbs that stretch over the water or the grass, avoiding such as may be easily approached from neighbouring trees. The nest has a hole at the side for the bird to enter. " 'Tis pretty," says Dampier, " to see twenty or thirty of them hanging round a tree."

In these savannas and primeval forests, an endless variety of birds and insects engaged the attention of the young seaman, to which we cannot now advert. The creeks, rivers, and lagoons, as well as the open shores, were equally prolific of fishes unknown in the English waters. No place in the world was better stored with alligators than the Bay of Campeachy. These the buccaneers, who scrupled at no sort of food, never ate save in cases of great necessity, as even their intrepid stomachs were offended by the strong musky flavour of the flesh of this hideous creature. The alligators of the Bay were generally harmless when not molested; though accidents sometimes occurred, of which one is recorded by Dampier that merits notice. In the height of the dry season, when in those torrid regions all animated nature pants with consuming thirst, a party of the wood-cutters, English and Irish, went to hunt in the neighbourhood of a lake called Pies Pond in Beef Island, one of the smaller islands of the Bay. To this pond the wild cattle repaired in herds to drink, and here the hunters lay in wait for them. The chase had been prosecuted with great success for a week, when an Irishman of the party, going into the water during the day, stumbled upon an alligator, which seized him by the knee. His cries alarmed his companions, who, fearing that he had been seized by the Spaniards, to whom the island belonged, and who chose the dry season to hunt and repel their unwelcome neighbours, instead of affording assistance, fled from the huts which they had erected. The Irishman seeing no appearance of help, with happy presence of mind quietly waited till the alligator loosened its teeth to take a new and surer hold; and when it did so, he snatched away his knee, interposing the butt-end of his gun in its stead, which the animal seized so firmly that it was jerked out of the man's hand and carried off. He then crawled up a neighbouring tree, again shouting after his comrades, who now found courage to return. His gun was found next day dragged ten or twelve paces from the place where it had been seized by the alligator.

At the same place, Pies Pond in Beef Island, Dampier had a remarkable escape from an alligator. Passing with some of his comrades through a small savanna, where the water lay two or three feet deep, in search of a bullock to shoot for supper, a strong scent of an alligator was perceived, and presently Dampier stumbled over one and fell down. He cried out for help, but his companions ran towards the woods to save themselves. No sooner had he scrambled up to follow them, than in the agitation of the moment he fell a second and even a third time, expecting every instant to be devoured, and yet escaped untouched; but he candidly says, " I was so frighted, that I never cared to go through the water again as long as I was in the Bay."

On the first Saturday after he commenced woodcutter Dampier followed his employers in the humble capacity of raising and driving the cattle out of the savannas into the woods, where the hunters lay in wait to shoot them. The following Saturday his ambition took a higher flight. He thought it more honourable to have a shot himself than to drive the game for others; and, after going five miles by water and one by land to the hunting-ground, he gave his companions the slip, and rambled so far into the woods that he lost himself, going at every step further astray through small strips of savanna and skirts of woodland—a maze of plain and forest which seemed interminable. The rest of this youthful adventure, from which Dampier drew a beneficial lesson for the regulation of his future life, cannot be better narrated than in his own words:—" This was in May (the dry season), and it was between ten o'clock and one when I began to find that I was, as we call it, *marooned*, or lost, and quite out of the hearing of my comrades' guns. I was somewhat surprised at this ; but, however, I knew that I should find my way out as soon as the sun was a little lower. So I sat down to rest myself, resolving, however, to run no further out of my way, for the sun being so near the zenith I could not distinguish how to direct my course. Being weary and almost faint for want of water, I was forced to have recourse to the wild pines, and was by them supplied, or else I must have perished with thirst. About three o'clock I went due north, or as near as I could judge, for the savanna lay east and west, and I was on the south side of it.

"At sunset I got out into the clear open savanna, being about two leagues wide in most places, but how long I know not. It is well stored with bullocks, but by frequent hunting they grow shy, and remove further up into the country. There I found myself four or five miles to the west of the place where I had straggled from my companions. I made homewards with all the speed I could; but being overtaken by the night I lay down on the grass a good distance from the woods, for the benefit of the wind to keep the mosquitoes from me; but in vain, for in less than an hour's time I was so persecuted, that though I endeavoured to keep them off by fanning myself with boughs, and shifting my quarters three or four times, yet still they so haunted me that I could get no sleep. At daybreak I got up and directed my course to the creek where we landed, from which I was then about two leagues. I did not see one beast of any sort whatever in all the way, though the day before I saw several young calves that could not follow their dams; but even these were now gone away, to my great vexation and disappointment, for I was very hungry. But, about a mile further, I espied ten or twelve quaums perching on the boughs of a cotton-tree. These were not shy: therefore I got well under them, and, having a single bullet but no shot about me, fired at one of them and missed it, though I had often before killed them so. Then I came up with and fired at five or six turkeys with no better success, so that I was forced to march forward, still in the savanna, toward the creek; and when I came to the path that led to it through the woods, I found to my great joy a hat stuck upon a pole, and when I came to the creek another. These were set up by my consorts, who had gone home in the evening, as signals that they would come and fetch me. Therefore I sat down and waited for them; for although I had not above three leagues home by water, yet it would have been very difficult, if not impossible, for me to have got thither overland, by reason of those vast impassable thickets abounding everywhere along the creek's side, wherein I have known some puzzled for two or three days, and have not advanced half a mile, although they laboured extremely every day. Neither was I disappointed of my hopes, for within half an hour after my arrival in the creek my consorts came, bringing every man his bottle of water and his gun, both to hunt for game and to give me notice by firing, that I might hear them; for I have known several men lost in the like manner, and never heard of afterwards."

Dampier had the more reason to congratulate himself on the issue of this adventure, that shortly before the captain and six of the crew of a Boston ship had wandered into the woods, part of whom were never again heard of. The captain, who was found in a thicket in a state of extreme exhaustion, stated that his men had dropped one by one, fainting for thirst in the parched savannas.

When his first month's service was ended, Dampier received as pay the price of a ton of wood, with which he bought provisions, and entered into a new engagement, on the footing of comradeship, but with other partners. Of the former company to which he had been attached, some went to Beef Island to hunt bullocks for their skins, which they prepared for sale by pegging them strongly down to the ground, turning first the fleshy and then the hairy side uppermost, till they were perfectly dry. It required thirty-two pegs, each as thick as a man's arm, to stretch one hide; afterwards, they were hung in heaps upon a pole, that they might not touch the ground, and from time to time well beat with sticks to drive out the worms which bred in the skins and spoiled them. Before being shipped off, they were soaked in salt water to kill the remaining worms. While still wet they were folded up, left thus for a time, and once more thoroughly dried and packed for exportation.

To this trade Dampier preferred wood-cutting. His partners were three Scotchmen, Price Morrice, Duncan Campbell, and a third, who is called by his Christian name of George only. The two latter were persons of education, who had been bred merchants, and liked neither the employment nor the society of the Bay; they therefore only waited the first opportunity of getting away by a logwood-ship. The first vessel that arrived was from Boston, and this they freighted with forty tons of dye-wood, which it was agreed Duncan

Campbell should go to New England to sell, bringing back flour and other things suited to the market of the Bay, to exchange for hides and logwood; while George remained making up a fresh cargo against Campbell's return. And here Dampier makes an observation on the character of his associates, which deserves to be noticed as the result of the experience of a man who had seen and reflected much upon life and manners. "This," he says, "retarded our business, for I did not find Price Morrice very intent on work; for 'tis like he thought he had logwood enough. And I have particularly observed there, and in other places, that such as had been well-bred were generally most careful to improve their time, and would be very industrious and frugal when there was any probability of considerable gain. But, on the contrary, such as had been inured to hard labour, and got their living by the sweat of their brows, when they came to have plenty, would extravagantly squander away their time and money in drinking and making a bluster."

To make up for the indolence of his comrade Dampier kept the closer to work himself, till attacked by a very singular disease. A red and ill-conditioned swelling or boil broke out upon his right leg, which he was directed to poultice with the roasted roots of the white lily. This he persisted in doing for some days, "when two white specks appeared in the centre of the boil, and on squeezing it two small white worms spurted out, about the thickness of a hen's quill and three or four inches long."

These were quite different from the Guinea-worm, common in some of the West India Islands, and in the time of Dampier very common in Curaçoa. From the latter he afterwards suffered severely.

Shortly after his recovery from this attack the Bay was visited by one of those tremendous hurricanes known only in tropical countries, which raged for twenty-four hours without intermission. This was in June 1676. Two days before the storm came on the wind "whiffled" about to the south and back again to the east, but blew faintly, while the weather continued very fair, though it was remarked that the men-of-war birds came trooping towards the shore in great numbers, and hovered over the land. The hunters and logwood-cutters, among their numerous superstitions, augured the arrival of ships from the appearance of those birds, and imagined that as many birds as hovered overhead so many vessels might be expected. At this time there appeared whole flocks.

It was noticed by Dampier that for two days the tide kept ebbing, till the creek by which the woodmen's huts stood was left nearly dry. In it there was commonly at ebb-tide seven or eight feet of water, but now scarcely three remained even in the deepest places. At four o'clock, in the afternoon following this strange ebbing of the waters, the sky looked very black, the wind sprung up at south-east, fresh and rapidly increasing, and in less than two hours blew down all the cabins of the woodmen save one: this they propped with posts, and as it were anchored by casting ropes over the roof, which were then made fast on both sides to stumps of trees. In this frail shed they all huddled together while the hurricane raged abroad. It rained in torrents during the whole period of the tempest; and in two hours after the wind had risen the water flowed so fast into the creek that it was as high as the banks. Though the wind now blew off-shore, the waters continued to rush in; nor did the rain abate; and by ten o'clock next morning the banks of the creek were overflowed.

The situation of the woodmen now became perilous. They brought their canoe to the side of the hut, and fastened it to the stump of a tree as a means of escape—this being their only hope of safety, as beyond the banks which edged the creek the land fell, and there "was now no walking through the woods because of the water. Besides, the trees were torn up by the roots, and tumbled down so strangely across each other that it was almost impossible to pass through them." In this violent tempest many fish were either cast alive upon the shore or found floating dead in the lagoons. It was remarkable that the hurricane, as was afterwards ascertained, did not extend ninety miles to windward.

Of four ships riding at anchor at One-Bush Key, three were driven from their moorings, and one of them was carried up into the woods of Beef Island.

The wood-cutters suffered in many ways. The whole country was laid under water to a considerable depth, there being three feet even on the highest land; so that they could not for some time prosecute their labours. Much of their provision was destroyed, and what remained they had no way of cooking save in their canoes.

As soon as the storm abated, Dampier's company embarked in the canoe and made for One-Bush Key, about four leagues distant, hoping to procure assistance from the ships there. These, as has been noticed, had all been driven from their anchors save one; and the kindness of the crew of this fortunate vessel had already been severely taxed by an influx of the flooded woodcutters from different points. Dampier and his companions could get "neither bread nor punch, nor so much as a dram of rum, though they offered to pay for it." From this inhospitable quarter they rowed for Beef Island, their singular landmark being the flag of a ship displayed in the woods. The vessel herself was found two hundred yards from the sea, from which she had cut her way in the storm, levelling the trees on each side, and making a clear path before her through the forest. In this transit the stumps had gone through her bottom, and there was no way of saving her. Meanwhile she held together, and the forlorn woodmen were well entertained with victuals and punch, and invited to remain for the night; but hearing a signal-gun fired from a distant lagoon, they concluded that one of the ships was driven in there by distress, and rowed off to her assistance. With a Captain Chandler, whom they found here greatly in want of their services, Dampier and his partners laboured for two days, and then went to Beef Island to hunt for cattle. This island is about seven leagues long, and in breadth from three to four: at the east end "low drowned land;" the middle is one large savanna, bordered with trees; the south side, between the savannas and the mangrove-belt or swampy ground, is very rich.

But the social condition of Beef Island, at the time specified, is more an object of interest than its natural productions. It had been lately settled by a colony of Indians. "It is no new thing," says Dampier, "for the Indians of these woody parts of America to fly away, whole towns at once, and settle themselves in the unfrequented woods to enjoy their freedom; and if they are accidentally discovered, they will remove again; which they can easily do, their household goods being little else but their hammocks and their calabashes. They build every man his own house, and tie up their hammocks between two trees, wherein they sleep till their houses are made. The woods afford them some subsistence, such as pecaree and waree; but they that are thus strolling, or *marooning* as the Spaniards call it, have plantain-walks that no man knows but themselves, and from thence have their food till they have raised plantation-provision near their new-built town. They clear no more ground than what they actually employ for their subsistence. They make no paths; but when they go far from home they break now and then a bough, letting it hang down, which serves as a mark to guide them in their return. If they happen to be discovered by other Indians inhabiting among the Spaniards, or do but distrust it, they immediately shift their quarters to another place,—this large country affording them good fat land enough, and very woody, and therefore a proper sanctuary for them."

It was some of these fugitive Indians that came to settle at Beef Island, where, besides gaining their freedom from the Spaniards, they might see their friends and acquaintances, that had been taken some time before by the privateers and sold to the log-wood-cutters, with whom some of the women lived still, though others had been conducted by them to their own habitations. It was these women, after their return, that made known the kind entertainment they met with from the English, and persuaded their friends to leave their dwellings near the Spaniards and settle on this island. They had been here almost a year before they were discovered by the English, and even then were accidentally found out by the hunters as they followed their game. "They were not very shy all the time I was there," continues Dampier; "but I know that upon the least disgust they would have been gone." This avoidance of their "kind entertainers," the English, does not look as if the Indians had been peculiarly anxious to cultivate their further acquaintance. The poor Indians were undoubtedly equally anxious to conceal themselves and their plantations from the Spaniards, from whom they fled, and the English hunters and logwood-cutters, whom they shunned.

John d'Acosta, a Spaniard of the town of Campeachy, who held a grant of this island, managed better than any of his countrymen in securing his property from the depredations of the buccaneers. In the dry season he spent usually a couple of months here with his servants, "hocksing" cattle for their hides and tallow. Beef was to him of course of small value; and happening at one time to encounter the logwood-men hunting in his savannas, he requested them to desist, saying that firing made the cattle wild; but that if they wanted beef he would supply them with as much as they pleased by *hocksing*. They accepted the offer, and acted with honour to John d'Acosta, who soon became very popular among them, though their friendship did him no good with his own countrymen. He was thrown into prison upon suspicion of conniving with the buccaneers, and forfeited his right to Beef Island, which henceforth the Spaniards abandoned to the English hunters and freebooters.

The manner of hunting wild cattle, termed *hocksing* or *houghing*, was peculiar to the Spaniards, the English always using fire-arms in the chase. The Spanish *hocksers*, in the course of many years' practice, became dexterous at their art. They were always mounted on good horses, which were as diligently and early trained to the sport as the rider, and as well aware when to advance and retreat with advantage. The hunter was armed with a hocksing-iron in the shape of a crescent, about seven inches in length, and having a very sharp edge. This was fastened to a pole about fourteen feet in length, which the hunter laid over the horse's head, the instrument projecting forward. Riding up to his prey, with this he strikes, and seldom fails to hamstring it, when the horse instantly wheels to the left to avoid the attack of the wounded animal. If the stroke has not quite severed all the sinews, the animal soon breaks them himself by continually attempting to leap forward. While limping thus, and somewhat exhausted, the hunter rides up to him again, and at this time attacks him in front, striking the iron into the knee of one of his fore legs. The animal usually drops, when the hunter dismounts, and with a sharp-pointed knife strikes into the head a little behind the horns so dexterously that at one stroke the head drops as if severed from the neck, and the poor beast is dead. The hunter remounts and pursues other game while the skinners take off the hide.

The English hunters had so greatly thinned the numbers of wild cattle on Beef Island, that it was now dangerous for a single man to hunt them, or to venture through the savannas, so desperate and vicious had they become. An old bull, once shot at, never failed to remember the attack and to offer battle; and the whole herd sometimes drew up in array to defend themselves. The account which Dampier gives of the tactics of the wild cattle almost borders upon the marvellous, though he is one of the most veracious and unpretending of travellers, rather diminishing than exaggerating the dangers he had passed and the wonders he had seen. The old bulls led the van, behind them were ranged the cows, and next in order the young cattle. Wherever the hunters attempted to break the line, the bulls opposed their embattled front, wheeling round in every direction to face the enemy. The aim of the hunter was therefore rather an animal detached from the herd than a general or open attack. If the prey was desperately wounded, in its rage it made for the hunter; but if only slightly, it scampered off. These assaults of the infuriated animals were sometimes attended by fatal accidents.

The hurricane had deprived Dampier of his slender stock of provisions, and having neither money nor credit to obtain a fresh supply from the traders who arrived from Jamaica, he was forced, for immediate subsistence, to join a company of "privateers" then in the Bay. With these buccaneers he continued for nearly a year, rambling about the Bay of Campeachy, visiting its numerous creeks, islands, and rivers, and making with them frequent descents upon Indian villages and Spanish settlements. At these places they obtained supplies of Indian corn, which, with the beef for which they hunted, turtle, and *manatee*, formed their principal subsistence, Dampier, in every passing hour, adding to his stores of knowledge.

The manatee or sea-cow, as seen by Dampier in the Bay of Campeachy, the river Darien, at Mindanao, and on the coast of New Holland, he describes as of the thickness of a horse, and in length ten or twelve feet. The mouth is like that of a cow; the lips are very thick, the eyes no bigger than a pea, and the ears two small holes. It frequents creeks, inlets, and mouths of rivers, and never leaves the water for any length of time. It lives on a sort of grass which grows in the sea. The flesh is white, sweet, and wholesome. The tail of a young cow was esteemed a delicate morsel by the buccaneers, and so was a sucking-calf, which they cooked by roasting. The tough thick skin of the manatee they applied to various uses.

The Mosquito Indians were peculiarly dexterous in fishing, and also in striking manatee and catching turtle; for which purpose the buccaneers always tried to have one or two natives of the Mosquito Shore attached to their company as purveyors on their cruises.

In the river of Tobasco, near its mouth, abundance of manatee was found, there being good feeding for them in the creeks. In one creek which ran into the land for two or three hundred paces, and where the water was so shallow that the backs of the animals were seen as they fed, they were found in great numbers. On the least noise they dashed out into the deep water of the river. There was also a fresh-water species resembling those of the sea, but not so large. The banks of the creek which they frequented were swampy and overgrown with trees, and the same place afforded great abundance of land-turtle, the largest Dampier ever saw save at the Gallapagos Islands in the South Sea, the very head-quarters of turtle. On the borders of the Tobasco lie ridges of dry rich land, covered with lofty "cotton and cabbage-trees, which make a pleasant landscape," and in some places guava-trees, bearing large and finely-flavoured fruit; there were also cocoa-plums and grapes. The savannas, on which herds of deer and bullocks were seen feeding, especially in the mornings and evenings, were fenced with natural groves of the guava. Dampier appears to have been delighted with the aspect of this "delicious place." While he was here, a party hunting in the savannas late in the evening shot a deer. One of them, while skinning the animal, was shot dead by a comrade, who in the twilight mistook him for another deer.

For above twenty miles up the river there was no settlement; after which there was a small fort, with a garrison consisting of a Spaniard, and eight or ten Indians whom he commanded, whose business was rather to spread alarm into the interior if the buccaneers approached, than to resist their attacks. Their precautions were, however, useless when opposed to the address and activity of the buccaneers, who had frequently pillaged the towns and villages on this river, though latterly they had sometimes been repulsed with loss. In some of these towns there were merchants and planters, cocoa-walks being frequent on both sides of the river. Some parts along the banks were thickly planted with Indian towns, each having a *padre*, and also a *cacique*, or governor. These Indians were free labourers in the cocoa-walks of the Spanish settlers, though a few of them had plantations of maize, plantain-walks, and even small cocoa-walks of their own. Some of the natives were bee-hunters, searching in the hollow trees in the woods for hives, and selling the wax and honey. These Indian bee-hunters were so ingenious as to supply the wild bees with trees artificially hollowed, and thus increased the number of hives and the profits of their traffic. "The Indians inhabiting these villages live like gentlemen," says Dampier, "in comparison of many near any great towns, such as Campeachy or Merida; for there even the poorer and rascally sort of people that are not able to hire one of these poor creatures, will by violence drag them to do their drudgery for nothing, after they have worked all day for their masters."

The Indians of the villages on the Tobasco lived chiefly on maize, which they baked into cakes; and from which they also made a sort of liquor, which, when allowed to sour, afforded a pleasant refreshing draught. When a beverage for company was wanted, a little honey was mixed with this drink. A stronger liquor was made of parched maize and anotta, which was drunk without straining. The Indians reared abundance of turkeys, ducks, and fowls,—the padre taking such strict account of the tithe that it was necessary to procure his license before they durst kill one. They also raised cotton, and manufactured their own clothing, which for both sexes was decent and becoming.

Under the sanction of the village-priest all marriages were contracted,—the men marrying at fourteen, the women at twelve. If at this early age they had made no choice, then the padre selected for them. These early marriages were one means of securing the power and increasing the gains of the priest; and the young couples themselves were contented, happy, and affectionate. They inhabited good houses, lived comfortably by the sweat of their brows, and on holy eves and saints' days enjoyed themselves under the direction of their spiritual guides, who permitted them the recreation of pipe and tabor, hautboys and drums, and lent them vizards and ornaments for the mummings and other amusements which they practised. The village churches were lofty, compared with the ordinary dwelling-houses, and ornamented with coarse pictures of tawny or bronze-coloured saints and madonnas, recommended to the Indians by the tint of the native complexion. To their good padres, notwithstanding the tithe-fowls, the Indian flocks were submissive and affectionate.

We cannot here follow the minute account which Dampier has given of all the rivers of Campeachy during his cruise of eleven months around this rich country. The farthest west point which he visited was Alvarado, to which the buccaneers with whom he sailed went in two barks, thirty men in each. The river flows through a fertile country, thickly planted with Spanish towns and Indian villages. At its mouth was a small fort, placed on the declivity of a sand-bank, and mounted with six guns. The sand-banks are here about two hundred feet high on both sides.

This fort the buccaneers attacked; but it held out stoutly for five hours, during which time the country was alarmed, and the inhabitants of the adjoining town got off in their boats, carrying away all their money and valuables, and the best part of their goods. The buccaneers lost ten men killed or desperately wounded; and when they landed next morning to pillage, it being dark before the fort yielded, little booty was found. Twenty or thirty bullocks they killed, salted, and sent on board, with salt-fish, Indian corn, and abundance of poultry. They also found and brought away many tame parrots of a very beautiful kind, yellow and scarlet curiously blended; the fairest and largest birds of their kind Dampier ever saw in the West Indies. "They prated very prettily."

Though little solid booty was obtained, what with provisions, chests, hen-coops, and parrots' cages, the ships were filled and lumbered; and while in this state, seven Spanish *armadilloes* from Vera Cruz, detached in pursuit of the buccaneers, appeared coming full sail over the bar into the river. Not a moment was to be lost. Clearing their decks of lumber, by throwing all overboard, the buccaneers got under full sail, and drove over the bar at the river's mouth, before the enemy, who could with difficulty stem the current, had scarcely reached it. The Spanish vessels were to windward, and a few shots were of necessity exchanged; and now commenced one of those singular escapes from tremendous odds of strength of which buccaneer history is so full. The *Toro*, the admiral of the Spanish barks, was of itself more than a match for the freebooters. It carried ten guns and one hundred men, while their whole force was now diminished to fifty men in both ships, one of which carried six, the other two guns. Another of the Spanish vessels carried four guns, with eighty men, and the remaining five, though not mounted with great guns, had each sixty or seventy men armed with muskets. "As soon," says Dampier's journal, "as we were over the bar, we got our larboard tacks aboard, and stood to the eastward as nigh the wind as we could lie. The Spaniards came quartering on us, and our ship being the headmost the *Toro* came directly towards us, designing to board us. We kept firing at her, in hopes to have lamed either a mast or a yard; but failing, just as she was sheering aboard we gave her a good volley, and presently clapped the helm aweather, wore our ship, and got our starboard tacks aboard, and stood to the westward, and so left the *Toro;* but were saluted by all the small craft as we passed them, who stood to the eastward after the *Toro,* that was now in pursuit and close to our consort. We stood to the westward till we were against the river's mouth, then we tacked, and by the help of the current that came out of the river we were near a mile to windward of them all. Then we made sail to assist our consort, who was hard put to it; but on our approach the *Toro* edged away toward the shore, as did all the rest, and stood away for Alvarado; and we, glad of the deliverance, went away to the eastward, and visited all the rivers in our return again to Trist."

These visits produced little booty. They also searched the bays for *munjack,* "a sort of bitumen which we find in a lump washed up by the sea, and left dry on all the sandy bays of the coast." This substance the buccaneers, who were compelled to find substitutes for many necessary things, tempered with tallow or oil, and employed as pitch in repairing their ships and canoes.

On the return of Dampier to the island of Trist, the effects of the dismal hurricane of the former year had disappeared, and he resumed his labours among the woodmen. This employment was probably more profitable than his buccaneering cruise; as in the course of the following season he was able to visit England, intending to return to the Bay when he had seen his friends. He sailed for Jamaica in April 1678, and in the beginning of August reached London.

Cutting dye-wood was still a profitable though a laborious trade; and Dampier shrewdly remarks, "that though it is not his business to say how far the English had a right to follow it, yet he was sure that the Spaniards never received less damage from the persons who usually followed that trade than when they had exchanged the musket for the axe, and the deck of the privateer for the logwood-groves."

During his short residence in England at this time Dampier must have married; for though a trifling matter of this kind is too unimportant to be entered in a seaman's journal, we long afterwards, while he lay off the Bashee or Five Islands, learn that he had left a wife in England, as, in compliment to the Duke of Grafton, he named the northernmost of the Bashee group Grafton's Isle, "having," as he says, "married my wife out of his duchess's family, and leaving her at Arlington House at my going abroad."

CHAPTER III.

ADVENTURES WITH THE BUCCANEERS.

AFTER spending five or six months with his wife and his friends, Dampier, in the beginning of 1679, sailed as a passenger for Jamaica, intending immediately to return to his old trade and companions in the Bay of Campeachy. He took out goods from England, which he meant to exchange at Jamaica for the commodities in request among the wood-cutters. Instead, however, of prosecuting this design, Dampier remained in Jamaica all that year, and by some means was enabled to purchase a small estate in Dorsetshire. This new possession he was about to visit, when he was induced to engage in a trading voyage to the Mosquito Shore. It promised to be profitable, and he was anxious to realize a little more ready money before returning to England to settle for life. He accordingly sent home the title-deeds of his estate, and embarked with a Mr. Hobby.

Soon after leaving Port-Royal, they came to anchor in a bay at the west end of the island, in which they found Captains Coxon, Sawkins, Sharp, and "other privateers," as Dampier gently terms the most noted buccaneer commanders of the period. Hobby's crew deserted him to a man to join the buccaneer squadron; and the Mosquito voyage being thus frustrated, Dampier "was the more easily persuaded to go with them too."

Their first attempt was on Porto Bello, of which assault Dampier gives no account, and he might not have been present at the capture. Two hundred men were landed, and, the better to prevent alarm, at such a distance from the town that it took them three days to march upon it, as during daylight they lay concealed in the woods. A negro gave the alarm, but not before the buccaneers were so close upon his heels that the inhabitants were completely taken by surprise, and fled in every direction. The buccaneers plundered for two days and two nights, in momentary expectation of the country rising upon them, and overpowering their small number, but, from avarice and rapacity, they were unable to tear themselves away.

To the shame of the Spaniards they got clear off, and divided shares of one hundred and sixty pieces of eight a-head. Inspired by this success, they resolved immediately to march across the Isthmus. They knew that such strokes of good fortune as this at Porto Bello could not longer be looked for on the eastern shores of America, and for some time their imaginations had been running upon the endless wealth to be found in the South Sea. They remained for about a fortnight at the Samballas Isles, and during this time, preparatory to their grand attempt, endeavoured to conciliate the

Indians of the Darien by gifts of toys and trinkets and many fair promises. They also persuaded some of the Mosquito-men to join them, who on account of their expertness in fishing, and striking turtle and manatee, besides their warlike qualities, were useful auxiliaries either in peace or war. Of this tribe, so long the friends, and, as they named themselves, the subjects of Britain, Dampier has given an exceedingly interesting account. In his time the clan or sept, properly called Mosquito-men, must have been very small, as he says the fighting-men did not amount to one hundred. They inhabited a tract on the coast near Cape Gracios Dios, stretching between Cape Honduras and Nicaragua. "They are," says our navigator, who appears partial to these Indians, "very ingenious at throwing the lance, *fisgig*, harpoon, or any manner of dart, being bred to it from their infancy; for the children, imitating their parents, never go abroad without a lance in their hands, which they throw at any object till use hath made them masters of the art. Then they learn to put by a lance, arrow, or dart; the manner is thus:—Two boys stand at a small distance, and dart a blunt stick at one another, each of them holding a small stick in his right hand, with which he strikes away that which is darted at him. As they grow in years they become more dexterous and courageous; and then they will stand a fair mark to any one that will shoot arrows at them, which they will put by with a very small stick no bigger than the rod of a fowling-piece; and when they are grown to be men they will guard themselves from arrows though they come very thick at them, provided they do not happen to come two at once. They have extraordinary good eyes, and will descry a sail at sea, and see anything, better than we. Their chiefest employment in their own country is to strike fish, turtle, or manatee. For this they are esteemed and coveted by all privateers, for one or two of them in a ship will maintain one hundred men; so that when we careen our ships we choose commonly such places where there is plenty of turtle or manatee for these Mosquito-men to strike, and it is very rare to find a privateer destitute of one or more of them, when the commander and most of the crew are English; but they do not love the French, and the Spaniards they hate mortally.

"They are tall, well-made, raw-boned, lusty, strong, and nimble of foot, long-visaged, lank black hair, look stern, hard-favoured, and of a dark copper complexion. When they come among the privateers they get the use of fire-arms, and are very good marksmen. They behave themselves very bold in fight, and never seem to flinch nor hang back; for they think that the white men with whom they are know better than they do when it is best to fight, and, let the disadvantage of their party be never so great, they will never yield nor give back while any of their party stand. I could never perceive any religion nor any ceremonies or superstitious observations among them, being ready to imitate us in whatsoever they saw us do at any time. Only, they seem to fear the devil, whom they call *Willesaw;* and they say he often appears to some among them, whom our men commonly call their priests, when they desire to speak with him on urgent business. They all say they must not anger him, for then he will beat them; and he sometimes carries away these their priests. They marry but one wife, with whom they live till death separates them. At their first coming together the man makes a very small planta-tion......They delight to settle near the sea, or by some river, for the sake of striking fish, their beloved employment; for within land there are other Indians with whom they are always at war. After the man hath cleared a spot of land, and hath planted it, he seldom minds it afterwards, but leaves the managing of it to his wife, and he goes out a-striking. Sometimes he seeks only for fish, at other times for turtle or manatee, and whatever he gets he brings home to his wife, and never stirs out to seek for more till it is eaten. When hunger begins to bite, he either takes his canoe and seeks for more game at sea, or walks out into the woods and hunts for pecaree and waree, each a sort of wild-hogs, or deer, and seldom returns empty-handed, nor seeks any more as long as it lasts. Their plantations have not above twenty or thirty plantain-trees, a bed of yams and potatoes, a bush of pimento, and a small spot of pine-apples, from which they make a sort of drink, to which they invite each other to be merry.

Whoever of them makes pine-drink treats his neighbours, providing fish and flesh also."

At their drinking-matches they often quarrelled, but the women prevented mischief by hiding their weapons. The Mosquito-men were kind and civil to the English, who endeavoured to retain the regard of such useful allies. For this purpose it was necessary to let them have their own way in everything, and to return home the moment they desired it, for if contradicted there was an end of their services; and though turtle and fish abounded, they would manage to kill nothing. They called themselves, as has been noticed, subjects of the King of England, and liked to have their chiefs nominated by the Governor of Jamaica, which island they often visited. Pity that in subsequent periods the fidelity and regard of this brave and ingenious tribe were so ill and ungratefully requited by their powerful and ungenerous allies.

The buccaneers commenced their march across the Isthmus on the 5th April 1680, about three hundred and thirty strong, each man armed with a hanger, fusil, and pistol, and provided with four cakes of the bread which they called dough-boys. Their generalissimo was Captain Sharp; and the men, marshalled in divisions, marched in something like military order, with flags and leaders. They were accompanied by those Indians of Darien who were the hereditary enemies of the Spaniards, whom they had subsidized with the hatchets, knives, beads, and toys, with which they provided themselves at Porto Bello. These auxiliaries furnished them with plantains, venison, and fruit, in exchange for European commodities. The march was easily performed, and in nine days' journey they reached Santa Maria, which was taken without opposition, though this did not prevent the exercise of cruelty. The Indians cruelly and deliberately butchered many of the inhabitants. The plunder obtained falling far short of the expectations of the buccaneers, made them the more desirous to push forward. They accordingly embarked on the river of Santa Maria, which falls into the Gulf of St. Michael, in Indian canoes and pirogues, having previously, in their summary way, deposed Captain Sharp, and chosen Captain Coxon commander.

On the same day that they reached the Bay, whither some of the Darien chiefs still accompanied them, they captured a Spanish vessel of thirty tons burden, on board of which a large party planted themselves, happy after the march, and being cramped and huddled up in the canoes, again to tread the deck of a ship of any size. At this time they divided into small parties, first appointing a rendezvous at the island of Chepillo, in the mouth of the river Cheapo. Dampier was with Captain Sharp, who went to the Pearl Islands in search of provisions.

In a few days the buccaneers mustered for the attack of Panama, and on the 23rd April did battle for the whole day with three Spanish ships in the road, of which two were captured by boarding, while the third got off. The action was fierce and sanguinary: of the buccaneers, eighteen men were killed and thirty wounded. The resistance was vigorous and brave, and the Spanish commander with many of his people fell before the action terminated. Even after this victory the buccaneers did not consider themselves strong enough to attack the new city of Panama, but they continued to cruise in the Bay, making valuable prizes. In the action with the Spanish ships Captain Sawkins had greatly distinguished himself by courage and conduct; and a quarrel breaking out among the buccaneers, while Coxon returned to the North Sea, he was chosen commander. He had not many days enjoyed this office, when, in an attack on Puebla Nueva, he was killed leading on his men to the assault of a breast-work; and on his death Sharp, the second in command, showing faint heart, the buccaneers retreated. New discontents broke out, and the party once more divided, not being able to agree in the choice of a leader; of those who remained in the South Sea, among whom was Dampier, Sharp was chosen commander. For some months he cruised off the coast of Peru, occasionally landing to pillage small towns and villages; and on Christmas-day anchored in a harbour of the Island of Juan Fernandez to rest and refit. Here they obtained abundance of crayfish, lobsters, and wild-goats, which were numerous.

Sharp, who had always been unpopular, was once more formally deposed, and Captain Watling elected in his stead.

Having enjoyed themselves till the 12th of January, the buccaneers were alarmed by the appearance of three vessels, which they concluded to be Spanish ships of war in pursuit of them. They put off to sea in all haste, in the hurry leaving one of their Mosquito Indians named William upon the island.

They again cruised along the coast, and the attack of the Spanish settlements by hasty descent was resumed. In attempting to capture Arica, Captain Watling was killed, and the buccaneers were repulsed, having had a narrow escape from being all made prisoners. For want of any more competent leader, Sharp was once more raised to the command; and the South Sea had so greatly disappointed their hopes, that it was now agreed to return eastward by recrossing the Isthmus. But another quarrel broke out: one party would not continue under Sharp, and another wished to try their fortunes further on the South Sea. It was therefore agreed that the majority should retain the ship, the other party taking the long-boat and canoes. Sharp's party proved the more numerous. They cruised in the South Sea, off the coast of Patagonia and Chili, for the remainder of the season of 1681, and early in the following year returned to the West Indies by doubling Cape Horn, but durst not land at any of the English settlements. Sharp, soon afterwards going home, was tried in England with several of his men for piracy, but escaped conviction.

In the minority which broke off from Sharp was

William Dampier, who appears at this time to have been little distinguished among his companions. The party consisted of forty-four Europeans and two Mosquito Indians. Their object was to recross the Isthmus, —an undertaking of no small difficulty, from the nature of the country and the hostility of the Spaniards. Before they left the ship they sifted a large quantity of flour, prepared chocolate with sugar, as provision, and entered into a mutual engagement, that if any man sank on the journey he should be shot by his comrades, as but one man falling into the hands of the Spaniards must betray the others to certain destruction. In a fortnight after leaving the ship near the island of Plata, they landed at the mouth of a river in the Bay of St. Michael, where, taking out all their provisions, arms, and clothing, they sank their boat. While they spent a few hours in preparing for the inland march, the Mosquito-men caught fish, which afforded one plentiful meal to the whole party; after which they commenced their journey late in the afternoon of the 1st of May. At night they constructed huts in which they slept. On the 2nd they struck into an Indian path, and reached an Indian village, where they obtained refreshments; but were uneasy on understanding the closeness of their vicinity to the Spaniards, who had placed ships at the mouths of the navigable rivers to look out for them, and intercept their return eastward. Next day, with a hired Indian guide, they proceeded, and reached the dwelling of a native, who received them with sullen churlishness, which in ordinary times the buccaneers would ill have brooked; "though this," says Dampier, "was neither a time nor place to be angry with the Indians, all our lives lying at their hands." Neither the temptation of dollars, hatchets, nor long-knives, would operate on this intractable Indian, till one of the seamen, taking a sky-coloured petticoat from his bag, threw it over the lady of the house, who was so much delighted with the gift that she soon wheedled her husband into better humour, and he now not only gave them information, but found them a guide. It rained hard and frequently on both days, but they were still too near the Spanish garrisons and guard-ships to mind the weather or to dally by the way. The country was found difficult and fatiguing, without any trace of a path, the Indians guiding themselves by the rivers, which they were sometimes compelled to cross twenty or thirty times in a day. Rainy weather, hardship, and hunger soon expelled all fear of the Spaniards, who were, besides, not likely to follow their foes into these intricate solitudes.

On the 5th they reached the dwelling of a young Spanish Indian,—a civilized person, who had lived with the Bishop of Panama, and spoke the Spanish language fluently. He received them kindly, and though unable to provide for the wants of so many men, freely gave what he had. At this place they rested to dry their clothes and ammunition, and to clean their fire-arms. While thus employed, Mr. Wafer, the surgeon of the

INDIANS OF DARIEN.

Page 312.

buccaneers, who had been among the malcontents, had his knee so much scorched by an accidental explosion of gunpowder, that, after dragging himself forward during another day, he was forced to remain behind his companions, together with one or two more who had been exhausted by the march. Among the Indians of the Darien, Wafer remained for three months, and he has left an account which is considered the best we yet possess of those tribes.

The march was continued in very bad weather, this being the commencement of the rainy season, and thunder and lightning frequent and violent. As the bottoms of the valleys and the river-banks were now overflowed, instead of constructing huts every night for their repose, the travellers were often obliged to seek for a resting-place, and to sleep under trees. To add to their hardships their slaves deserted, carrying off whatever they could lay their hands upon.

Before leaving the ship, foreseeing the difficulties of the journey, and the necessity of perpetually fording the rivers, Dampier had taken the precaution to deposit his journal in a bamboo closed at both ends with wax. In this way his papers were secured from wet, while the journalist frequently swam across the rivers which so greatly impeded the progress of the march. In crossing a river, where the current ran very strong, one man, who carried his fortune of three hundred dollars on his back, was swept down the stream and drowned; and so worn out were his comrades that, fond as they were of gold, they would not at this time take the trouble to look for or burden themselves with his.

It was the eighteenth day of the march before the buccaneers reached the river Conception, where they obtained Indian canoes, in which they proceeded to La Sound's Key, one of the Samballas Islands, which were much frequented by buccaneers. Here they entered a French privateer, commanded by Captain Tristian; and, with better faith than buccaneers usually displayed, generously rewarded their Indian guides with money, toys, and hatchets, and dismissed them. The buccaneers of this time were somewhat less ferocious in manners than those under Morgan and Lolonnois, though it never entered into their thoughts that there could be any wrong in robbing the Spaniards. Sawkins and Watling maintained stricter discipline than had been customary in former periods, approximating their discipline and regulations to those of privateers or ships of war. They even made the Sabbath be observed with outward signs of respect. On one occasion when Sawkins's men, who like all buccaneers were inveterate gamblers, played on Sunday, the captain flung the dice overboard.

In two days after Dampier and his friends had gone on board the French vessel, it left La Sound's for Springer's Key, another of the Samballas Islands, where eight buccaneer vessels then lay, of which the companies had formed the design of crossing to Panama. From this expedition they were, however, diverted by the dismal report of the newly-arrived travellers; and the assault of other places was taken into consideration. From Trinidad to Vera Cruz the buccaneers had now an intimate knowledge of every town upon the coast, and for twenty leagues into the interior; and acquaintance with the strength and wealth of each, and with the number and quality of the inhabitants. The preliminary consultations now held lasted for a week, the French and English not agreeing; but at last they sailed for Carpenter River, going first towards the Isle of St. Andreas. In a gale the ships were separated; and Dampier being left with a French captain, conceived such a dislike to his shipmates that he, and his fellow-travellers in crossing the Isthmus, induced a countryman of their own, named Captain Wright, to fit up and arm a small vessel, with which they cruised about the coast in search of provisions, still, however, keeping their jackals, the Mosquito-men, who caught turtle while the buccaneers hunted in the woods for peccaries, warce, deer, quaums, parrots, pigeons, and curassow birds, and also monkeys, which in times of hardship they esteemed a delicate morsel. At one place several of the men were suddenly taken ill from eating land-crabs which had fed upon the fruit of the manchineel-tree. All animals that fed on this fruit were avoided by the freebooters as unwholesome, if not poisonous. In selecting unknown wild-fruits the buccaneers were guided by the birds, freely eating whatever kind had been pecked, but no bird touched the fruit of the manchineel.

On returning to La Sound's Key from this cruise, they were joined by Mr. Wafer. He had been for three months kindly entertained by an Indian chief, who had offered him his daughter in marriage, and grudged him nothing save the liberty of going away. From this kind but exacting chief he escaped under pretence of going in search of English dogs to be employed in hunting, the Indian being aware of the superiority which dogs gave the Spaniards in the chase. Mr. Wafer had been painted by the women of the Darien, and his own clothes being worn out, he was now dressed, or rather undressed, like the natives; whom, under this disguise, he resembled so much that it was some time before Dampier recognized his old acquaintance the surgeon.

From the Samballas they cruised towards Carthagena, which they passed, having a fair view of the city, and casting longing eyes upon the rich monastery on the steep hill rising behind it. This monastery, dedicated to the Virgin, is, says Dampier, " a place of incredible wealth, by reason of the offerings made here continually; and for this reason often in danger of being visited by the privateers, did not the neighbourhood of Carthagena keep them in awe. 'Tis, in short, the very Loretto of the West Indies, and hath innumerable miracles related of it. Any misfortune that befalls the privateers is attributed to this Lady's doing; and the Spaniards report that she was abroad that night the *Oxford* man-of-war was blown up at the isle of Vaca, and that she came home all wet; as belike she often returns with her clothes dirty and torn with passing through woods and bad ways when she has been upon an expedition, deserving doubtless a new suit for such eminent pieces of service."

The company of Captain Wright pillaged several small places about Rio de la Hacha and the Rancheries, which was the head-quarters of a small Spanish pearl-fishery. The pearl-banks lay about four or five leagues off the shore. In prosecuting this fishery, the Indian divers, first anchoring their boats, dived, and brought up full the baskets previously let down; and when their barks were filled, they went ashore, and the oysters were opened by the old men, women, and children, under the inspection of a Spanish overseer.

In a short time afterwards the buccaneers captured, after a smart engagement, an armed ship of twelve guns and forty men, laden with sugar, tobacco, and marmalade, bound to Carthagena from St. Jago in Cuba. From the disposal of this cargo, some insight is afforded into the mysteries of buccaneering. It was offered first to the Dutch governor of Curaçoa, who having, as he said, a great trade with the Spaniards, could not openly admit the freebooters to this island, though he directed them to go to St. Thomas, which belonged to the Danes, whither he would send a sloop with such commodities as the buccaneers required, and take the sugar off their hands. The rovers, however, declined the terms offered by the cautious Dutchman, and sailed from St. Thomas to another Dutch colony, where they found a better merchant. From hence they sailed for the isle of Aves, which, as its name imports, abounded in birds, especially boobies and men-of-war birds. The latter bird was about the size of a kite, black, with a red throat. It lives on fish, yet never lights in the water, but soaring aloft like the kite, "when it sees its prey, darts down, snatches it, and mounts, never once touching the water."

On a coral reef off the south side of this island the Count d'Estrées had shortly before lost the French fleet. Firing guns in the darkness to warn the ships that followed him to avoid the danger on which he had run, they imagined that he was engaged with the enemy, and crowding all sail ran upon destruction. The ships held together next day, till part of the men got on shore, though many perished in the wreck. Dampier relates that those of the ordinary seamen who got to land died of fatigue and famine, while those who had been buccaneers and were wrecked here, "being used to such accidents, lived merrily, and if they had gone to Jamaica with £30 in their pockets, could not have enjoyed themselves more; for they kept a gang by themselves, and watched when the ships broke up to get the goods that came out of them; and though much was staved against the rocks, yet abundance of wine and brandy floated over the reef, where they waited to take it up." The following anecdote of the wrecked crew is horribly striking:—"There were about forty Frenchmen on board one of the ships, in which was good store of liquor, till the after-part of her broke, and floated over the reef, and was carried away to sea, with all the men drinking and singing, who, being in drink, did not mind the danger, but were never heard of afterwards."

In a short time after, this island was the scene of a clever buccaneering trick, which Dampier relates with some glee. The wreck of the French fleet had left Aves Island a perfect arsenal of masts, yards, timbers, and so forth, and hither the buccaneers repaired to careen and refit their ships, and among others Captain Pain, a Frenchman. A Dutch vessel of twenty guns, despatched from Curaçoa to fish up the guns lost on the reef, descried the privateer, which she resolved to capture before engaging in the business of her voyage. The Frenchman abandoned his ship, which he saw no chance of preserving, but brought ashore some of his guns, and resolved to defend himself as long as possible. While his men were landing the guns, he perceived at a distance a Dutch sloop entering the road, and at evening found her at anchor at the west end of the island. During the night, with two canoes, he boarded and took this sloop, found considerable booty, and made off with her, leaving his empty vessel as a prize to the Dutch man-of-war.

At this island Dampier's party remained for some time, careened the largest ship, scrubbed a sugar-prize formerly taken, and recovered two guns of the wreck of D'Estrées' fleet. They afterwards went to the Isles of Rocas, where they fell in with a French ship of thirty-six guns, which bought ten tons of their sugar. The captain of this vessel was a Knight of Malta. To Dampier both he and his lieutenant were particularly attentive and kind, and offered him every encouragement to enter the French navy. This he declined from feelings of patriotism.

Here he saw, besides men-of-war birds, boobies, and noddies, numbers of the tropic-bird. It was as big as a pigeon, and round and plump as a partridge, all white, save two or three light-gray feathers in the wing. One long feather or quill, about seven inches in length, growing out of the rump, is all the tail these birds have. They are never seen far without the tropics, but are met with at a great distance from land. After taking in what water could be obtained, they left Rocas and went to Salt Tortuga, so called to distinguish it from Dry Tortuga near Cape Florida, and from the Tortuga of the first buccaneers, near Hispaniola, which place was now, however, better known as Petit Guaves. They expected to sell the remainder of their sugar to the English vessels which came here for salt; but not succeeding, they sailed for Blanco, an island north of Margarita, and thirty leagues from the Main. It was an uninhabited island, flat and low, being mostly savanna, with a few wooded spots, in which flourished the *lignum vitæ*. Iguanas, or guanoes, as they were commonly called in the West Indies, abounded on Blanco. They resembled the lizard species, but were bigger, about the size of the small of a man's leg. From the hind quarter the tail tapers to a point. If seized by the tail near the extremity, it broke off at a joint, and the animal escaped. They are amphibious creatures. Both their eggs and flesh were highly esteemed by the buccaneers, who made soup of the latter for their sick. There were many species found here, living on land or water, in the swamps, among bushes, or on trees. Green-turtle frequented this island in numbers.

From Blanco they returned to Salt Tortuga, and went from thence, after four days, to the coast of the Caraccas on the Main.

While cruising on this coast, they landed in some of the bays, and took seven or eight tons of cocoa, and afterwards three barks, one laden with hides, another with brandy and earthenware, and a third with European goods. With these prizes they returned to the Rocas to divide the spoil; after which Dampier, and other nineteen out of a company of sixty, took one of the captured vessels, and with their share of the plunder held their course direct for Virginia, which was reached in July 1682.

Of the thirteen months which our navigator spent in Virginia he has left no record; but from another portion of his memoirs it may be gathered that he suffered from sickness during most of the time. His disease was not more singular than was the mode of cure practised by a negro Esculapius, whose appropriate fee was a white cock. The disease was what is called the Guinea-worm. "These worms," says Dampier, "are no bigger than a large brown thread, but (as I have heard) five or six yards long, and if it break in drawing out, that part which remains in the flesh will putrify, and endanger the patient's life, and be very painful. I was in great torment before it came out. My leg and ankle swelled, and looked very red and angry, and I kept a plaster to it to bring it to a head. Drawing off my plaster, out came about three inches of the worm, and my pain abated presently. Till then I was ignorant of my malady, and the gentlewoman at whose house I lodged took it (the worm) for a nerve, but I knew well enough what it was, and presently rolled it upon a small stick. After that I opened it every morning and evening, and strained it out gently, about two inches at a time, not without pain." The negro doctor first stroked the place affected; then applied some rough powder to it, like tobacco-leaves crumbled; next muttered a spell; blew upon the part three times; waved his hands as often, and said that in three days it would be well. It proved so, and the stipulated fee of the white cock was gladly paid.

The next adventure of Dampier was the circumnavigation of the globe—a voyage and ramble extending to about eight years, which, in point of interest and variety, has never yet been surpassed. To it we dedicate the following chapter.

CHAPTER IV.

CIRCUMNAVIGATION OF THE GLOBE.

AMONG the companions of Dampier in his journey across the Isthmus, and in his subsequent cruise, was Mr. John Cook, a Creole, born in St. Christopher's, and a man of good capacity. He had acted as quartermaster, or second in command, under Captain Yanky, a French flibustier, who at this time held a commission as a privateer. By the ordinary laws of the buccaneers, when a prize fit for a piratical cruise was taken, the second in command was promoted to it; and in virtue of this title Cook obtained an excellent Spanish ship. At this, however, the French commanders were secretly discontented, and on the first opportunity they seized the ship, plundered the crew, who were Englishmen, of their arms and goods, and turned them ashore. The French captain, Tristian, either took compassion on some of the number, or hoped to find them serviceable, for he carried eight or ten of them with him to Petit Guaves, among whom were Cook and Davis. They had not lain long here when Captain Tristian and part of his men being one day on shore, the English party, in revenge of the late spoliation, overmastered the rest of the crew, took the ship, and sending the Frenchmen ashore, sailed for Isle à la Vache, where they picked up a straggling crew of English buccaneers, and before they could be overtaken, sailed for Virginia, where Dampier now was, taking two prizes by the way, one of which was a French ship laden with wine. Having thus dexterously swindled Tristian out of his ship, which might, however, be considered as but a fair act of reprisal, and having afterwards committed open piracy on the French commerce, the West Indies was no longer a safe latitude for these English buccaneers. The wines were therefore sold with the other goods, and two of the ships; and the largest prize, which carried eighteen guns, was new-named the *Revenge*, and equipped and provisioned for a long voyage. Among her crew of seventy men were almost all the late fellow-travellers across the Isthmus, including William Dampier, Lionel Wafer the surgeon, Ambrose Cowley, who has left an account of the voyage, and the commander, Captain John Cook. Before embarking on this new piratical expedition, they all subscribed certain rules for maintaining discipline and due subordination, and for the observance of sobriety on their long voyage.

They sailed from the Chesapeake on the 23rd August 1683, captured a Dutch vessel, in which they found six casks of wine and a quantity of provisions, and near the Cape de Verd Islands encountered a storm which raged for a week, "drenching them all like so many drowned rats." After this gale they had the winds and weather both favourable, and anchored at the Isle of Sal, one of the Cape de Verd group, so named from its numerous salt-ponds.

A Portuguese at this place, by affecting the mystery which gives so much zest to clandestine bargains, prevailed with one of the buccaneers to purchase from him a lump of what he called ambergris, which Dampier believed to be spurious. Of the genuine substance Dampier relates that he was once shown a piece which had been broken off a lump weighing one hundred pounds, found in a sandy bay of an island in the Bay of Honduras. It was found by a person of credit, a Mr. Barker of London, lying dry above high-water mark, and in it a multitude of beetles. It was of a dusky black colour, the consistence of mellow ordinary cheese, and of a very fragrant scent.

At the Isle of Sal, Dampier first saw the flamingo. It was in shape like the heron, but larger, and of a red colour. The flamingoes kept together in large flocks, and standing side by side by the ponds at which they fed, looked at a distance like a new brick wall. Their flesh was lean and black, but not unsavoury nor fishy-tasted. A knob of fat at the root of the tongue "makes a dish of flamingoes' tongues fit for a prince's table."

From this island they went to St. Nicholas, where the governor and his attendants, though not quite so tattered as those seen at the Isle of Sal, were not very splendidly equipped. Here they dug wells, watered the ship, scrubbed its bottom, and went to Mayo to obtain provisions, but were not suffered to land, as, about a week before, Captain Bond, a pirate of Bristol, had entrapped the governor and some of his people, and carried them away.

From the Cape de Verd Isles the *Revenge* intended to keep a direct course to the Strait of Magellan; but by adverse weather was compelled to steer for the Guinea coast, which was made in November, near Sierra Leone. They anchored in the mouth of the river Sherborough, near a large Danish ship, which they afterwards took by stratagem. While in sight of the Dane, which felt no alarm at the appearance of a ship of the size of the *Revenge*, most of the buccaneer crew remained under deck, no more of the hands appearing above than were necessary to manage the sails. Their bold design was to board the ship without discovering any sign of their intention, and the *Revenge* advanced closely, still wearing the semblance of a weakly-manned merchant-vessel. When quite close, Captain Cook in a loud voice commanded the helm to be put one way, while by previous orders and a preconcerted plan the steersman shifted it into a quite opposite direction; and the *Revenge*, as if by accident, suddenly fell on board the Dane, which by this dexterous manœuvre was captured with only the loss of five men, though a ship of double their whole force. She carried thirty-six guns, and was equipped and victualled for a long voyage.

This fine vessel was, by the exulting buccaneers, named the *Bachelor's Delight*, and they immediately burned the *Revenge*, that she " might tell no tales," sent their prisoners on shore, and steered for Magellan Strait.

On the voyage to the Strait, the *Bachelor's Delight* encountered frequent tornadoes, accompanied by thunder, lightning, and rain. Many of the men were seized with fever, and one man died. Having little fresh animal food of any kind, they caught sharks during the calms between the gusts of the tornadoes, which they prepared by first boiling and afterwards stewing them with pepper and vinegar. About the middle of January they lost one of the surgeons, who was greatly lamented, as there now remained but one for the long voyage which was meditated. On the 28th they made John Davis's Southern Islands, or the Falkland Isles, then, however, more generally known as the Sebald de Weert Islands.

In the course of their voyage, Dampier, who possessed more geographical and nautical knowledge than his companions, had been persuading Captain Cook to stop here to water, and afterwards to prosecute the voyage to Juan Fernandez by doubling Cape Horn, avoiding the Strait altogether, which, he judiciously says, "I knew would prove very dangerous to us, the rather because our men being privateers, and so more wilful and less under command, would not be so ready to give a watchful attendance in a passage so little known. For although these men were more under command than I had ever seen any privateers, yet I could not expect to find them at a moment's call, on coming to an anchor, or weighing anchor." The Falkland Islands are described by Dampier as rocky and barren, without trees, and having only some bushes upon them. Shoals of small lobsters, which coloured the sea red in spots for a mile round, were seen here. They were only of the size of the tip of a man's little finger, yet perfect in shape, and naturally of the colour that other lobsters assume after they are boiled.

The advice of Dampier was not taken; but westerly winds prevented Cook from making the entrance of the Strait, and on the 6th February they fell in with the Strait of Le Maire, high land on both sides, and the passage very narrow. They ran in for four miles, when a strong tide setting in northward "made such a short cockling sea," which ran every way, as if in a place where two opposing tides meet; sometimes breaking over the poop, sometimes over the waist and the bow, and tossing the *Bachelor's Delight* "like an eggshell."

In the same evening they had a breeze from west-north-west, bore away eastward, and having the wind fresh all night, passed the east end of Staten Island next day. Our navigator, on the 7th at noon, found the latitude to be 54° 52′ S., and the same night they lost sight of Tierra del Fuego, and saw no other land till they entered the South Sea. In doubling Cape Horn they were so fortunate as to catch twenty-three barrels of rain-water, besides an abundant supply for present consumption.

On the 3rd March they entered the South Sea with a fair fresh breeze, which from the south had shifted to the eastward. On the 9th they were in latitude 47° 10', and on the 17th in latitude 36°, still bearing for Juan Fernandez. On the 19th a strange sail was seen to the southward, bearing full upon them, which was mistaken for a Spaniard, but proved to be the *Nicholas* of London, commanded by Captain Eaton, fitted out as a trader, but in reality a buccaneer ship. Captain Eaton came on board the *Bachelor's Delight*, related his adventures, and, like a true brother, gave the company water, while they spared him a supply of bread and beef. Together they now steered for Juan Fernandez, and on the 23rd anchored in a bay at the south end of the island, in twenty-five fathoms water. From Eaton they had heard of another London vessel, the *Cygnet*, commanded by Captain Swan, which was really a trader, and held a license from the then Lord High Admiral of England, the Duke of York, afterwards James II. With this ship the *Nicholas* had entered the South Sea, but they had been separated in a gale.

It may be remembered that when Captain Watling and his company escaped from Juan Fernandez three years before, they had left a Mosquito Indian on the island, who was out hunting goats when the alarm came. This Mosquito man, named William, was the first and the true Robinson Crusoe, the original hermit of this romantic solitude. Immediately on approaching the island, Dampier and a few of William's old friends, together with a Mosquito-man named Robin, put off for the shore, where they soon perceived William standing ready to give them welcome. From the heights he had seen the ships on the preceding day, and, knowing them to be English vessels by the way they were worked, he had killed three goats, and dressed them with cabbage of the cabbage-tree, to have a feast ready on the arrival of the ships. How great was his delight, as the boat neared the shore, when Robin leaped to the land, and running up to him, fell flat on his face at his feet. William raised up his countryman, embraced him, and in turn prostrated himself at Robin's feet, who lifted him up, and they renewed their embraces. "We stood with pleasure," says Dampier, "to behold the surprise, tenderness, and solemnity of their interview, which was exceedingly affecting on both sides; and when these their ceremonies of civility were over, we also that stood gazing at them drew near, each of us embracing him we had found here, who was overjoyed to see so many of his old friends, come hither, as he thought, purposely to fetch him."

At the time William was abandoned, he had with him in the woods his gun and knife, and a small quantity of powder and shot. As soon as his ammunition was expended, by notching his knife into a saw he cut up the barrel of his gun into pieces, which he converted into harpoons, lances, and a long knife. To accomplish this he struck fire with his gun-flint and a piece of the barrel of his gun, which he hardened for this purpose in a way he had seen practised by the buccaneers. In this fire he heated his pieces of iron, hammered them out with stones, sawed them with his jagged knife, or ground them to an edge, and tempered them; "which was no more than these Mosquito-men were accustomed to do in their own country, where they make their own fishing and striking instruments without either forge or anvil, though they spend a great deal of time about them." Thus furnished, William supplied himself with goat's flesh and fish, though, till his instruments were formed, he had been compelled to eat seal. He built his house about a half-mile from the shore, and lined it snugly with goat-skins, with which he also spread his couch or *barbecue*, which was raised two feet from the floor. As his clothes wore out he supplied this want also with goat-skins, and, when first seen, he wore nothing save a goat's skin about his waist. Though the Spaniards, who had learned that a Mosquito-man was left here, had looked for William several times, he had always, by retiring to a secret place, contrived to elude their search.

The island of Juan Fernandez was hilly, and intersected by small pleasant valleys; the mountains were partly savanna and partly woodland; the grass of the flat places being delicate and kindly, of a short thick growth, unlike the coarse sedgy grass of the savannas of the West Indies. The cabbage-tree was found here, and well-grown timber of different kinds, though none that was fit for masts. There were in the island two bays, both at the east end, where ships might anchor, and into each of them flowed a rivulet of good water. Water was also found in every valley. Goats, which according to Dampier were originally brought to the island by the discoverer, were now found in large flocks, and seals swarmed about the island "as if they had no other place in the world to live in, every bay and rock being full of them." Sea-lions were also numerous, and different kinds of fish were found. The seals were of different colours—black, gray, and dun—with a fine thick short fur. Millions of them were seen sitting in the bays, going or coming into the sea, or, as they lay at the top of the waves, sporting and sunning themselves, covering the water for a mile or two from the shore. When they come out of the sea "they bleat like sheep for their young; and though they pass through hundreds of others' young, yet they will not suffer any of them to suck." The sea-lion is shaped like a seal, but is six times as big, with "great goggle eyes," and teeth three inches long, of which the buccaneers sometimes made dice.

The buccaneers remained for sixteen days at this island getting in provisions, and for the recovery of the sick and those affected with scurvy, who were placed

SEA LIONS.
Page 334.

on shore, and fed with vegetables and fresh goat's flesh, which regimen was found beneficial. On the 8th April they sailed for the American coast, which they approached in 24° S.; but stood off at the distance of fourteen or fifteen leagues, that they might not be observed from the high grounds by the Spaniards.

The nautical and geographical observations of Dampier in this tract of the Pacific are important. The land from the 24th to the 10th degree south was of prodigious height. "It lies generally in ridges parallel to the shore, and three or four ridges, one within another, each surpassing the other in height; those that are farthest within land being much higher than the others. They always appear blue when seen at sea." To the excessive height of the mountain-ridges Dampier imputes the want of rivers in this region.

The first capture of the buccaneers, made on the 3rd of May, was a Spanish ship bound for Lima, laden with timber from Guayaquil; from which they learned that it was known in the settlements that pirates were on the coast.

On the 9th they anchored at the Isle of Lobos de la Mar with their prize. Lobos de la Mar is properly a cluster of small islets, divided by narrow channels. They are sandy and barren, destitute of water, and frequented by sea-fowl, penguins, and a small black fowl that our navigator never saw save here and at Juan Fernandez, which made holes in the sand for a night-habitation. This black fowl made good meat.

At this place the ships were scrubbed, and the prisoners rigidly examined, that from their information the voyagers might guide their future proceedings. Truxillo was the town at last fixed upon for making a descent. The companies of both ships were mustered, for Eaton and Cook had now agreed to hunt in couples, and the arms were proved. The men amounted to one hundred and eight fit to bear arms, besides the sick. Before they sailed on this expedition, three ships were seen steering northward. Cook stood after one of them, which made for the land, and Eaton pursued the other two to sea, and captured them on the same day. They contained cargoes of flour from Lima for the city of Panama, whither they carried intelligence, from the governor, of the formidable buccaneer force which now threatened the coast. One of the ships carried eight tons of quince-marmalade. The buccaneers were deeply mortified to learn that they had narrowly missed a prize containing eight hundred thousand pieces of eight, which had been landed at an intermediate port, upon a rumour that English ships were cruising off the coast of Peru.

The design against Truxillo was now abandoned, as they learned that it had lately been fortified, and a Spanish garrison established for its defence; and on the evening of the 19th they sailed with their flour-prizes for the Galapagos Islands, which they descried on the 31st, "some appearing on the lee-bow, some on the weather-bow, and others right ahead." The Galapagos Islands were still very little known at the time the buccaneers made this visit. They lie under the equator, are numerous, and were uninhabited, and abounded in iguanas and large land-turtle; otherwise they are rocky and barren, and mostly destitute of water, though in some of them this article, so essential to the mariner, was found of excellent quality both in brooks and ponds. Several of the isles are seven or eight leagues long, and from three to four broad, and partially wooded. Land-turtle were found here in such multitudes that Dampier says "five hundred or six hundred men might subsist on them for several months without any other sort of provision." Some of them weighed from one hundred and fifty to two hundred pounds, and were two feet or two feet six inches over the calipee, and sweet as a young pullet. The islands also abounded in sea-turtle,—the creeks and shallows being filled with the turtle-grass on which the green-turtle feed. The sea-turtle were of four kinds—the green-turtle, the loggerhead, the trunk-turtle, and the hawksbill; on the back of this last species is found the shell so much valued in commerce. The largest of them afforded about three pounds and a half of this shell.

At the Galapagos Isles the buccaneers remained for ten days, and deposited a store of their prize-flour against future necessity. Salt was found here, pigeons abounded, the sea teemed with fish, and the leaves of the *mammee*-tree furnished them with vegetables; so that the Galapagos were in all respects well adapted for a buccaneer station.

By the advice of an Indian, one of their prisoners, the buccaneers were induced to visit Ria Lexa, his native place, where he promised them a rich harvest in plunder.

At Juan Fernandez, Captain Cook had been taken ill; he now died somewhat suddenly as they stood off Cape Blanco, and, as a mark of respect, was buried on shore. While his men were digging the grave they were seen by three Spanish Indians, who held aloof, but asked them many questions; "and one man," says Dampier, "did not stick to sooth them up with as many falsehoods, purposely to draw them into our clutches; and at length drilled them by discourse so near that our men laid hold on all three at once." One escaped before the burial of Cook was over, and the other two were taken on ship-board. When examined, notwithstanding their pretended simplicity, they confessed that they had been sent out as spies by the governor of Panama, who had received intelligence of the buccaneer squadron.

The voyagers were informed by these prisoners that large herds of cattle were reared in this neighbourhood, which was welcome news to seamen who had seen no fresh meat since their run from the Galapagos. Two boats were immediately sent to the shore with an Indian guide to bring off cattle; but the enterprise appeared dangerous, and Dampier with twelve men returned on board. Those who were more foolhardy, and who even slept on shore, found themselves next morning watched by forty or fifty armed Spaniards, and their boat burned. The cowardly Spaniards, afraid to come forward, still lurked in their ambush; and one of the seamen on landing, having noticed an insulated rock which just appeared above water, they made off for this fortress, and holding fast by each other, and wading to the neck, they reached the rock, while the Spanish shot whistled after them. In this perilous condition they had remained for seven hours, the tide, which was at the ebb when they took refuge here, rising around them, and gaining on the rock so rapidly, that, had not help come from the ships, in another hour they must have been swept away. The Spaniards, who relished bush-fighting better than the open field, meanwhile lay in wait for the catastrophe; but when the canoe from the English ships bore off the men, they offered no resistance.

The quarter-master, Edward Davis, was now elected commander in the room of Captain Cook; and after taking in water, and cutting lancewood for handles to their oars, they bore away for Ria Lexa, and on the 23rd July were opposite the harbour. The situation of the town is known by a high-peaked volcanic mountain, which rises within three leagues of the harbour, but may be seen at the distance of twenty leagues. A small flat island, about a mile long and a quarter of a mile broad, forms the harbour, in which two hundred sail can ride. It may be entered by a channel at each end.

The Spaniards had here also got the start of their enemy. They had thrown up a breastwork on a strong position, and stationed sentinels to give instant alarm; and the buccaneers, who wished to surprise and plunder, and not to fight against great odds, deemed it prudent to steer for the Gulf of Amapalla, an arm of the sea running inland eight or ten leagues, and made remarkable by two headlands at the entrance,—Point Casivina on the south side, in latitude 12° 40″ N., and on the north-west Mount St. Michael.

At a previous consultation it had been agreed that Captain Davis should advance first, in two canoes, and endeavour to seize some Indians to labour at careening the ships, and also a prisoner of better condition, from whom intelligence might be obtained. On the Island of Mangera the padre of a village, from which all the other inhabitants had fled, was caught while endeavouring to escape, and with him two Indian boys. With these Davis proceeded to Amapalla, where, having previously gained over or frightened the priest, he told the Indians drawn up to receive him that he and his company were Biscayners, sent by the King of Spain to clear the seas of pirates, and that his business in the bay of this island was only to careen his ships. On this assurance Davis and his men were well received, and they all marched together, strangers and natives, to church, which was the usual place of public assembly, whether for business or amusement. The images in the churches here, like those in the Bay of Campeachy, were painted of the Indian complexion; and the people, under the sway of their padres, lived in much the same condition as the tribes described on the banks of the Tobasco, cultivating maize, rearing poultry, and duly paying the priest his tithe. Here, too, they were indulged in masques and other pastimes, with abundance of music, on saints' eves and holidays. "Their mirth," says Dampier, "consists in singing, dancing, and using as many antic gestures. If the moon shine, they use but few torches; if not, the church is full of light. They meet at these times all sorts of both sexes. All the Indians that I have been acquainted with who are under the Spaniards seem to be more melancholy than other Indians who are free; and at these public meetings, when they are in the greatest of their jollity, their mirth seems to be rather forced than real. Their songs are very melancholy and doleful; so is their music."

In attending them to the church under the guise of friendship, Davis intended to ensnare these unsuspecting people and make them all his prisoners, till he had dictated his own terms of ransom, the padre having, probably from compulsion, promised his aid in entrapping his flock. This hopeful project was frustrated by one of the buccaneers rashly and rudely pushing a man into the church before him. The alarm was given, the Indian fled, and his countrymen "sprung out of the church like deer." Davis and his men immediately fired, and killed a leading man among the natives.

The buccaneers were, however, afterwards assisted by several of the natives in storing the ships with cattle plundered from an island in the gulf belonging to a nunnery in some distant place; and, from some feelings of remorse, on leaving this quarter Davis presented the islanders of Amapalla with one of his prize-ships, and a considerable part of the cargo of flour which it contained. The ships here broke off consort-ship. The crews had quarrelled,—Davis's party, in right of priority in marauding, claiming the larger share of the spoils. Eaton left the gulf on the 2nd of September, and Davis, with whom Dampier continued, on the day following, having previously set the padre on shore. They stood for the coast of Peru, having almost every day tornadoes accompanied with thunder and lightning,—weather of this kind generally prevailing in these latitudes from June to November. When these gusts were over, the wind generally shifted to the west. Near Cape San Francisco they had settled weather and the wind at south. About this place they again fell in with Eaton, who had encountered terrible storms—"such tornadoes as he and his men had never before seen; the air smelling very much of sulphur, and they fancying themselves in great danger of being burned by the lightning." Captain Eaton had touched at Cocos Island, where he laid up a store of flour, and took in water and cocoa-nuts. Cocos Island, as described by Eaton, is nearly surrounded by rocks; but at the north-east end there is one small and secure harbour,—a brook of fresh water flowing into it. The middle of the island is high, and, though destitute of trees, looks verdant and pleasant from the abundance of an herb which the Spaniards called *gramadiel* growing upon the high grounds. Near the shore all round the island were groves of cocoas.

At the Island of La Plata—so named, according to Dampier, from Sir Francis Drake having divided upon it the plunder of the plate-ship the *Cacafuego*—the buccaneers found water, though but a scanty rivulet, and plenty of small sea-turtle. Captain Eaton's company would again have joined their former consorts; but Dampier relates that Davis's men, his own comrades, were still so unreasonable that they would not consent to new-comers having an equal share of what they pillaged; so the *Nicholas* held southward, while the *Bachelor's Delight* steered for Point Santa Elena in 2° 15′ S., pretty high but flat land, naked of trees and overgrown with thistles. There was no fresh water on the Point, and this article the inhabitants brought from four leagues' distance, from the river Colanche, the innermost part of the bay. Water-melons, large and very sweet, were the only things cultivated on the Point. Pitch was the principal commodity of the inhabitants. It boiled out of a hole in the earth, at five paces above high-water mark, and was found plentifully at flood-tide. When first obtained it was like thin tar, but was boiled down to the consistence of pitch.

Davis's men landed at Manta, a village on the mainland, about three leagues to the east of Cape San Lorenzo, where they made two old women prisoners, from whom they learned that many buccaneers had lately crossed the Isthmus from the West Indies, and were cruising off the coast in canoes and pirogues. The viceroy had taken every precaution against this new incursion. On all the uninhabited islands the goats had been destroyed; ships were burned to save them from the buccaneers; and no provisions were allowed to remain at any place on the coast, but such as might be required for the immediate supply of the inhabitants. Davis returned to La Plata, at a loss what course to take; when, on the 2nd October, he was joined by the *Cygnet* of London, commanded by Captain Swan, who, ill-treated by the Spaniards, and disappointed of peaceful traffic, for which he had come prepared with an expensive cargo, had been compelled by his men to receive on board a party of buccaneers, and in self-defence to commence freebooter. Before he had adopted this course some of his men had been killed by the Spaniards at Baldivia, where he had attempted to open a trade. With this small buccaneer party, which had come by the Darien, plundering by the way, Swan fell in near the Gulf of Nicoya. It was led by Peter Harris, the nephew of a buccaneer commander of the same name who had been killed in the battle with the Spanish ships in the Bay of Panama three years before. Harris took command under Swan, in a small bark wholly manned by buccaneers.

This was a joyful meeting of old associates; and the departure of Eaton was now deeply regretted, as their united force might have insured success to more important undertakings than any they had yet ventured to contemplate. While the ships were refitting at La Plata, a small bark, which Davis had taken after the Spaniards had set it on fire, was sent out to cruise, and soon brought in a prize of four hundred tons burden, laden with timber, and gave intelligence that the viceroy was fitting out a fleet of ten frigates to sweep them from the South Seas. Again the loss of Eaton was felt, and this bark was despatched to search for him on the coast of Lima. It went as far as the Isle of Lobos. Meanwhile Swan's ship, which was still full of English goods, was put in better fighting trim, and made fit to accommodate her additional crew. The supercargo sold his goods on credit to every buccaneer who would purchase, taking his chance of payment, and the bulky commodities which remained were pitched overboard,— silks, muslins, and finer goods, and iron bars, which were kept for ballast, being alone retained. In lieu of these sacrifices, the whole buccaneers on board the *Cygnet* agreed that ten shares of all booty should be set aside for Swan's owners.

The men-of-war were now scrubbed and cleaned, a

small bark was equipped as a fire-ship; and the vessel which had been cruising after Eaton not having returned, the squadron sailed without it on the 20th October, and on the 3rd November landed at Payta, which was found nearly abandoned, but left without "money, goods, or a meal of victuals of any kind." They anchored before the place, and demanded ransom for its safety, ordering in the meanwhile three hundred pecks of flour, three thousand pounds of sugar, twenty-five jars of wine, and one thousand of water, to be brought off to the ships; but, after wasting six days, they obtained nothing, and in revenge burned the town. The road of Payta was one of the best in Peru—roomy, and sheltered from the south-west by a point of land. The town had no water except what was carried thither from Colan, from whence the place was also supplied with fruits, hogs, plantains, and maize. Dampier says that on this coast, from about "Cape Blanco to 30° S.; no rain ever falls that he ever observed or heard of." He calls this range "the dry country." Wafer states that heavy nightly dews fertilize the valleys. The country around it was mountainous and sterile.

From information obtained here, it was gathered that Captain Eaton had been before them, and had burned a large ship in the road, and landed all his prisoners. They also learned that a small vessel, which they concluded to be their own bark, had approached the harbour, and made some fishermen bring out water.

Harris's small vessel being found a heavy sailer, was burned before leaving Payta, from which the squadron steered for Lobos de Tierra, and on the 14th anchored near the east end of the island, and took in a supply of seals, penguins, and boobies, of which they ate "very heartily, not having tasted flesh in a great while before." To reconcile his men to what had been the best fare of the crews of Drake, Cavendish, and the earlier navigators, Captain Swan commended this food as of extraordinary delicacy and rarity, comparing the seals to roasting pigs, the boobies to pullets, and the penguins to ducks. On the 19th the fleet reached Lobos de la Mar, where a letter was found deposited at the rendezvous by the bark, which was still in search of Eaton. It was now feared he had sailed for the East Indies, which turned out to be the fact.

Here the Mosquito-men supplied the companies of both ships with turtle; while the seamen laboured to clean and repair, and provide them with fire-wood, preparatory to an attempt upon Guayaquil. For this place they sailed on the morning of the 29th. According to Dampier, Guayaquil was then one of the chief ports of the South Seas. The commodities it exported were hides, tallow, cocoa, sarsaparilla, and a woollen fabric named Quito cloth, generally used by the common people throughout all Peru. The buccaneers left the ships anchored off Cape Blanco, and entered the bay with their canoes and a bark. They captured a small vessel laden with Quito cloth, the master of which informed them of a look-out being kept at Puna, which lay in their way, and that three vessels with negro slaves were then about to sail from Guayaquil. One of these vessels they took shortly afterwards, cut down her mainmast, and left her at anchor, and next morning captured the other two, though only a few negroes were picked out of this to them useless cargo.

From mismanagement, and disagreement between the commanders and the men in the two ships, the expedition against Guayaquil misgave. It was imagined that the town was alarmed and prepared to receive them warmly; and after having landed, lain in the woods all night, and made their way with considerable difficulty, they abandoned the design before one shot had been fired, and while the place lay full in view of them at a mile's distance without manifesting any appearance of opposition being intended.

Dampier, whose ideas took a wider and bolder range than those of his companions, deeply lamented their ill conduct upon the fair occasion which offered at this time of enriching themselves at less expense of crime than in their ordinary pursuits. "Never," he says, "was there put into the hands of men a greater opportunity to enrich themselves." His bold and comprehensive plan was, with the one thousand negroes found in the three ships, to have gone to Santa Martha and worked the gold-mines there. In the Indians he reckoned upon finding friends, as they mortally hated the Spaniards; for present sustenance they had two hundred tons of flour laid up at the Galapagos Islands; the North Sea would have been open to them; thousands of buccaneers would have joined them from all parts of the West Indies, and, united, they might have been a match for all the force Peru could muster, masters of the richest mines in this quarter and of all the west coast as high as Quito. Whether Dampier unfolded this "golden dream" at the time does not appear. The buccaneers, at all events, sailed to La Plata, where they found the bark, and divided the cloth of Quito equally between the companies of Swan and Davis, converting the vessel in which it had been taken into a tender for the *Cygnet*.

This ship had since joining depended almost wholly upon the *Bachelor's Delight* for provisions, as it had neither Mosquito purveyors nor a store of flour; and the original buccaneer company of Davis now murmured loudly at feeding the cowards who they alleged had balked the attempt on Guayaquil. But neither could afford to part consortship, and they sailed in company on the 23rd December to attack Lavelia, in the Bay of Panama. In this cruise, from the charts and books found in their prizes, they supplied the ignorance and deficiencies of the Indian and Spanish pilots whom they had as prisoners on board, these drafts being found surer guides. Their object was in the first place to search for canoes—the want of boats being greatly felt—in rivers where the Spaniards had no trade with the natives, nor settlements of any kind, as concealment was most important to the success of their operations. From the equinoctial line to the Gulf of St. Michael the coast abounded in unfrequented rivers where boats might be found. When five days out from La Plata, they made a sudden descent upon a village named Tomaco, where they captured a vessel laden with timber, in which was a Spanish knight with a crew of eight Spaniards, and also took, what the buccaneers valued much more, a canoe with twelve jars of old wine. A canoe with a party that rowed six leagues further up the river, which Dampier names St. Jago, came to a house belonging to a Spanish lady of Lima, whose servants at this remote station traded with the natives for gold. They fled; but the buccaneers found several ounces of gold left in their calabashes. The land on the banks of this river was a rich black mould, producing tall trees. The cotton and cabbage trees flourished here on the banks; and a good way into the interior, Indian settlements were seen, with plantations of maize, plantain-walks, hogs, and poultry. At Tomaco a canoe with three natives visited the strangers, whom they did not distinguish from Spaniards. They were of middling stature, straight, and well-limbed, "long-visaged, thin-faced, with black hair, ill-looked men of a very dark copper complexion." The buccaneers presented them with wine, which they drank freely.

On the 1st of January the *Cygnet* and *Bachelor's Delight* sailed for the Island of Gallo, carrying with them the Spanish knight, Don Pinas, and two canoes. On the way one of their boats captured the packet-boat from Lima, and fished up the letters which the Spaniards when pursued had thrown overboard attached to a line and buoy. From these despatches they learned the welcome and important fact of the Governor of Panama hastening the sailing of the triennial plate-fleet from Callao to Panama, previous to the treasure being conveyed across the Isthmus to Porto Bello on mules. To intercept this fleet would enrich every man among them at one stroke; and to this single object every faculty was now bent. As a fit place to careen their ships, and at the same time lie in wait for their prey, they fixed upon the Pearl Islands, in the Bay of Panama, for which they sailed from Gallo on the morning of the 7th—two ships, three barks, a fireship, and two small tenders, one attached to each ship.

On the 8th they opportunely captured a bark with flour, and then "jogged on with a gentle gale" to Gorgona, an uninhabited island, well-wooded and watered with brooklets issuing from the high grounds. Pearl-oysters abounded here. They were found in from four to six fathoms water, and seemed flatter in the shell than the ordinary eating oyster. The pearl was found at the head of the oyster, between the shell and the meat, sometimes one or two pretty large in size, and at other times twenty or thirty seed-pearls. The inside of the shell was "more glorious than the pearl itself."

Landing most of their prisoners at Gorgona, the squadron, now consisting of six sail, steered for the Bay of Panama, and anchored at Galera, a small, barren, uninhabited island, from which they again sailed on the 25th to one of the southern Pearl Islands, as a place more suitable to hale up and clean the ships. While this was in progress, the small barks cruised, and brought in a prize laden with beef, Indian corn, and fowls, which were all highly acceptable. They next took in water and fire-wood, and were at last in fit order to fight as well as to watch the plate-fleet, which they did cruising before Panama, between the Pearl Islands and the Main, where, says Dampier, "it was very pleasant sailing, having the Main on one side, which appears in divers forms. It is beautified with many small hills, clothed with wood of divers sorts of trees, which are always green and flourishing. There are some few small high islands within a league of the Main, scattered here and there one, partly woody, partly bare, and they as well as the Main appear very pleasant." Most of the Pearl Islands were wooded and fertile; and from them were drawn the rice, plantains, and bananas which supplied the city of New Panama, "a fair city standing close by the sea, about four miles from the ruins of the old town," encompassed behind with a fine country of hill and valley, beautified with groves and spots of trees appearing like islands in the savannas. The new city had been walled in since the visit which Dampier had made it with Sawkins,

Coxon, and Sharp, and the walls were now mounted with guns pointing seaward.

As Davis lay nearly opposite the city, its supplies from the islands were completely cut off, while his people every day fished, hunted, or pillaged among them. At this time Davis negotiated for an exchange of prisoners, giving up forty, of whom he was very glad to be rid, in return for one of Harris's band and a man who had been surprised by the Spaniards while hunting in the islands. Attention to the safety of the meanest individual of their company was at all times one of the fundamental principles of the buccaneers; and it is stated on good authority that, when they first hunted in the wilds of Hispaniola, if at nightfall one comrade was missing, all business was suspended till he was either found or his disappearance satisfactorily accounted for.

The Lima fleet proved tardy in making its appearance, and the buccaneers again moved, and came to anchor near Taboga, an island of the bay abounding in cocoa and mammee, and having fine brooks of pure water gliding through groves of fruit-trees. About this time they were nearly ensnared by a stratagem of the Spaniards, who, under pretence of clandestine traffic, sent a fire-ship among them at midnight; but the treachery was suspected in time, and avoided. This fire-ship had been fitted up by the same Captain Bond of whom they had heard at the Cape de Verd Islands. He was an English pirate who had deserted to the Spaniards.

The squadron, which had been scattered through the night from alarm of the fire-ship, had scarcely returned to its station, and looked about for the cut anchors, when the freebooters were thrown into fresh consternation by seeing many canoes, full of armed men, passing through an island channel and steering direct for them. They also bore up; but the strangers proved to be a party of two hundred and eighty buccaneers, French and English, in twenty-eight canoes, who had just crossed the Isthmus on an expedition to the South Sea. The English seamen, eighty in number, entered with Swan and Davis; and the flour prize was given to the French flibustiers, who entered it under the command of Captain Groignet, their countryman. These strangers announced another party of one hundred and eighty, under Captain Townley, all English, who were at this time constructing canoes to bring them down the rivers into the South Sea; and on the 30th of March these joined the fleet, not, however, in canoes, but in two ships which they had taken as soon as they entered the bay, laden with flour, wine, brandy, and sugar. The squadron was further increased by the arrival of a vessel, under the command of Mr. William Knight; and the Indians of Santa Martha brought intelligence that yet another strong party, French and English, were on the way. These also arrived, to the number of two hundred and sixty-four men, with three commanders; one of whom, Le Picard, was a veteran who had served under Lolonnois and Morgan at Porto Bello.

The buccaneer force now amounted to about one thousand men, and the greatest want was coppers to cook provisions for so many. The few kettles which they had were kept at work day and night, and a foraging party was sent out to bring in coppers.

From intercepted letters it was ascertained that the Lima fleet was now at sea; and the design upon the city was suspended till the plate-ships were first secured, though, as it chanced, in counting on their easy capture, the buccaneers reckoned without their host.

It was now the latter end of May, and for six months the buccaneers had concentrated their attention on this single enterprise. Their fleet now consisted of ten sail; but, save the *Bachelor's Delight*, which carried thirty-six guns, and the *Cygnet*, which was armed, none were of force, though all were fully manned. The Spanish fleet, it was afterwards learned, mustered fourteen sail—two of forty guns, one of thirty-six, another of eighteen, and one of eight guns, with large companies to each ship. Two fire-ships attended the Spanish fleet.

Before the buccaneers had finished consultation on their plan of operations the Spanish fleet advanced upon them, and battle was resolved on. And, "lying to windward of the enemy," says Dampier, "we had it not in our choice whether to fight or not. It was three o'clock in the afternoon when we weighed, and being all under sail, we bore down right afore the wind on our enemies, who kept close on a wind to come to us; but night came on without anything besides the exchanging of a few shot on each side. When it grew dark the Spanish admiral put out a light as a signal for his fleet to come to an anchor. We saw this light at the admiral's top for about half an hour, and then it was taken down. In a short time after we saw the light again, and being to windward we kept under sail, supposing the light had been in the admiral's top; but, as it proved, this was only a stratagem of theirs, for this light was put out the second time at one of the barks' topmast-head, and then she was sent to leeward, which deceived us, for we thought still the light was in the admiral's top, and by that means ourselves to windward of them." At daybreak the buccaneers found that by this stratagem the Spaniards had got the weather-gage of them, and were bearing down full sail, which compelled them to run for it; and a running fight was maintained all day, till, having made a turn almost round the bay, they anchored at night whence they had set out in the morning. Thus terminated their hopes of the treasure-ships, though it was afterwards learned that the plate had been previously landed. The French captain, Groignet, had kept out of the action, for which he and his crew were afterwards cashiered by their English associates. The common accusation which the English buccaneers brought against their allies was reluctance to fight; while the latter blamed their indecent contempt of the Catholic religion, displayed as often as they entered the Spanish churches, by hacking and mutilating everything with their cutlasses, and firing their pistols at the images of the saints. Next morning the Spanish fleet was seen at anchor three leagues to the leeward, and as the breeze sprung up it stood away for Panama, contented with safety and the small advantage obtained on the former day. The buccaneers were equally well satisfied to escape a renewed engagement, and after consultation they bore away for the Keys of Quibo to seek Harris, who had been separated from them in the battle or flight. At this appointed rendezvous they met their consort, and a fresh consultation made them resolve to march inland and assault Leon, first securing the port of Ria Lexa.

The assault and conquest of these places offers nothing of interest or novelty; they were carried by the united buccaneer force, amounting to six hundred and forty men, with eight vessels, three of them being tenders, and one a fire-ship. In this assault Dampier was left with sixty men to guard the canoes in which the party had been landed. At Leon they lost a veteran buccaneer of the original breed, whom Dampier thus eulogizes:—" He was a stout, old, gray-headed man, aged about eighty-four, who had served under Oliver (Cromwell) in the Irish rebellion; after which he was at Jamaica, and had followed privateering ever since. He would not accept the offer our men made him to tarry ashore, but said he would venture as far as the best of them; and when surrounded by the Spaniards, he refused to take quarter, but discharged his gun amongst them, keeping a pistol still charged; so they shot him dead at a distance. His name was Swan. He was a very merry, hearty old man, and always used to declare he would never take quarter."

A Mr. Smith, a merchant or supercargo, who had sailed with Captain Swan from London to trade in the South Sea, was made prisoner on the march to Leon. This city, situated near the Lake of Nicaragua, Dampier describes as one of the most healthy and pleasant in all South America. No sooner were the buccaneers masters of it than they demanded a ransom of three hundred thousand dollars, which was promised but never paid; and becoming suspicious that the Spaniards were dallying with them merely to gain time and draw their force to a head, the town was set on fire, and they returned to the coast, first supplying themselves with beef, flour, pitch, tar, cordage, and whatever Leon and Ria Lexa afforded. One Spanish gentleman, who had been released on engaging to send in one hundred and fifty head of cattle, redeemed his parole with scrupulous honour. Mr. Smith was exchanged for a female prisoner, and Ria Lexa was left burning.

The buccaneer squadron now separated, and the fraternity broke into several small detachments—Dampier choosing to follow Captain Swan, who intended first to cruise along the shores of Mexico, the country of the mines, and then, sailing as high as the southwest point of California, cross the Pacific, and return to England by India. This plan presented many temptations to Dampier, whose curiosity and thirst of knowledge were insatiable; and he might also have shared in the hopes of his comrades, who promised themselves a rich booty in the towns in the neighbourhood of the mines before they turned their faces westward. Captain Townley had kept by Swan when they separated from Eaton, and each ship had now a tender belonging to it. They put to sea on the 3rd September, and encountered frequent and fierce tornadoes till near the end of the month. Early in October they were off the excellent harbour of Guatalco, the mouth of which may be known by a great hollow rock, from a hole in which every surge makes the water spout up to a considerable height, like the blowing of a whale.

From the sea the neighbouring country looked beautiful. Here they found some provisions, and landed their sick for a few days.

The *Cygnet* and her consort advanced slowly along the coast, landed near Acapulco, plundered a carrier who conducted sixty laden mules, and killed eighteen beeves. They next passed on to Colima, their object being that tempting prize which for generations had quickened the avarice of maritime adventurers—the Manilla ship—for which they kept watch at Cape Corrientes. After quitting Ria Lexa many of the men had been seized with a malignant fever; and as the same kind of disease broke out in Davis's squadron, it was with some feasibility imputed to infection caught at the place mentioned, where many of the inhabitants had been carried off by a disorder of the same kind some months before the buccaneers visited the town.

To victual the ship for the long voyage in view was one main object of the continued cruise of Captain Swan on this coast; but the attempts made for this purpose were often baffled with loss, and so much time had now elapsed that it was concluded the Manilla ship had eluded their vigilance. About the beginning of January, Townley left them in the Bay of Vanderas, and returned towards Panama, carrying home a few Indians of the Darien who had accompanied Swan thus far. The Mosquito-men remained in the *Cygnet*.

To obtain provisions, Swan captured the town of St. Pecaque, on the coast of New Galicia, where large stores were kept for supplying the slaves who worked in the neighbouring mines. He brought off on the first day a considerable quantity of provisions on horseback, and on the shoulders of his men. These visits were repeated, a party of buccaneers keeping the town, till the Spaniards had collected a force. Of this Captain Swan gave his men due warning, exhorting them, on their way to the canoes with the burdens of maize and other provisions which they carried, to keep together in a compact body; but they chose to follow their own course, every man straggling singly while leading his horse or carrying a load on his shoulders. They accordingly fell into the ambush the Spaniards had laid for them, and, to the amount of fifty, were surprised and mercilessly butchered. The Spaniards, seizing their arms and loaded horses, fled with them, before Swan, who heard the distant firing, could come to the assistance of his men. Fifty-four Englishmen and nine blacks fell in this affair, which was the most severe the buccaneers had encountered in the South Sea. It is in consonance with the spirit of that age to find Dampier relating that Captain Swan had been warned of this disaster by his astrologer.* Many of the men had also, he states in his manuscript journal, foreboded this misfortune, and in the previous night, while lying in the church of St. Pecaque, " had been disturbed by grievous groanings, which kept them from sleeping."

This disheartening affair determined Swan and his diminished company to quit this coast, and they accordingly steered for Cape St. Lucas, the south point of California, to careen and to refresh themselves before crossing the Pacific; but by adverse winds they were compelled to put into a bay at the east end of the middle island of the Tres Marias, where they found iguanas, racoons, rabbits, pigeons, and deer, fish of various kinds, turtle, and seals. There they careened the ship, divided and stowed the provisions between it and the tender, and went over to the mainland for water, having previously landed the prisoners and pilots, who were now of

* It was then customary, before undertaking a voyage, to consult an astrologer.

no use save to consume provisions. That they were abandoned on an uninhabited island is said to have been in revenge of the fatal affair of St. Pecaque.

While they lay here, Dampier, who had escaped the contagious fever, languished under a dropsical complaint, of which several of the men had died. The method of cure was singular, but the patient believed it successful. " I was," he says, " laid and covered all but my head in the hot sand. I endured it near half an hour, and was then taken out and laid to sweat in a tent. I did sweat exceedingly while I was in the sand, and I do believe it did me much good, for I grew well soon after."

While careening the ship, Swan had more fully laid before his company his plan of going to the East Indies, holding out to them hopes of plunder in a cruise among the Philippines. Dampier describes many of them as so ignorant that they imagined it impossible to reach India from California; others entertained more reasonable fears of their provisions failing before they could reach the Ladrones. Maize, and the fish which the Mosquito-men caught, some of which were salted for store, now constituted the whole provision of above one hundred and fifty men, and of this but a short allowance could be afforded daily, calculating on a run of at least sixty days.

On the 31st March, having all agreed to attempt the voyage, and consented to the straitened allowance, the *Cygnet* and the tender commanded by Captain

Teat sailed from the American coast, steering southwest till she arrived at 13° N., in which parallel she held due west for the Ladrones. The men received but one meal a day; and there was no occasion, Dampier says, to call them to their victuals, which were served out by the quartermaster with the exactness of gold. Two dogs and two cats which were on board soon learned to attend daily for their respective shares.

The *Cygnet* enjoyed a fair fresh-blowing trade-wind, and went on briskly, which was some consolation for scanty fare. At the end of twenty days they had made so much progress that the men began to murmur at being still kept upon such short allowance; and by the time they reached Guahan they were almost in open mutiny, and had, it was said, resolved to kill and eat Swan in the first place, and afterwards, in regular order, all who had promoted this voyage. In the long run of five thousand miles, they had seen no living thing, whether bird, fish, or insect, save in longitude 18°, a flock of boobies, presumed to be the denizens of some cliffs or islands, though none were seen. On the 21st of May, near midnight, they had the happiness of coming to anchor on the west side of Guahan, about a mile from the shore, after a run which Dampier calculated at seven thousand three hundred and two miles. At this island the Spaniards had a small fort and a garrison of thirty men. Presuming that the *Cygnet* was a Spanish vessel from Acapulco, a priest came off, and was detained as a hostage till terms of obtaining provisions were arranged; and as these were dictated by fair principles of exchange, no difficulty was experienced, both the Spaniards and the few natives on the island gladly bringing their goods to a safe and profitable market.

The natives and the Spaniards here lived in a state of constant hatred, if not in open hostility; and Captain Eaton, who had touched at Guahan on his voyage to India, after parting with Davis on the coast of Peru, had been instigated by the governor to plunder and practise every cruelty upon the islanders. This advice neither himself nor his men were slow to follow. "He gave us leave," says Cowley's manuscript narrative of the voyage, " to kill and take whatever we could find in one half of the island where the rebels lived. We then made wars," as Cowley chooses to term wanton, unprovoked aggression, " with these infidels, and went on shore every day, fetching provisions, and firing among them wherever we saw them; so that the greater part of them left the island. The Indians sent two of their captains to treat with us, but we would not treat with them. The whole land is a garden."

Dampier reckons that at this time there were not above one hundred Indians on the whole island, as most of those who had escaped slaughter destroyed their plantations, and went to other islands remote from the tender mercies of the Spaniards and their new allies the buccaneers. While a friendly and brisk trade was going on between the shore and the *Cygnet*, the

MALAY PROA.
Page 369.

Acapulco vessel came in sight of the island, but was warned off in time by the governor, without, luckily for herself, having been descried by the buccaneers. In the eagerness of flight she ran upon a shoal, where her rudder was struck off, nor did she get clear for three days. As soon as the natives informed the buccaneers of this prize they "were in a great heat to be after her;" but Swan, who disliked his present vocation, and still hoped to open an honest traffic at Manilla, though he found it prudent, under present circumstances, to keep this design secret, persuaded, or as probably frightened his wild crew out of this humour by representing the dangers of the chase.

Suitable presents were exchanged between the governor and the priest and the English captain, and preparations were made to depart. Here Dampier first saw the bread-fruit—the staff of life of so many of the insulated tribes of Polynesia. Of the *flying-proas*, or sailing-canoes of these islands, so often described, he expresses the highest admiration. "I believe," he says, "they sail the best of any boats in the world." One that he tried would, he believed, "run twenty-four miles an hour;" and one had been known to go from Guahan to Manilla, a distance of four hundred and eighty leagues, in four days.

It took the *Cygnet* nineteen days to reach the coast of Mindanao, for which she sailed on the 2nd June; and after beating about through several channels and islands, she came to anchor on the 18th July opposite the river's mouth, and before the city of Mindanao. They hoisted English colours, and fired a salute of seven or eight guns, which was returned from the shore by three. The island of Mindanao was divided into small states, governed by hostile sultans—the governor of this territory and city being the most powerful of their number. The city stood on the banks of the river, about two miles from the sea. It was about a mile in length, but narrow, and winded with the curve of the stream. The houses were built on posts, from fourteen to twenty feet high; and as this was the rainy season they looked as if standing in a lake, the inhabitants plying about from house to house in canoes. They were of one story, which was divided into several rooms, and were entered by a ladder or stair placed outside. The roofs were covered with palm or palmetto leaves. There was a piazza, generally lying in a state of great filth, under each house, some of them serving for poultry-yards and cellars. " But at the time of the land-floods all is washed very clean." The floors were of wicker-work of bamboo.

Captain Swan had many reasons for desiring to cultivate the friendship of the ruling powers at Mindanao. Immediately after the *Cygnet* came to anchor, Rajah Laut, the brother and prime minister of the sultan, and the second man in the state, came off in a canoe, rowed with ten oars, to demand whence they were. One of the sultan's sons, who spoke the Spanish language, accompanied his uncle. When informed that the strangers were English, they were welcomed, though Rajah Laut appeared disappointed that they were not come to establish a factory, for which proposals had already been made to him by the East India Company. The conversation was carried on by Mr. Smith, the late prisoner at Ria Lexa, and the sultan's son, who, with his uncle, remained all the while in the canoe. They promised to assist the English in procuring provisions, and were rowed off without more passing at this time.

Dampier regrets that the offer of a settlement here was not accepted, " by which," he says, " we might better have consulted our own profit and satisfaction than by the other roving loose way of life. So it might probably have proved of public benefit to our nation, and been a means of introducing an English settlement and trade, not only here but through several of the Spice Islands which lie in its neighbourhood." They had not lain long here when they received another invitation to settle in a different island, the sultan of which sent his nephew to Mindanao to negotiate secretly with Captain Swan.

The *Cygnet's* company had not been aware of the dignity of their first visitors till they were gone, when the government officer informed them; who, according to the custom of the ports of China and other parts in the East, came on board to measure the ship—a practice of which Dampier could not conceive the reason, unless the natives wished to improve their knowledge of ship-building.

In the same afternoon Captain Swan sent Mr. More, one of the supercargoes, to the city with a present for the sultan, consisting of three yards of scarlet cloth, three yards of broad gold lace, a Turkish scimitar, and a pair of pistols; and to the Rajah Laut, the dignitary they had already seen, three yards of the same cloth with silver lace. After some preliminary ceremonies, the English envoy was at night admitted to an audience, to which he was conducted by armed men, accompanied by servants bearing torches. The sultan, with ten privy councillors all seated on carpets, awaited his arrival. The present was graciously accepted, a conference took place in Spanish, after which Mr. More and his attendants, being first treated with supper, returned on board. Next day Captain Swan was invited on shore, whither he went, preceded by two trumpeters. He was conducted to an audience, and entertained with betel and tobacco. Two letters were shown him, sent by East India merchants to the sultan, demanding liberty to build a factory and fort, and specifying the terms of traffic, rates of exchange, and of weights and measures. One letter was beautifully written, and between each line there was drawn a line of gold. Another letter, left by a Captain Goodlud, who had lately visited Mindanao, and directed generally to any of the English who might touch there, concluded, "Trust none of them, for they are all thieves; but *tace* is Latin for a candle."

After the interview with the sultan, Captain Swan

visited Rajah Laut, who, being rather in disgrace with his brother at this time, had not been present at the audience. He entertained the English captain with boiled fowls and rice, and strongly urged him to bring the ship into the river, as stormy weather was at this season to be expected. He also advised him to warn his men against offending the natives by infringing their customs, and altogether appeared very familiar and friendly. To impress Swan with an idea of his justice, he ordered a man who had formerly robbed Captain Goodlud to be now punished; and the miserable wretch was accordingly publicly exposed bound to a post, and stripped naked, with his face opposite the scorching sun, while he was shifted round and kept in torture, following its course all day, stung by the gnats and mosquitoes. This was a usual mode of punishment. His life was at nightfall left at the mercy of the English captain, who informed Rajah Laut that he had no right to take cognizance of any crime which had not been committed by his own men and in his own ship.

The letters from the Company's agents, by convincing Swan that there was a serious intention of establishing a factory at this place, gave him confidence to enter the river, trusting also to the friendly professions of Rajah Laut. The *Cygnet* was accordingly lightened of part of her cargo, and with the help of sixty native fishermen, Rajah Laut directing their operations in person, she crossed the bar with the first spring-tide, and was moored within the mouth of the river. The buccaneers remained here so long upon a footing of daily intimate intercourse with the townspeople, that Dampier has been enabled to give a very full and minute account of the Mindanaians. A singular custom of the country facilitated easy intercourse with the natives, though seamen, having their pockets stored with gold and their ships with desirable commodities, who are neither suspected of any sinister intention by the people nor viewed with jealousy by the government, have rarely found the half-civilized tribes of the Indian islands difficult of access.

The custom common in the South Sea Islands of exchanging names and forming a comradeship with a native, whose house is thenceforward considered the home of the stranger, extended in Mindanao to the other sex, and "an innocent platonic female friend, named a *pagally*," was offered to each of the Englishmen, besides his male comrade. These friendships were, however, not so perfectly disinterested as not to require the cement of presents on the one side and flatteries on the other. In Mindanao, as in more refined parts of the world, those who were best dressed and furnished with gold most readily obtained companions and pagallies. Under the sanction of this singular national custom the wives of the greatest men might choose friends among the strangers, or be selected as pagallies, and allowed to converse in public with the persons who distinguished them by their choice.

On their first arrival—for they soon declined in favour, owing probably to their own reckless and dissolute manners—the seamen could not pass along the streets without being compelled to enter the houses, where they were presented with betel and tobacco, the cordial hospitality of the givers atoning for the scantiness of this Oriental entertainment. To express the vivacity and degree of their affection, the natives would place the forefingers of both hands close together, saying the English and themselves were like this; the Dutch were signified by holding the same fingers six inches apart, and the Spaniards at double that distance. Captain Swan, who still had a large quantity of iron and lead, as well as other goods belonging to his owners, meanwhile traded with Rajah Laut, at whose house he dined every day till he established himself at a dwelling which he hired in the town. Those of the buccaneers who had money also took houses on shore, lived a jovial life among their comrades and pagallies, and hired female servants from their masters as temporary housekeepers.

The most important division of this island, the largest save Luconia of the Philippine group, was, as has been mentioned, under the sway of the Sultan of Mindanao, who was often at war with the tribes that occupied the interior and the opposite coasts, and were less civilized and wealthy than his subjects. The soil of the island was deep and black, producing great varieties of timber; and among others the tree named by the natives the *libby*, from the pith of which sago is manufactured. Rice was raised in some places, and on the hilly land potatoes, yams, and pumpkins. The fruits were the plantain, which Dampier names the "king of fruits," guavas, bananas, musk, and water-melons, betel-nuts, cocoa-nuts, jacas, durions, cloves, nutmegs, oranges, etc. From the fibres of the plantain the common people of Mindanao manufactured the only cloth which they wore, making webs of seven or eight yards long. The betel-nut, so much esteemed in most places of India, grew here on a tree like the cabbage-tree, but smaller. At the top of these trees the nuts grow on a tough stem, as thick as a man's finger, in clusters of forty or fifty. The fruit resembles the nutmeg, but is rather larger and rounder. When to be chewed, the nut was cut into four bits, one of which was wrapped up in an areca-leaf spread with a soft paste made of lime. Every native carried his lime-box by his side, into which he dipped his finger, spread his areca-leaf, wrapped up his nut, and proceeded to chew. Where there are no betel-vines the leaves are imported for this purpose. The nut is most admired when young, and while it is green and juicy. It tastes rough in the mouth, dyes the lips red and the teeth black, but at the same time preserves them. Those who are not accustomed to its use become giddy at first, especially if the nuts are old.

The religion of the Mindanaians was the Mohammedan; and the children were taught to read and write, though business was generally transacted by Chinese, the natives being indifferent accountants. Besides what was supposed their native language, they spoke a dialect of the Malay, which was among them the language of commerce. Many of them also understood Spanish, as the Spaniards had only been expelled during the reign of the present sultan's father. Rajah Laut both spoke and wrote Spanish; and had, from reading and conversation, acquired a considerable knowledge of European countries. The natives were of middle size, with small limbs, particularly the females. They had straight bodies, with small heads. Their faces were oval, but those of the women were round. Their foreheads were low, with small black eyes, short low noses, their lips thin and red, their skins tawny, but inclining to a brighter yellow than some of the other Indians, especially among the women. Young females of rank were often much fairer than the other women, and their noses rose to a more aristocratic prominence than those of meaner females. In female children the nose, or rise between the eyes, was sometimes scarcely perceptible. The natives all walked with a stately air, and the women, though barefooted, had very small feet. The nail of the left thumb was allowed to grow very long. The men wore a small turban, the laced ends hanging down, with trowsers and a frock, but neither stockings nor shoes. The women tied up their hair in a knot, which hung down on the crown of the head. They wore a petticoat, and a frock that reached below the waist, with very long sleeves, which, pushed up, sat in puckered folds, and were a source of great pride to the wearers. They were also adorned with ear-rings and bracelets, which the pagally would sometimes beg from her English friend. The clothing of the higher class was made of long cloth, but the lower universally wore the *saggan* or plantain-cloth. They used no chairs, but sat cross-legged on the floor or on mats. The common food of the people was sago or rice, with occasionally a fish or two; but the better classes had often fowls and buffaloes' flesh. In some things their habits were very filthy, and in others very cleanly. Like all Oriental tribes they washed themselves frequently in the rivers, and took great delight in swimming, to which exercise both sexes are accustomed from infancy. The trades practised here were those of goldsmiths, blacksmiths, and carpenters, every man being more or less of a carpenter, and handling with dexterity their scanty tools, which consisted of the axe and the adze alone, saws and planes being altogether unknown. Yet the ships and barks they built were stout and serviceable, and in them the natives made war, or traded to Manilla, and sometimes to Borneo and other distant places, exchanging the gold and bees'-wax found in the interior of the island for calicoes, silks, and muslins. They had also a traffic with the Dutch in tobacco, which in Mindanao was of excellent quality, and sold so low as twelve pounds for a rial. The Mindanaians were resolute in fight, though they avoided the open field, erecting forts and small works, on which they mounted guns. These forts they would defend and besiege for months together, sometimes making a sally. Their weapons were lances, swords, and what Dampier calls hand-cressets, resembling a bayonet, which they wore at all times, whether in war, at work, or pastime. When likely to be overcome, they sell their lives dearly, and seldom either give or take quarter, the conqueror hewing down his antagonist without mercy.

The people here were liable to a leprous disease, the skin becoming blotched and scurfy, and rising in white scales from the continual rubbing induced by intolerable itchiness. Some had the skin white, in spots over their body, though smooth; and these Dampier conjectured were patients who had been cured. Polygamy was common. The sultan had one queen and twenty-nine inferior wives, of whom one was called the war-queen, as she always attended her lord to battle. The daughter of the sultan by his queen was kept in strict seclusion; but his other children in patriarchal numbers roamed about the streets, often begging things which they fancied from the buccaneer seamen. It was said that the young princess had never seen any man save her father the sultan, and Rajah Laut; though all the other women were occasionally allowed to appear abroad in pageants, or upon public festivals.

The sultan was an absolute prince, who, in Oriental fashion, encouraged the industry and commercial enterprise of his subjects by borrowing sums, however small, which he discovered they had accumulated by trade. By way of varying this system of arbitrary exaction, he would at other times first compel them to purchase goods belonging to himself, which had probably been confiscated, and afterwards find some occasion of state to reclaim those goods for the public service. He was a little man, now between fifty and sixty, and altogether inferior to his brother and grand vizier, the Rajah Laut, who, though only equal in trickery, was superior to all his compeers in capacity and intelligence. It was he who led the military forces of the sultan, managed the foreign policy, and regulated the internal affairs of Mindanao. Without the license of Rajah Laut no one could either buy or sell, nor could the common fishermen enter or leave the port without his permission. The Rajah Laut was altogether the hero of Mindanao, the women in the public dances and festivals singing his praises and celebrating his exploits.

Besides being the wet season, it was Ramadan time when the *Cygnet* came to anchor in the river, and amusement and pleasure were nearly suspended in Mindanao; but as soon as this solemn period was past, the Rajah Laut entertained his friend Captain Swan every night with dances, those bands of regularly-trained dancing-women being seen here which are common over all India. But all the females of Mindanao were fond of dancing, which they practised in a ring of forty or fifty, who joined hand-in-hand, singing in chorus, and keeping time, and, though they never moved from the same spot, making various gestures, throwing forward one leg, and clapping their hands at the close of the verse. The Rajah Laut was in return entertained by Captain Swan's men, who performed English dances to the music of violins, in a ball-room fitted up with gold and silver lace, and illuminated by a profusion of wax-candles. Dampier relates the very natural mistake into which the rajah fell regarding one of these quarter-deck performers. John Thacker, a common buccaneer, though he could neither read nor write, had acquired the accomplishment of dancing about some " of the music-houses of Wapping," and coming into the South Sea with Captain Harris, had been so fortunate in acquiring booty that he now wore fine clothes, and by his superior dress and dancing was supposed by the natives to be a person of noble extraction. When the rajah, to satisfy his curiosity on this important point, put the question to one of the company, the seaman replied humorously, that the conjecture as to Jack's quality was quite correct; and that most of the ship's company were of like extraction, at least all who wore good clothes and had money, those meanly clad being but common seamen. The rajah from this time portioned out his civilities according to the garb of his new friends.

Captain Swan was by this time deeply chagrined at the result of his voyage. Most of his crew were turbulent and lawless—those who had money revelling on shore, and continually involving themselves in quarrels with the natives, while those who were poor were growling on board at the privations they suffered and the time wasted in inaction. In the number of the penniless was Dampier, who had no means of recreation and no source of enjoyment save the faculty of a powerful and quick observation, and the delight of entering his remarks in his journal. The single and undivided object of the rest of the crew of the *Cygnet* was gold,— the plunder of the Manilla ship; nor durst the commander reveal his dislike to their project. About the same time that his crew grew violently discontented, he became himself suspicious of the good faith of his friend Rajah Laut, who for the iron and lead which he had procured continued to pay with fair promises.

Beef was one of the articles which the rajah had promised to the English, and a party went a-hunting with him, but found no prey. Dampier, a practised hunter, was always of these parties, and used the opportunities they afforded to extend his knowledge of the country. In these distant hunting-excursions the rajah carried his wives, children, and servants along with him in the proas of the country, which were fitted up with rooms. They settled at some village in the neighbourhood of the hunting-ground, the chief and his family occupying one end of the house and the Englishmen the other. While he and his men, who always hunted from dawn till late in the afternoon, were abroad, the Englishmen were frequently left at home with the women and children. Though these ladies never quitted their own apartment while the chief remained at home, he was no sooner gone than they usually flocked to the strangers' room, asking a thousand questions about the condition of the women and the fashions and customs of England. These were the subject of long and earnest argument among themselves, some condemning and others applauding the custom, which all allowed to be singular, of even the king and chiefs having but one wife. Among the proselytes to monogamy was the war-queen or wife, the lady who enjoyed the privilege of attending the rajah to battle; and her reasons, if they did not convince, at least silenced her opponents.

During this excursion, Dampier, from the conversation of the women, considerably increased his acquaintance with the character and customs of the people. They bathed daily, and washed after every meal; and if they became unclean from touching accidentally any forbidden thing, they underwent scrupulous purification. Though associating so intimately with the English, they did not like to drink with nor after them. Wild-hogs abounded, but swine's flesh, and every part of that filthy animal, was held in the utmost abhorrence by the Mindanaians; and though they invited the seamen to destroy the animals that came to the city during the night to feed on garbage under the houses, they were ordered to take the swine on board, and those who had touched these abominable creatures were ever afterwards loathed and avoided by the natives, and forbidden their houses.

This superstitious dislike was carried to so great a length, that the Rajah Laut returned in a rage a pair of shoes made in the English fashion, of leather he had furnished, and in which he had taken great pride, till he learned that the thread with which they were sewed had been pointed with hog's bristles. The shoemaker got more leather, and made a quite unexceptionable pair, with which the rajah was satisfied.

At this hunting-village, in the evenings, the women danced before the rajah; and before the party broke up to return to Mindanao, he entertained the Englishmen with a jar of "rice-drink," a fermented liquor, on which he and his attendants got very merry. He drank first himself, and then his men; "and they all," says Dampier, "were as drunk as swine before they suffered us to drink."

That balance in human affairs which pervades all conditions was now turning the scale in favour of the less fortunate portion of the *Cygnet's* crew. The Mindanaians, though hospitable and kind, were, when offended, vindictive and deadly in their resentments. The conduct of these dissolute and openly profligate seamen had given them deep offence, and sixteen of the buccaneers were in a short time taken off by poison, to which more afterwards fell victims. The islanders were skilled in subtle poisons, which had not their full operation till a long while after they were administered. Some of the men, after they were conscious of having been poisoned, lingered on for months. When they died, their livers were found black, dry, and shrivelled "like cork."

The ship had not lain long in the river when it had been discovered that her bottom was eaten with worms, which bred in such great numbers in this place that shortly before a Dutch vessel had been destroyed by them in two months, while the Rajah Laut became heir to her great guns. It began to be suspected that he entertained the hope of being equally fortunate in a legacy from the *Cygnet*, as he had given no intimation of a danger which the Mindanaians always avoided by placing their barks and boats in a dry-dock the moment they came into port, even when only returned from fishing. He shook his head and seemed displeased when he saw that the sheathing of the vessel had prevented serious damage, and gravely remarked, "that he never did see a ship with the cunning device of two bottoms before." Dampier had seen the same kind of worms in myriads in the Bay of Campeachy and in the Bay of Panama, and in smaller numbers in Virginia. They are never seen far out at sea.

This alarming damage was repaired in time, though, taken with other circumstances, it strengthened the suspicions of Captain Swan, and excited the discontent of the men by increasing their alarm. Rajah Laut also, if he did not absolutely refuse, still delayed to furnish the beef and rice necessary to their subsistence, and which were to be the price of the commodities with which Captain Swan had so largely furnished him.

His English friend had also lent the rajah twenty ounces of gold, to defray the expenses of a solemn ceremonial observed shortly before, when his son had been circumcised. This splendid ceremony, at which the English assisted, had been celebrated with music, dances, the singular war-dance of the country, banquets, pageants, and processions by torchlight. The rajah, in a manner not uncommon in Eastern countries, not only refused to repay the gold, but when urged, insisted that it had been a present, and finally demanded payment for all the victuals Swan and his men had consumed at his hospitable board.

While the rajah thus refused to discharge his debts, the buccaneer crew clamoured to be gone, and becoming openly mutinous, a party of them resolved to carry off the ship. Neither Dampier, who happened to be on board, nor the surgeon's mate, approved of this treacherous design, but they were reluctantly compelled to go with the rest, leaving Captain Swan and thirty-six men at Mindanao, from whence the *Cygnet* sailed on the 14th January 1687, intending to cruise off Manilla. A buccaneer of Jamaica, named Read, was chosen commander. The first intimation Swan had of his abandonment was the gun which was fired as the ship got under way. To his own irresolution, bad temper, and want of firmness, Dampier imputes this misfortune. If, when apprised of the design of the mutineers, he had come on board and behaved with prudence and courage, he might have brought back the greater part of the men to their duty, and taken his own measures with the ringleaders, to some of whom he had certainly given just cause of discontent.

After leaving Mindanao, the *Cygnet*, with a crew now reduced by various causes to eighty men, coasted to the westward. They fell in with a great many "keys," or small low islets, between which and Mindanao there was a good channel. On the east of these keys they anchored and obtained green-turtle. At different places they cut ratans, such as were used in England for walking-canes. They saw here large bats, "seven or eight feet from tip to tip" of the extended wings, which regularly at dusk took their flight from the smaller islands to the main island in swarms like bees, and returned like a cloud before sunrise. On the 23rd they reached Luconia, having captured a Spanish vessel, laden with rice and cotton cloth, bound for Manilla. The master had been boatswain of the Acapulco ship which had escaped them at Guahan, and which now lay safe in port. Nothing, therefore, of consequence could be hoped for this season, and to beguile the time, and wait a more favourable opportunity, they resolved to sail for the Pulo Condore or "Islands of Calabashes," a group of small islands off the coast of Cambodia. They anchored at Condore on the 14th March. Two of the cluster are pretty large and high. They were tolerably well wooded, and on the largest of them was found a tree from which the inhabitants extracted a pith or viscid juice which they boiled up into good tar, and which, if kept boiling long enough, became pitch. The mangoes of which the Indian pickle is made were found here. They were now ripe, and were betrayed to the seamen by their delicious fragrance. The grape-tree was also seen, with the wild or spurious nutmeg, and many sorts of beautiful birds, as parrots, paroquets, pigeons, and doves. The inhabitants of Pulo Condore resembled the Mindanaians, but were darker in complexion. Their chief business was to make tar of the pith of the trees mentioned above, which they exported to Cochin-China, from which these islanders were originally a colony. The oil of the turtle was another article of their commerce with their mother-country. The islanders were idolaters. In a temple Dampier saw the image of an elephant and of a horse, which they were supposed to worship.

At this place the buccaneers remained for a month; after which they cruised in the Gulf of Siam and in several parts of the China Seas, taking all barks that fell in their way, whether Spanish, Portuguese, or native vessels. From the crew of a junk belonging to the island of Sumatra they learned that the English had established a factory on that island. The surgeon and Dampier, who had accompanied "this mad crew" against their inclination, "and were sufficiently weary of them," would have escaped here, and taken their chance of getting to this or some other English factory, but they were constrained to remain in the *Cygnet.*

The next destination of the buccaneers was the

Ponghou Islands, which in no respect answered their purpose of quiet and security. At the place where they anchored there were a large town and a Tartar garrison.

In the charts which they possessed there were laid down, marked by the figure 5, a group of islands situated between Luconia (the cynosure of their hopes) and Formosa; and these, which offered a tolerably convenient station, they hoped might be either uninhabited or only peopled by tribes from whom they might with impunity plunder provisions, without danger of the outrage being heard of in the Philippines. They steered for them, and on the 6th August reached the interesting group now known as the Bashee Islands. They approached by the westernmost and largest of the group, on which they had the felicity to see goats browsing; but safe anchorage was not obtained till next day in a bay at the east side of the easternmost island. The sails were not furled when a hundred small boats swarmed round the *Cygnet*, each carrying from three to six men, with whom the deck was soon crowded. The pirates, alarmed by the numbers of the islanders, got their fire-arms in readiness; but iron, the most precious of metals with the savage, for which he freely and gladly gives gold in exchange, wondering at the folly or simplicity that induces the European to the unequal barter, and leaving the philosopher to decide which gains most by the bargain,—iron was the only thing that captivated the Basheeans, who quickly picked up all the little pieces they could find, but were otherwise perfectly quiet and orderly. Waxing bolder by indulgence, one of them tried to wrench out an iron pin from the carriage of a gun. He was laid hold of, and his cries made all his countrymen scamper off in a fright. The man was, however, kindly treated, and, being first made sensible of his error in attempting to steal, was presented with a piece of iron, with which he swam to his comrades. Thus reassured, the islanders returned, and a brisk trade was opened, which was renewed daily. Ever after this slight check they continued honest, and they had always been civil. A hog was now got for two or three pounds of iron, a fat goose for an old iron hoop, and the liquor of the islands, the *Bashee*-drink, from the name of which the pirates gave the whole group their general appellation, for old nails, spikes, and bullets.

These five islands were more particularly named:— 1. Orange Island, so called by the Dutchmen among the crew in honour of their native prince. It is the largest and most westerly of the group, and was uninhabited. 2. Grafton Island was so named by Dampier in compliment to the noble family in whose household he had, as has been mentioned, left his wife. 3. Monmouth Island was named by the seamen after the unfortunate Duke of Monmouth, the son of Charles II. The other two were called the Goat and the Bashee Island, from the number of goats seen on the one, and the abundance of the beverage which gained the approbation of the seamen that was made on the other. The two latter are small islands, lying to the south, in the channel which divides Orange Island from Grafton and Monmouth Islands. Monmouth Island is high, and so fenced with steep rocks and precipitous cliffs that the buccaneers did not land upon it as they did upon all the other islands. Grafton and Monmouth Islands were thickly inhabited, and on Bashee there was one village. The natives were " short squat people, generally round-visaged, with low foreheads and thick eyebrows; their eyes small and hazel-coloured, yet bigger than those of the Chinese; short low noses; their lips and mouths middle-proportioned; their teeth white; their hair black, thick, and lank, which they wore cut short—it will just cover their ears, and so is cut round very even," says Dampier, and to this fashion they seemed to attach great importance. Their skins are a dark copper colour. They wear neither hat, cap, turban, nor anything to keep off the heat of the sun. The men had a cloth about their middle, and some wore jackets of plantain-leaves, "as rough and bristly as a bear's skin." The women were clothed with a short cotton petticoat which fell below the knees, of "a thick stubborn" cloth that they manufactured themselves. Both men and women wore large ear-rings of a yellow glistering metal, found in the mines in their own mountains, resembling gold, but paler in colour. These rings, and this metal, completely baffled the science of the pirates, who had rather an instinctive love of gold than much knowledge of its natural properties. When first polished the rings made of this yellow metal looked peculiarly brilliant; but they soon faded and became quite dim, when it was necessary to throw them into the fire, first casing them in a soft paste made of a red earth. After being heated red hot they were cooled in water, and the paste rubbed off, when the glistering lustre was found renewed. Our navigator was, unfortunately, too poor to be able to purchase any of this metal; or rather too honest to reckon any part of the iron belonging to Captain Swan's owners, of which there was still a good quantity on board, his property, though his companions were much less scrupulous. The language of the people of the Bashee Isles was quite strange to the pirates, though they were now tolerably well acquainted with the Malay tongue, the dialect of Mindanao, and the Chinese language.

No foreign commodities of any kind were seen among the Basheeans, nor anything that could have been introduced by sea, save a few bits of iron and pieces of buffalo-hides. In all points they appeared an unmixed race, in their dispositions singularly mild, amiable, and peaceful. Their islands produced plantains, bananas, pumpkins, and plenty of yams, which made the principal part of their food. They had no grain of any kind, and consequently but few fowls, which Dampier never saw in plenty where there was not either maize, rice, or grain of some sort. Some cotton-plants were seen, and sugar-canes, from the boiled juices of which

the natives made the liquor so agreeable to their visitors.
The boiled juice, with which a small black berry was
mixed, was allowed to ferment for three or four days,
and when it had settled, was poured off clear from the
lees, and was fit to drink. It was much like English
beer, both in taste and colour, and, as Dampier verily
believed, a perfectly wholesome beverage, many of the
men who drank it copiously every day, and were often
drunk with it, being never once sick in consequence of
their liberal potations. The natives sold it cheaply,
and when the seamen visited at their houses freely
gave them Bashee-drink, and sometimes bought a jar
from a neighbour to entertain their guests. These
purchases were made with small crumbs of the glistering metal above described, which, wrapped in plantain-leaves, served as a substitute for coin. Though cleanly
in their persons and habitations, the inhabitants of the
Bashee Isles were in some respects very filthy in their
eating. They were not seen at this time to kill any
animals for their own use; but of the goats purchased
by the buccaneers they begged the skin and garbage,
and when the surly seamen threw them into the sea,
they would take them out. With the hogs they never
meddled. The goat's skin they broiled and gnawed,
and of the paunch made what to them appeared a
delicious dish. The whole crude contents of the stomach
were emptied into a pot, and stewed with any small
fish they had caught, which they took what Dampier
thought very superfluous trouble in cleaning and minc-

ing, considering the nature of the substances with which the fish were mixed. This mess was eaten as the people of the Philippines did their rice, he being reckoned the best-bred among the Mindanaians who, wetting his hands to prevent the boiled rice from sticking to them, could most dexterously roll up and swallow the largest ball. The people of these islands had another singular dish made of locusts, which at this season attacked the potato-leaves in multitudes, and in their ravages spared no green thing. They were about an inch and a half in length, and as thick as the tip of a man's little finger, with large thin wings and long small legs. The Basheeans caught them in small nets, a quart at one sweep. When enough were obtained for a dish, they were parched in an earthen pot over the fire, till the legs and wings dropped off, when from brown they became red. Their bodies were succulent, though the heads crackled under the teeth of the eater.

The dwellings of the islanders, and the places upon which they had perched them, were among the most singular features of their social condition. In describing them we adopt the words of Dampier: "These people made but low, small houses. The sides, which were made of small posts wattled with boughs, are not above four feet and a half high; the ridge-pole is about seven or eight feet high. They have a fireplace at one end of their houses, and boards placed on the ground to lie on. They inhabit together in small villages built on the sides and tops of rocky hills, three or four rows of houses one above another, under such steep precipices that they go up to the first row with a wooden ladder, and so with a ladder still from every story up to that above it, there being no other way to ascend. The plain on the first precipice may be so wide as to have room both for a row of houses, which stand all along the edge or brink of it, and a very narrow street running along before their doors between the row of houses and the foot of the next precipice, the plain of which is in a manner level with the roofs of the houses below, and so for the rest. The common ladder to each row, or street, comes up at a narrow passage, left purposely about the middle of it, and the street being bounded with a precipice also at each end, it is but drawing up the ladder if they be assaulted, and then there is no coming at them from below but by climbing a perpendicular wall. And that they may not be assaulted from above, they take care to build on the side of such a hill whose back hangs over the sea, or is some high, steep, perpendicular precipice, altogether inaccessible." These precipices and regular terraces appeared quite natural. Grafton and Monmouth Islands abounded in these rocky fortresses, in which the natives felt themselves secure from pirates, and from enemies whether foreign or domestic.

The boats of the islanders were ingeniously constructed, somewhat like Deal yawls, and some of them so large that they could carry forty or fifty men.

They were impelled by twelve or fourteen oars on each side. Though scantily provided with iron, the Basheeans could work this metal, employing the same sort of bellows, remarkable for rude ingenuity, which Dampier had seen at Mindanao. This primitive bellows was formed of two hollow cylinders, made of the trunks of trees, like our wooden water-pipes. They were about three feet long, and were placed upright in the ground, near the blacksmith's fire, which was made on the floor. Near the bottom of each cylinder, on the side next the forge, a hole was bored, into which a tube was exactly fitted. These tubes met in a common centre or mouth opposite the fire. The bellows being thus prepared, a man stood between the hollowed trunks with a brush of feathers in each hand, which he worked alternately in the cylinders, like the piston of a pump, thus impelling the air through the small pipes below, which by this means kept up a blast that played continually upon the fire.

The men of the Bashee Islands, while the *Cygnet* lay there, were generally employed in fishing, leaving the plantations to the care of the women. Their weapons were wooden lances, of which only a few were headed with iron; their armour a buffalo's hide, as thick as a board, which covered them to the knees, having holes for the head and arms. No form of worship was observed among this tribe, nor did any one seem to have more authority than another. Every man had one wife, and ruled his own household,—the single wife appearing affectionate and happy, and the children respecting and honouring their parents. The boys went out to fish with their fathers, while the girls attended to domestic duties with their mothers. Their plantations were in the valleys, where each family had one; and thither the young girls, as soon as they were able for the task, descended every day from their rocky abodes to dig yams and potatoes, which they carried home on their heads for the use of the family.

In no part of the world had Dampier seen people so perfectly quiet and civil as these islanders. "They dealt justly and with great sincerity," he says, "and made us very welcome to their houses with Bashee-drink."

Meanwhile the cruise off Manilla was not forgotten. Eighty hogs were salted, and yams and potatoes laid up for sea-store. The crew had taken in water, and now only waited the settling of the eastern monsoon to take their departure. On the 24th September the wind shifted to the east, and by midnight blew so fiercely that they were driven to sea, leaving six of their men on the island. It was the 1st October before they were able to recover their anchoring-ground. The natives immediately rowed their comrades on board. As soon as the ship was out of sight, the islanders increased in hospitality and kindness to the strangers left among them. They only stipulated that the buccaneers should cut their hair in the Bashee fashion; and on this condition offered each of them a wife, and, as a dowry, a plantation and implements of labour.

The late storm, their long and profitless cruise, now extending with some of them to years, and the penalties to which their criminal acts made them all alike liable in every civilized country, combined to depress the spirits of the crew of the *Cygnet;* and once more every man heartily wished himself at home, "as they had done a hundred times before." They were, however, persuaded by the captain and master to try one more chance, and agreed to steer for Cape Comorin, for ever renouncing the long-indulged dream of capturing the Manilla ship. Dampier believed that the ultimate object of the pirate commanders was to cruise in the Red Sea, and by one more desperate effort to make or for ever mar their fortunes. Of all the company none was more heartily tired than our navigator, who had been betrayed into this voyage, and whose thoughts, since leaving Mindanao, had run continually on making his escape to some English settlement. To avoid the danger of meeting English or Dutch ships, with which, in taking the best and most direct course, they were in danger of falling in, they agreed, instead of steering for the Strait of Malacca, to go round the east side of the Philippines, and, keeping south to the Spice Islands, pass these, and enter the Indian Ocean about Timor. To Dampier all routes were alike. "I was well enough satisfied," he says, "knowing that the further we went the more knowledge and experience I should get, which was the main thing I regarded, and should also have the more variety of places to attempt an escape from them."

On the 3rd October they sailed from the Bashee Isles, leaving for the first time a somewhat favourable impression of their characters, and bearing away grateful and affectionate remembrances of this gentle and amiable tribe. They steered south-south-west, with the wind at west and fair weather; and passed certain islands which lie by the north end of Luconia. Leaving the coast of this island, and with it "all their golden prospects," they steered southward, keeping to the east of the Philippines, and on the 15th anchored between the two small islands named Candigar and Sarangan, near the south-east end of Mindanao; and next day, at the north-west end of the most easterly of the islands, found a fit place to careen and refit the ship. While they lay here the nephew of the sultan, who, in name of his uncle, had formerly been treating with Captain Swan to visit and garrison his island and take in a cargo of spice, came on board and requested a passage home, as they were understood to be going southward. From him they obtained intelligence of Captain Swan and their deserted comrades, who had been fighting under Rajah Laut with a hostile tribe in the interior. The Englishmen had conducted themselves so bravely in fight that they were now in high favour at Mindanao, though it was feared they had been found too powerful and useful as allies to be permitted easily to leave their new service. Swan had for some time been attempting, unsuccessfully, to hire a vessel to convey him to Fort St. George.

At this time Dampier took an opportunity of persuading the men to return to their duty, to carry the ship back to the river of Mindanao, and give her up to the true commander; but before this could be effected, one man, who seemed the most zealously to embrace the proposal, gave information, and Captain Read deemed it prudent to weigh anchor with all expedition, and without waiting the arrival of the prince, to whom a passage had been promised. Read held a course south-west, and once more disappointed the hopes of Dampier, who believed that, by carrying home the young chief, they might, at his uncle's island, establish a factory and a lawful traffic.

The ultimate fate of Captain Swan, of whom we are now to lose sight, was not a little painful. Two supercargoes or merchants of the ship, Harthop and Smith, died at Mindanao; and when the commander, after a series of vexations and disappointments, was going out to a Dutch vessel which lay in the river, hoping to get away at last, the boat was run down by the emissaries of Rajah Laut, and Swan and the surgeon were either drowned or killed in the water. The property of the English captain was immediately seized by the perfidious chief, who justified his conduct by imputing as crimes to the unfortunate Englishman the idle, impotent threats wrung from him by hope deferred, irritation, and grief.

The *Cygnet* continued her bootless voyage among the islands and channels of the Philippines on to the Spice Isles, and anchored off Celebes, where the seamen obtained a supply of turtle, and found among other shell-fish cockles of so monstrous a size that the meat of one of them made a meal for seven or eight persons. It was palatable and wholesome. Here they also found a vine, of which the leaves, pounded and boiled with lard, made an infallible sea-salve. One of the company had formerly learned its uses from the Indians of the Darien; and most of the seamen now laid up a store, such as had ulcers finding great benefit from its healing properties. On the 29th November they left this place; and after encountering the dangers of the shoals which surround Celebes, and experiencing fierce tornadoes, on the 1st December they saw, and on the 5th approached, the north-west end of the island of Bouton. On the evening of the 30th they had seen at a distance two or three water-spouts, but escaped them all.

An Indian, who spoke the Malay tongue, came on board at this time with some of the turtle-strikers, and informed them of a good harbour on the east side of Bouton, for which they sailed. They came to anchor within a league of Callasusung, a clean and handsome town, situated upon a hill in the middle of a fertile plain, surrounded with cocoa-trees. The people resembled the inhabitants of Mindanao, and their houses were built in the same style; but they appeared in all respects more "neat and tight." They were Mohammedans, and spoke the Malay language. The same description seems to fit every sultan whom the voyagers saw,—"a little man about forty or fifty, with a great many wives and children." Unaware of the exact character of his visitors, the Sultan of Bouton was pleased to hear that they were English, and made them a visit in a handsomely-ornamented proa, with a white silk flag displayed at the mast-head, edged with red, and having in the centre, neatly painted, the device of the prince,—a green griffin trampling upon a dragon or winged serpent.

They had no object in remaining here, and as a forlorn hope, or from curiosity, resolved to steer for New Holland, "to see what that country could afford them." In leaving Bouton they got among shoals, and it was about three weeks before they passed Timor and got clear of all the dangers of this chain. They stood off south, and on the 4th January fell in with the northwest coast of New Holland in 16° 50″. They ran close in, but found no safe anchoring ground, as the coast lay open to the north-east. They steered for about twelve leagues north-east by east, keeping close in by the shore, and reached a point three leagues to the eastward of which they found a deep bay with many islets, and finally anchored at about a mile from the land. Seeing people walking on the shore, a canoe was sent off, but the natives ran away and hid themselves; and though traces of fires were seen, no habitation could be discovered. Toys and trinkets were left on the shore at such places as the people were likely to find them.

The coast here was low and level, with sandbanks. No water could be found, though at several places old wells were seen dry in the sandy bays. Having failed of their object on the mainland, neither provisions nor water being found, nor a hope of them, some of the boats visited the islands in the bay, and surprised a party of the natives. The men at first threatened the intruders, and showed their lances and swords; but the noise of a single gun frightened them, and the women seemed in very great alarm. Screaming, they ran away with their children, while the men stood to parley. Those who, from sickness or feebleness, were unable to follow, lay still by their fires uttering doleful lamentations; but when it was seen that no harm was intended them, they became tranquil, and many of the fugitives returned.

The buccaneers had entertained no design against these wretched people more flagitious than to make them labour in carrying the water-casks to the boats. To this they tried to bribe them with ragged shirts and old breeches, finery which could have charmed some of the insular families of the Pacific, though they were totally disregarded by the inert natives of New Holland, whose first associations with European finery were connected with hard and compulsory labour. "We put them on them," says Dampier, speaking of the tattered rags of the buccaneers, "thinking this finery would make them work heartily for us; and our water being filled in barrels of about six gallons, we brought these new servants to the wells, and put a barrel on each of their shoulders to carry to the canoe. But all the signs we could make were to no purpose; for they stood like statues without motion, but grinned like so many monkeys, staring upon one another." It was found that they had not even strength sufficient for the task of being carriers of water; and Dampier believed that an English shipboy of ten years old would have been able to bear heavier burdens than these feeble savages. "So we were forced," he says, "to carry our water ourselves; and they very fairly put the clothes off again, and laid them down, as if clothes were only to work in. I did not perceive," he adds, "that they had any great liking to them at first; neither did they seem to admire anything we had." In the estimation of Dampier, the natives of New Holland were lower in the scale of humanity than any tribe of which he had ever heard, the Hottentots not excepted. "Setting aside their human shape," he says, "they differ but little from brutes. They are tall, straight-bodied, and thin, with long, small limbs. They have great heads, round foreheads, and great brows. Their eyelids are always half closed to keep the flies out of their eyes, so that they never open their eyes like other people; and therefore they cannot see far, unless they hold up their heads as if they were looking at something over them. They have great bottle-noses, pretty full lips, and wide mouths. The two fore teeth of their upper jaw are wanting in all of them, men and women, old and young. Whether they draw them out I know not; neither have they any beards. They are long-visaged, and of a very unpleasant aspect, having no one graceful feature in their faces. Their hair is black, short, and curled, like that of negroes; and the colour of their skins coal-black, like that of the negroes in Guinea. They have no sort of clothes, but a piece of the rind of a tree tied as a girdle about their waists, into which is thrust a handful of long grass or small green leafy boughs. They have no houses, lying in the open air without covering, the earth their bed, the heaven their canopy." They lived in groups or families of from twenty to thirty, men, women, and children; their only food being a small kind of fish which they caught at flood-tide in a sort of weirs. Few shell-fish were seen among them. Yet even these miserable people were redeemed to humanity by the possession of some good qualities. Whatever they caught was fairly divided. Were it little or much every one had a share of the bounty that Providence had sent, " the old and feeble who were unable to go abroad, as well as the young and lusty." This disinterestedness, with their bold defence of the women and children on the first appearance of the Europeans and the startling report of fire-arms, is, however, all that can be said in praise of apparently the most abject and wretched tribe of the great human family. When they had consumed what was caught, they lay down till next low water, and then all who were able to crawl, be it night or day, went to examine the weirs. No iron was seen among these people; but they had wooden swords, and a kind of lance like a long pole, sharpened at the upper end, and hardened by heat.

No sort of quadruped was seen here; but there were a few land and sea birds, and plenty of manatee and turtle, though the natives had never learned to strike them. They had neither boats, canoes, nor rafts, but could swim between the islands of the bay. No form of worship was discerned among them; and though they greedily devoured rice, manatee, or whatever was given them, their minds never once appeared awakened to any feeling of interest or curiosity. Four men who were caught swimming, and brought on board the ship, were sensible to nothing but the food which they devoured and the delight of getting away. The wonders around them, — the British ship and her strange company,—which would have charmed many of the tribes of Polynesia to an ecstasy of surprise, were unnoticed by the savages of this part of New Holland.

The Mosquito-men were busily employed during the time that the ship was cleaned and the sails repaired;

nor did Dampier miss the opportunity of once again persuading his messmates to go to some English factory and surrender the vessel and themselves. The threat of being left on this barren and melancholy coast, among the most wretched of the human race, compelled him to consult his prudence rather than his duty, and to wait a fairer chance of escape.

The destination of the *Cygnet* was still Cape Comorin; and on the 4th of May they made the Nicobar Islands, the chief commodities of which were ambergris and fruits, which the inhabitants disposed of to any European vessels that chanced to visit them. Dampier now openly expressed his intention of leaving the ship; and Captain Read, believing that he could not more effectually punish his refractory shipmate than by granting his wish, and leaving him at one of these islands, at once gave him leave to go on shore. Lest Read might change his mind, Dampier immediately lowered his bedding and chest, and got some one to row him to the land. He had not been long on shore when a party were sent from the ship to bring him back, and he complied, aware that if he persisted in going away against their will, the buccaneers would not hesitate to make a descent on the coast and kill some of the natives, who would in turn revenge themselves on him. On returning to the ship, he found that his spirited example had moved some of the other persons who had long entertained a similar design of effecting their escape, and three of them now joined his party, of whom the surgeon was one. The captain and crew refused on any terms to let the surgeon depart; but after some altercation Dampier and his two companions, on a fine clear moonlight night, were landed and left in a sandy bay of this unknown island. One of the seamen who rowed them ashore stole an axe and gave it to them, as the means of propitiating the natives or of buying provisions. They were speedily joined by four Acheenese previously found in a captured proa, whom Captain Read released before setting sail; and now they fancied themselves strong enough to row to Sumatra. A Portuguese, taken prisoner by the buccaneers long before, was also landed, and the party of eight considered itself able for defence if attacked by the natives, though no one offered to disturb them.

From the owner of an empty hut in which they slept they bought a canoe with the stolen axe, and, placing their goods in it, embarked for Acheen. It upset as soon as under way, and though no life was lost, their clothes were wetted, and what to Dampier was of far greater importance, the journals of many years and his drafts were damaged. Three days were spent in drying their things, and altering the canoe into a sailing-boat, which was expertly done by the Acheenese, who fitted her with a mast, outriggers, and a suit of mat-sails. With the natives, who watched all their movements, though more from curiosity than suspicion, they bartered rags and strips of cloth for mel-lory,—a fruit the size of the bread-fruit, shaped like a pear, with a tough, smooth, light-green rind, which Dampier asserts is confined to these islands. They also obtained cocoa-nuts, which the Acheenese gathered, and might have had hogs, but that they did not choose to disgust their Malayan friends, who were Mohammedans. Once more they embarked in their frail vessel, their only guides a pocket-compass, with which Dampier had provided himself, and a sketch of the Indian Seas, which, contemplating escape, he had previously, from a chart in the ship, copied into his pocket-book.

They had been out three days when the weather became threatening, and soon rose to a tempest. We shall employ the striking language of Dampier himself to describe what followed, nor, while it reveals so much of his true character and feelings, could a better specimen of his more elevated and earnest style be easily selected:—" The wind continued increasing all the afternoon, and the sea still swelled higher and often broke, but did us no damage; for the ends of the vessel being very narrow, he that steered received and broke the sea on his back, and so kept it from coming in, which we were forced to keep heaving out continually. The evening of this day was very dismal. The sky looked very black, being covered with dark clouds. The wind blew hard, and the seas ran high. The sea was already roaring in a white foam about us; a dark night coming on, no land to shelter us, and our little bark in danger to be swallowed by every wave; and, what was worst of all, none of us thought ourselves prepared for another world. I had been in many imminent dangers before now, but the worst of them all was but play-game in comparison with this. I had long before this repented me of that roving course of life, but never with such concern as now. I did also call to mind the many miraculous acts of God's providence towards me in the whole course of my life, of which kind I believe few men have met the like. And for all these I returned thanks in a peculiar manner, and once more desired God's assistance, and composed my mind as well as I could in the hopes of it; and, as the event showed, I was not disappointed of my hopes. Submitting ourselves therefore to God's good providence, and taking all the care we could to preserve our lives, Mr. Hall and I took turns to steer, and the rest to heave out the water; and thus we provided to spend the most doleful night I ever was in."

The pious trust of Dampier and his companions did not fail them. After enduring great hardship, they reached a small fishing-village in a river's mouth of the island of Sumatra, at which their companions, the Malays of Acheen, were previously acquainted. They were so much exhausted when they arrived here as to be unable to row their canoe to the village,—another example of the sudden prostration of strength to which persons who have been in imminent jeopardy are liable as soon as the danger appears to be past. The people of the place assisted them in, and a chief who came to see them, being given to understand that they were prisoners escaped like the Acheenese from pirates, treated them with great kindness. A house was provided for their reception, and far more provisions were sent to it than they could use, as they were all sick from excessive fatigue, and the cold and heat to which they had alternately been exposed, now scorching unsheltered in the noontide sun, and again bleaching in the chill rains of midnight. After resting for ten days, though not yet restored to health, they entreated to be allowed to proceed to Acheen to their countrymen; and they were provided with a large proa, and permitted to depart. On their arrival at Acheen they were strictly examined by the native magistrate, and then given up to the care of an Irish gentleman connected with the factory. The Portuguese died, and Ambrose, one of the Englishmen who left the *Cygnet*, did not long survive him. Dampier, originally robust, and whose constitution was now by his hardy mode of life almost invincible, recovered, though slowly; the remedies of a Malay doctor, to whose care he was committed, having proved worse than the original disease.

When his health was somewhat re-established, Dampier made a voyage to Nicobar with Captain Bowry, an English captain who traded to different parts of India. His next voyage was to Tonquin with Captain Weldon, with whom he afterwards went to

Malacca, and thence to Fort St. George, where he remained for five months, and then returned to Bencoolen, to a factory lately established by the English on what was at that time called the Westcoast. Here he also officiated for five months as gunner of the fort.

While at Acheen, after returning from Malacca, Dampier met with Mr. Morgan, a former shipmate in the *Cygnet*, from whom he learned the fortunes of the buccaneers. After he had left them at Nicobar, they steered for Ceylon, but by stress of weather were compelled to seek refreshments upon the coast of Coromandel. Half the crew at this time left the ship, part of whom afterwards found their way to Agra, and entered the service of the Mogul as guards; but upon the offer of a pardon from the English governor at Fort St. George, they repaired to that garrison. The *Cygnet* reached Madagascar, where the pirates entered the service of some petty prince then at war with a neighbouring chief.

We may here take a farewell glance of the buccaneers, and especially of those left by Dampier in the South Sea. In pursuing their old vocation they became more successful after the *Cygnet* crossed the Pacific. They captured many vessels, and revelled in the plunder of several towns; sometimes cruising together, but as often in detached bands. Townley was so far fortunate as to obtain with ease at Lavelia the treasure and merchandise landed from the Lima ship in the former year, for which Swan had watched so long in vain, and for which the whole buccaneer force had battled in the Bay of Panama. Townley afterwards died of wounds received in another attack. The French party stormed Granada; and Groignet, dying of his wounds, was succeeded by Le Picard. Harris followed Swan across the Pacific; and Knight, satiated with plunder, returned by Cape Horn to the West Indies, those of his party who had in gambling lost their share of the pillage remaining in the *Bachelor's Delight*. The narrative of the traverses of this vessel on the coasts of Peru and New Spain, written by Lionel Wafer, who remained with Davis while Dampier followed Swan, possesses considerable interest. Davis generally kept apart from the French freebooters, but joined them in an attack on Guayaquil, where the buccaneers amicably divided a rich booty. The French party, among whom, however, there were many Englishmen, afterwards made their way overland, and with great difficulty, from the Bay of Amapalla to the head of a river which falls into the Caribbean Sea, each man with his silver and gold on his back, the fortunate and cunning hiring as porters the comrades they had previously stripped at the gaming-table.

Davis, who during his long cruise had frequently remained for weeks at Cocos Island and the Galapagos group, now sailed from Guayaquil to these islands, to careen and victual his ship previous to leaving the

South Sea by Cape Horn. The Galapagos* were become to the buccaneers in the South Sea what Tortuga had been to their predecessors in the West Indies. In his run south from the Galapagos, Davis discovered Easter Island, though the merit of the discovery was afterwards claimed by the Dutch Admiral Roggewein, and is still a matter of dispute. Davis at this time left five of his men with five negro slaves on Juan Fernandez. They had lost every farthing which they possessed at the gaming-table, and were unwilling to leave the South Sea as poor as they entered it. The *Bachelor's Delight* successfully doubled Cape Horn, and Davis, who among the buccaneers stood high in point of character both for capacity and worth, reached the West Indies just in time to avail himself of the pardon offered by royal proclamation. Dampier afterwards in England met with his old commander, whom he highly esteemed.

Though the French flibustiers, countenanced by their government, continued to flourish during the war which followed the accession of William III. to the throne of England, and did brave service to their country in the West Indies, buccaneering, already severely checked, ceased among the English from this time, or shifted into the legitimate channel of privateer adventure; yet for more than twenty years a few

* The captain of an English ship, which made a voyage in the Pacific in 1794, one hundred and ten years after the retreat of the buccaneers from the South Sea, relates that he found the remains of their seats, made of turf and stones, empty jars like those in which the Peruvian wine is kept, and nails, daggers, and other articles left by them.

desperate characters, English or English Creoles, outlaws or deserters, pretending to be the true successors of the old rovers, who had strictly limited their depredations to the Spanish West Indies, continued to infest the commerce of every nation, and haunted every sea from Cape Wrath to the islands of the Indian Ocean, wherever robbery could be practised with impunity whether on land or water. The better to forward or conceal their designs, these lawless ruffians often allied themselves with native princes, as the new commander of the *Cygnet* had done at Madagascar. Of these degenerate descendants of the buccaneers of America, the numerous crew of a pirate-ship named the *Revenge*, which was captured among the Orkney Isles, suffered by the sentence of the Court of Admiralty so late as 1724.*

While Dampier was at Fort St. George an English vessel arrived from Mindanao laden with clove-bark, having on board an Indian prince he had formerly seen a slave at that place, and whom Mr. Moody, the supercargo of the ship, had purchased from his owner. This prince was from the islands named Meangis, which he said abounded in gold and cloves; and it had been a favourite speculation with Dampier to establish a factory and open a trade there, which might have been managed from Mindanao. This scheme was, however, blown to air; and Prince Jeoly, whom Dampier while

* We need scarcely remind the reader of Sir Walter Scott's romance "The Pirate."

at that island had proposed to purchase from his master to be his guide and introducer, was now on the way to England to be exhibited as a show. Mr. Moody, who had purchased Jeoly, was meanwhile appointed to the factory of Indrapoor, then just established on the west coast of Sumatra, and to induce Dampier to accompany him to this station, and take charge of the guns, promised that a vessel should be purchased in which he might realize his old scheme of going to Meangis with the native prince, and establishing a commerce in cloves and gold. Being afterwards unable to fulfil this promise, Moody not only released his friend from the engagement to serve at Indrapoor, but presented him with a half-share of the "painted prince," leaving him meanwhile under his charge. As Prince Jeoly was the first *tattooed* man ever seen in Europe, the account given of him by Dampier is still curious. The islands from which he came lay about twenty leagues from Mindanao, bearing south-east. They were three in number, small but fertile, and abounding, according to the report of the prince, in gold. The abundance of cloves and spice Jeoly, using a common Oriental figure, described by showing the hairs of his head. His father was rajah of the island on which they lived. On it were about thirty men and a hundred women, of whom five were Jeoly's wives. By one of his wives he had been "painted." He was tattooed down the breast, between the shoulders, and on the thighs; and also round the arms and legs in the form of broad rings and bracelets. The figures Dampier could not compare to either the outline of animals or plants, but they were full of ingenious flourishes, and showed a variety of lines and checkered work in intricate figures. Upon the shoulder-blades the lines and pattern were peculiarly elegant. Most of the men and women of Jeoly's island were thus "painted." They wore gold bracelets and anklets, had canoes, and lived upon potatoes, yams, fruits, and fish. They had also plenty of fowls. His native language was quite different from the Malayan, which he had acquired during his slavery. In passing with some of his relations from one island to another, their canoe had been driven by a violent tempest towards the coast of Mindanao, and they were all made prisoners by the Mindanaian fishermen, who stripped them of their golden ornaments, and sold them for slaves.

With his situation at the fort of Bencoolen Dampier found much reason to be dissatisfied, though the character of the governor was his principal grievance. But besides his disgust with this official, from whose treatment of others Dampier drew no favourable augury for himself, he began strongly to experience the stirrings of that longing after his native country to which every wanderer is at last subjected; and though his pecuniary affairs were in greater disorder than on the day he embarked with the buccaneers, and he had been glad to earn two dollars, his sole treasure, by teaching plain sailing to the lads of Weldon's ship, he sanguinely promised himself a fortune from Prince Jeoly, and hoped that in England he might be able to obtain a ship to carry back the chief to his native island, where, thus introduced, he could not fail to establish a lucrative trade in gold and spices. Mr. Moody had meanwhile disposed of the share which he retained of the unfortunate captive to the mate of an India ship bound for England, and with this vessel Dampier wished to return home himself, though the capricious and tyrannical governor, who had at first consented to his departure, at the time of the ship's sailing revoked the permission, nor yielded to any entreaties, though the captain and others importuned him to let the long-absent wanderer return to his country. The day before the ship sailed Dampier crept at midnight through a port-hole of the fort, abandoning all his property, save his journal and manuscripts, for the chance of freedom and of reaching home. The mate of the ship, his new partner in Jeoly, by previous agreement waited for him with a boat, and kept him concealed on board till the vessel sailed, which it did on the 25th January 1691.

The voyage, from the illness of the crew, proved tedious and troublesome, but it was completed at last; though the same bad fortune which had attended Dampier at so many turns of life deprived him of all advantage from bringing home Jeoly. He arrived in the Thames in utter poverty, and was compelled by necessity to sell his share of "the painted prince;"

thus for ever renouncing the romantic project of carrying him back to Meangis, which poor Jeoly was destined never again to revisit. After being seen by many "eminent persons," he caught the smallpox at Oxford, and died.

Of Dampier at this time we hear no more. The narrative of his eight years' ramble round the globe breaks off abruptly by saying, "We luffed in for the Downs, where we anchored September 16th, 1691."

All that can now be learned—all, perhaps, that is desirable or important—is, that in the following year Dampier published his "New Voyage round the World," and afterwards a Supplement; which he entitled "Voyages and Descriptions." The work was dedicated to Charles Montague, Esquire, President of the Royal Society, and a Commissioner of the Treasury, with whom it appears he had no previous acquaintance. Its intrinsic merits, the charm of the narrative, and the style, soon brought the author into notice, and the work ran rapidly through several editions, and was translated into French and Dutch. Among other distinctions, Captain Lemuel Gulliver, at that period a navigator of very great celebrity, hailed Dampier, from whom he borrowed many hints, as "Cousin."

CHAPTER V.

VOYAGE TO NEW HOLLAND.

IN 1699, the country being in profound peace, an expedition of discovery, highly honourable to the royal projector, was ordered by William III., the conduct of which the Earl of Pembroke, who was then at the head of the Admiralty, committed to Dampier, who was recommended solely by his qualifications as a seaman, his large experience, and evident capacity. The countries which he was particularly recommended to examine in this voyage were New Holland and New Guinea.

The vessel in which Dampier undertook the voyage to New Holland was a king's ship named the *Roebuck*, old and crazy before she left the port. She carried twelve guns, and a crew of fifty men and boys, with provisions for twenty months, and the equipments necessary to the accomplishment of a voyage undertaken for the future promotion of traffic, but of which the immediate object was discovery. Dampier, who had always been fond of natural history, at this time carried a draftsman with him. The *Roebuck* left the

Downs on the 14th January 1699, and proceeded prosperously to the Cape de Verd Islands, and afterwards to the coast of Brazil, where Dampier thought it necessary to put into some port, as he intended at the next stretch at once to reach New Holland. On the 25th March they anchored at Bahia de todos los Santos, where thirty large European vessels then lay, besides other ships and a multitude of craft. The governor was named Don John de Lancaster, and, claiming to be of high English extraction, was exceedingly courteous to the countrymen of his ancestors.

They sailed on the 23rd April, and on the following days caught small sharks, which they cooked in the buccaneer fashion, and called good fish. On their way to the Cape of Good Hope they saw nothing more remarkable than the carcass of a whale, about which hovered "millions" of sea-fowl, darkening the air far around. They also saw the stormy petrel, a bird resembling a swallow, but smaller, and which skims like a swallow. Seamen, naturalists say most unjustly, call them foul-weather birds, and at all times dislike their appearance. " In a storm they will hover under the ship's stern, in the wake or smoothness which the ship's passing has made on the sea; and there, as they fly gently, they pat the water alternately with their feet, as if they walked upon it, though still on the wing. Hence the seamen gave them their name, from Peter walking on the Lake of Gennesareth."

The voyage proceeded favourably. On 4th July

they frequently made soundings, and ninety leagues from New Holland often saw whales, and at thirty leagues bones of the scuttle-fish floating, and also seaweed. They were now close upon the western coast of New Holland, and constantly sounded. On the morning of the 1st August they descried land at the distance of six leagues, but were unable to find a safe harbour, and from foul weather were compelled to stand off till the 5th, when they again approached the same coast. Next morning they ran into an opening, keeping a boat sounding before the ship, and anchored at two miles from the shore, in the harbour named Dirk Hartog's Reede, from the first discoverer, who in 1616 had anchored here. To this bay Dampier gave the name of Sharks' Bay. He lays it down as in 25° S. at the mouth.

The land here is rather high, and from sea appears level, but is found to be gently undulating. On the open coast the shore is bluff; but in the bay the land is low, and the soil sandy, producing a species of samphire. "Farther in" (we now adopt Dampier's description) "it is a reddish mould, a sort of sand producing grass, plants, and shrubs. Of trees and shrubs are various sorts, but none above ten feet high. Some of the trees were sweet-scented, and reddish within the bark like sassafras, but redder. The blossoms of the different sorts of trees were of several colours, but mostly blue, and smelt very sweet and fragrant. There were also beautiful and fragrant flowers growing on the ground, unlike any I had ever seen elsewhere." There were eagles, but no other large birds; and of small singing-birds great variety, with fine shrill notes. Besides the ordinary sea-birds there were many strange kinds, quite new to the voyager. The kangaroo he describes as a sort of racoon, differing from those of the West Indies chiefly in the legs; what he calls the racoons of New Holland having very short fore-legs, with which they go jumping about. Of the iguanas of this country Dampier gives a striking description. They were inferior as food to those with which he had been familiar in the West Indies and the South Sea, and when killed and opened were very offensive in smell. Nothing can be more loathsome and disgusting than the picture he gives of this large species of lizard (*Scincus tropicurus*). In Sharks' Bay, besides an abundance of sharks, large green-turtle were found, both of which furnished welcome refreshment to the seamen. The fish were skate, rays, and other flat kinds, with mussels, oysters, and small shell-fish. "The shore was lined with strange and beautiful shells."

They had anchored at three different places to search for water; and on the 11th, for this purpose, and also to prosecute discovery, they stood further into the bay, but, after several abortive attempts, again bore out to sea, having previously scrubbed the ship. Sea-snakes were seen of different kinds,—one sort yellow with brown spots, about four feet in length and of the thickness of a man's wrist, with a flat tail; another kind smaller, shorter, and round, spotted black and yellow.

It was the 14th August when they sailed out of this bay or bight, and plied off and on northward, keeping about six or seven leagues from the shore, and frequently sounding. On the 15th they were in latitude 24° 41′ S.; on the 16th in 23° 22′, "jogging on northward," seeing in their progress many small dolphins and whales, and abundance of scuttle-fish shells and water-serpents. On the afternoon of the 18th, off a shoal in 22° 22″, of which Dampier kept clear, numerous whales were seen on all sides of the ship "blowing and making a very dismal noise." When the *Roebuck* got into deeper water these alarming fellow-voyagers left her.

On the 20th they were carried out of sight of land, which was recovered on the 21st, visible only from the mast, bearing south-east by east, and appearing at the distance of nine leagues like a bluff headland. Around this place was an archipelago of islands, of good height, which Dampier believed to be a range stretching from east-north-east to west-south-west for about twenty leagues, or probably to Sharks' Bay, and of considerable depth, which he presumed might possibly afford a passage to the great South Sea eastward. Next day he ran in among these islands, the boat sounding before. The water was of very unequal depth, and the arid appearance of the shores and yellow rusty colour of the rocks made them despair of finding water, though Dampier, hoping that they might either discover a new channel leading through to the mainland of New Holland or find some sort of rich mineral or ambergris, for which this was a favourable latitude, was unwilling to turn back. The island near which he rode he named Rosemary Island, as a plant that seemed of that kind grew here in abundance, but was destitute of smell. Two kinds of beans were found; the one growing on bushes, the other on a creeping plant that ran along the ground. Cormorants and gulls were seen, and a kind of white parrot, which flew in large flocks.

They left this place on the 23rd, and for some time coasted on with the land-breeze, having had, since leaving Sharks' Bay, fine clear weather, which still continued. Water-snakes, whales, noddies, and boobies were seen. On the 27th and 28th they were out of sight of land, which was recovered on the 30th in latitude 18° 21′ S., great smokes being seen on the shore. This night there was an eclipse of the moon.

Early next day an armed party of ten men landed to search for water, carrying with them pickaxes and shovels. Three tall black naked men were seen on the beach, but they went away. The boat, lying at anchor a little way out in the water to prevent seizure, was left in the care of two sailors, while the rest of the party followed the natives, who were soon joined by eight or nine men. They stood posted on an eminence, from which, however, they fled on the approach of the Englishmen.

From this height the party descried a savanna studded with what they at first fancied to be huts, but discovered to be only rocks and no water near them. They returned to the place at which they had landed, and began to dig, but were menaced by another party of natives collected on an adjoining height, who vociferated with angry gestures, as if they ordered the strangers to be gone. One of them at length ventured to approach, and the rest followed at a cautious distance. Dampier went forward to meet them, making signs of peace and friendship; but the leader fled, and the others kept aloof. The want of water made it absolutely necessary to establish a communication with the natives, whether by fair or violent means; and an attempt was made to catch some of them, a nimble young man who was with Dampier trying to run them down. As soon as he overtook them they faced about and fought him; and Dampier, who was himself assailed, was compelled to fire off his musket in defence of his man, who, though armed with a cutlass, was unable to beat back so many wooden lances. The first shot, intended to scare but not to injure, was treated, after a momentary alarm, with indifference or contempt. They tossed up their arms, exclaiming, "*Pooh, pooh, pooh!*" and pressed closer upon the seaman; and Dampier durst no longer withhold his fire. One native fell; his friends paused in alarm, and the young seaman escaped. "I returned back," says Dampier, "with my man, designing to attempt the natives no further, being very sorry for what had happened." The young Englishman was wounded in the cheek by a lance. Among the attacking party there was one young man who, from his appearance and dignity of demeanour, was imagined a chief or leader. Yet this impression was given by something distinct from either height of stature or personal beauty; for the New Hollander was neither so tall nor well-made as some of the others, but "a brisk young man," active and courageous. He was the only one of the group that was painted. A circle drawn with some sort of white pigment surrounded each of his eyes, and a white streak reached from the forehead to the tip of the nose. His breast and part of his arms were also stained, "not for beauty or ornament," it was very rationally concluded, "but that he seemed thereby to design the looking more terrible, this his painting adding very much to his natural deformity." Dampier imagined these New Hollanders to be of the same nation with those he had seen when the *Cygnet* had touched on this coast. "They were the same blinking creatures," he says, "with the most unpleasant looks and worst features of any people I had ever seen." He did not get near enough to discover if this tribe also wanted the two fore-teeth, as that tribe did. By the old fire-places quantities of shells were found of the kinds of shell-fish on which the other island-tribe lived; and their lances were similar in shape. The general features of the country at the places visited on this coast were the same as those already described—low, with chains of sand-hills, the land round the shore dry and sandy, bearing many shrubs with beautiful blossoms of various colours and of delicate fragrance. Farther on, the land was mixed woodland and savanna. The plains were studded with detached rocks resembling haycocks at a distance, some red and others white. By subsequent voyagers these have been taken for large ant-hillocks. Some animals were seen resembling hungry wolves, lean as skeletons.

Brackish water was at last obtained, which was employed to boil the oatmeal, in order to save what remained in the casks. Our navigator on the 5th September left this arid and sterile coast; on the 7th, in latitude 16° 9′ S., and out of sight of land, stood out to sea; and on the 8th, in 15° 37′, shaped his course for the island of Timor. On the 22nd he came to anchor in Coepang Bay, near the Dutch fort Concordia, but afterwards went to Laphao, a Portuguese settlement on the opposite side of the island.

After resting and refitting at this fine island, the voyage was prosecuted to New Guinea. The *Roebuck* sailed on the 20th December; and on the 1st January 1700, they descried the western coast of this country—high level land covered with thriving trees. Near the land they were assailed by tornadoes, and black clouds hovered over it, while at sea the weather was clear and settled. On the 7th they landed, caught at one haul above three hundred mackerel, and next day anchored in the mouth of a river, where they took in water. Fruits of unknown kinds were brought on board by the pinnace; and one of the men shot a stately landfowl about the size of the dunghill cock, sky-coloured, but with a white blotch and reddish spots about the wings, and a long bunch of feathers on the crown. From Freshwater Bay, which they named this place, they sailed out by White Island, which was in 3° 4′ S., and is distinguished by white cliffs. The *Roebuck* beat up to the northward against currents and adverse winds, and passed many islets and dangerous shoals, occasionally anchoring to obtain wood and water. At an island named by the natives Sabuda, in 2° 43′ S., Dampier found a tawny race closely resembling his old friends at Mindanao. Negroes were also seen here, of the curly-haired blacks which had originally obtained for this country the name of New Guinea. Some of these Oceanic negroes appeared to be slaves of the yellow or Malay race. The weapons were the same as in Mindanao, the lances pointed with bone. These islanders had a very ingenious way of making the fish rise. A block of wood carved like a dolphin was let down into the water by a line, to which a weight was attached in order to sink it. When they had waited the effect of their stratagem, the decoy was rapidly raised by the line, the fish followed it, and the strikers stood ready prepared.

Still plying northward, on the 4th February they reached the north-west cape of New Guinea, called by the Dutch Cape Mabo. A small wooded island lies off the cape, and to the north and north-east islets are numerous. The land is generally high, and covered with tall healthy timber. Near one of these islands, which, from the enormous size of the cockles found at it, he named Cockle Island, Dampier had almost run upon a shoal, but got off; and coming to anchor, despatched the boats to the island, from whence pigeons were brought, and cockles of the moderate weight of ten pounds. The shell alone of one formerly found weighed fifty-eight pounds. Bats of the large kind were seen here.

The *Roebuck* stood onward four or five leagues, shaping her course to the east, and at a small wooded island found ordinary-sized cockles in prodigious abundance, and numerous pigeons. On the 7th they anchored at an island finely wooded with tall "straight trees fit for any use," which Dampier loyally named King William's Island. From the time of passing Cape Mabo till the 12th, the *Roebuck*, owing to easterly winds, had not advanced above thirty leagues to the eastward. When they got to 2° S. the easterly winds increased, and, as they approached the Equinoctial, hung still more easterly. On the afternoon of the 12th the wind shifted to a more favourable point, with heavy rain, which continued for some days. They descried, at the distance of six leagues from the shore, two headlands about twenty miles apart, one to the east, the other to the west. The last they named the Cape of

Good Hope. On the morning of the 15th they were in danger of running upon an island not laid down in their charts, which Dampier, in commemoration of the escape, named Providence Island. Large trees and logs were this day seen floating, which Dampier concluded had come out of some of the rivers of New Guinea. On the 16th they crossed the Line. The *Roebuck* was steered for an island seen on the 25th at the distance of fifteen leagues, supposed to be that called Vischer's Island by the Dutch; but as it was to him unknown land, Dampier named it Matthias Island. It was about ten leagues long, hilly and wooded, but intersected by savannas and open places. Another island—low, level land, seven or eight leagues to the eastward of this— was named Squally Island, as they here encountered tornadoes so violent and frequent that they durst not venture to stand in.

Dampier afterwards stood for the mainland, encountering frequent and violent squalls, and steered for a part of the coast where he saw many smokes arising. The islands he had at first passed were those now known as the Admiralty Islands. His course had lain to the northward of them.

The land he approached was mountainous and well-wooded, with large plantations and cleared patches lying on the hill-sides. The discoverer wished to have some intercourse with the natives here, and was glad to see boats and proas come off in great numbers. They approached near enough to make signs and to be heard, but their language was totally unknown to the voyagers. They could not be induced to approach the ship any closer—not even by the allurement of beads, knives, or glasses, though some beads floated to them in a bottle were readily picked up, and they seemed pleased with the gift. They often struck their left breast with the right hand, and held a black truncheon over their heads, as if in token of friendship. It was impossible, from the state of the current, to get the ship into the bay to which the natives pointed; and when she wore off, they appeared angry, though they still followed in their proas, which were now increased to a formidable fleet. The bays were also lined with men. The crew got ready their small-arms; and when the ship fairly stood out, the natives became so ill-pleased that they launched showers of stones after her from slings. One gun was fired off, and some of the slingers were conjectured to be killed or wounded. Dampier named this place Slingers' Bay.

Next day the *Roebuck* passed an island where smokes were seen and men in the bays, who followed in three canoes, but could not overtake the ship. This island is the Gerrit Denys or Gerard Dynas of the Dutch. It is high, mountainous, and wooded. The hill-sides were covered with plantations, and in the sheltered bays there were cocoa-nut trees. It seemed very populous; the natives were black, with crisp hair, which they shaved in different figures, and dyed of various hues. They were strong and well-limbed, with broad round faces and large flat noses; yet the expression of their countenance, when not disfigured by their singular taste in ornament, was not unpleasant. Besides being painted, they wore some kind of ornament through their noses, about four inches long, and as thick as a man's thumb. Their ears were perforated with large holes filled with similar decorations. The weapons seen were swords, lances, slings, bows and arrows. The proas were ingeniously built, and ornamented with carved figures, though they had neither sail nor anchor, and the natives were expert and fearless in managing them. Their language was clear and distinct. The black truncheon, used as at Slingers' Bay, or a fresh-gathered leafy bough, was their symbol of friendship. These they placed upon their heads, to which they often lifted their hands.

Dampier next day reached Anthony Kaan's Island, which in its external features and social condition closely resembled the neighbouring group. It lies in 3° 25″ S. As the *Roebuck* held along the coast, other natives approached; and three ventured on board, to whom the captain gave a knife, a looking-glass, and beads, showing them pumpkins and cocoa-nut shells, and by signs requesting them to bring similar things to the ship. They understood this language, and out of one of the canoes took three cocoa-nuts, which they presented to him. When nutmegs and gold-dust were shown them, they appeared to intimate that such things were to be obtained on their island. The natives here, like those already seen, were black, tall, strong, and well made, with crisp hair, and their nose and ears were ornamented in the same fashion as those seen the former day.

Dampier's next stage was St. John's, an island about ten leagues long, abounding in plantations and cocoa-nut trees, with groves of palms by the shores and in the bays. All these islands appeared so populous that the navigator feared to send a party on shore for wood or water, unless he could have found anchoring ground where the ship might have been brought up to protect them, and he now again stood for the mainland of New Guinea to supply his wants. On the 8th he approached the coast so near that smokes were seen, with the land high and wooded, and thinly interspersed with savannas. Canoes came off to the ship, in which were natives exactly resembling those they had last seen. A headland lay to the south, in latitude 5° 5′ S., from which point Dampier concluded that the shore trended to the westward, as no land was seen beyond it. This headland he named Cape St. George, the meridian distance of which from Cape Mabo is twelve hundred and ninety miles. An island off this cape he named St. George's Island, and the bay between it and the west point St. George's Bay. Great quantities of smoke arose in sight, and next day a volcano was discovered burning. The south-west cape of the bay Dampier named Cape Orford, in compliment to his noble patron. It is a bluff point, of medium height, and flat at the top. In advancing on the 14th, a cluster of islands were seen in a bay in which Dampier hoped to find anchorage. He ran in, and saw smokes, and, having got up with the point of the bay, houses, plantations, and cocoa-nut trees. He approached within a few miles of the shore, and several proas, with about forty men, came out to view the ship, but would not venture on board. The ship now lay becalmed, and as other proas full of men approached from different points, one of them of very large size, the commander became uneasy. He made the first party signs to return to the shore; but they either could not understand or would not obey, and he "whistled a shot over their heads," which made them pull away. Two boats, which had started from different points, intended, it was apprehended, to effect a junction and attack the ship. Of these, one was a large boat, with a high head and stern, painted, and full of men. At this formidable bark Dampier fired another shot, which made it sheer off, though it afterwards pulled but the more vigorously to join the other advancing boat. To prevent this junction, and overawe the natives in their suspected design, the gunner was directed to fire a shot between these boats as they approached each other; which he did with so true an aim, using round and partridge shot, that they instantly separated and made for the shore with all speed. The *Roebuck*, which had been for a short time becalmed, bore after them into the bay with a gentle favouring breeze; and when it reached the point, a great many men were seen lurking about the rocks and peeping out. Another shot was fired against the point, as a necessary measure of intimidation. The shot grazed between the ship and the point, flew over it, and grazed a second time very near the ambushed party. A number of the natives were still seen sitting under the cocoa trees, whom Dampier, who knew the people here to be inhospitable, distrustful, and treacherous (a character which the Oceanic negroes had obtained from all previous navigators), deemed it necessary to scare and disperse; and a third gun was fired among the wood, but over their heads, before the boat was sent out to sound. The *Roebuck* followed the boat, and found good anchorage at a quarter of a mile from the shore, and opposite the mouth of a small river, where they hoped to find water, the true and only object of all this seeming harshness. A group stationed on a small point at the river's mouth was scattered by the former means, though this shot and all that were fired were aimed aside and harmless. The seamen then rowed for the shore, and before they landed, the Indians rushed into the water, and placed cocoa-nuts in their boat as a present or a propitiatory offering.

Water was obtained—one boat's crew keeping watch while the other filled the casks—and an attempt was made to commence a trade by exchanging axes and hatchets for yams, potatoes, and other articles. The natives were not insensible to the value of the goods offered in exchange, but they would part with nothing save cocoa-nuts, which they climbed the trees to gather, and gave to the seamen, at the same time making signs to them to be gone.

Having obtained a tolerable quantity of both wood and water, Dampier held a consultation with his officers on the propriety of putting to sea, or of remaining here some time longer, to fish, and endeavour to obtain hogs, goats, yams, and whatever refreshments the place afforded. It was agreed to remain. While the men were employed in cutting wood, a party of about forty natives, men and women, passed near them. They at first appeared frightened, but were somewhat reassured by the signs of friendship made by the sailors, and passed quietly on. The men were finely bedecked with feathers of gay colours stuck in their hair, and carried lances; while the women trudged behind totally naked, save for a few green boughs stuck into the string tied round their waists. On their heads they carried large baskets full of yams. "And this," says Dampier, "I have observed of all savages I have known—that they make their women carry the burdens, while the men walk before without any other load than their arms and ornaments."

When the boats went next ashore, some of the seamen entered the dwellings of the natives, who, instead of becoming more familiar on further acquaintance, got more and more shy and distrustful. They had now gathered all the cocoas, and driven away their hogs to a place in the bottom of the bay. Dampier himself landed, carrying with him articles proper for presents and trade; but he was unable to inspire the natives with any degree of confidence. Few of them approached him, and those with reluctance; and a promise which an Indian made of bringing cocoa-nuts was probably never intended to be kept. He visited three different villages, and uniformly found the huts abandoned and the furniture and live-stock carried off. When Captain Dampier returned to the ship, he found all the officers and men most importunate to obtain his permission to visit the place whither the hogs had been driven. They extorted a reluctant consent, and departed, furnished with commodities for traffic, strictly enjoined to deal fairly with the natives, and for their own security to act with caution. The bay was two miles distant, and Dampier, who had great misgivings of the consequences of the enterprise, prepared, in case of the worst, to assist them with the ship's guns, as the natives were now seen assembling on the shore in large groups, prepared to resist the landing, shaking their lances and using threatening gestures. The English displayed their tempting wares, and made signs which were disregarded by the natives, some of whom plunged into the sea with their lances and targets to commence the attack. But the seamen were resolved in every event to obtain provisions; and since fair means were repulsed, they made no scruple at using violence and severity. The first fire of the muskets made the greater part of the warriors run off, though a few stood with great resolution, still in the attitude of repelling the landing. The boldest at last dropped his target—it was conjectured that he was hit in the arm—and the whole took to flight. Dampier acknowledges that "some felt the smart of our bullets, but none were killed; our design being rather to fright than to kill them." The seamen shot nine hogs, besides wounding many that escaped, and in the evening made a second trip and brought off eight more. As a sort of compensation for the injury done, Dampier sent a captured canoe back to the shore, and deposited in it two axes, two hatchets, six knives, six looking-glasses, four bottles, and a quantity of beads.

This bay, in 6° 10′ S., and one hundred and fifty-one miles west of Cape St. George, Dampier named Port Montague, in honour of the President of the Royal Society. Of the appearance and nature of the country here he makes a very favourable report. "It is mountainous and wooded, with rich valleys and pleasant fresh-water brooks." The rivers abounded in fish; cocoa-nut trees sprung and throve on every island, and many fruits of unknown kinds were seen. Ginger was among the spontaneous productions.

The *Roebuck* was now well supplied with wood and water, and the hogs had been salted as soon as brought on board. On the 22nd March they left Port Montague, and on the 24th, in the evening, saw high land bearing north-west, "half-west, and no land visible more to the west." They steered west-north-west, coasting along under easy sail, and at two o'clock saw a pillar of fire. At daylight this was discovered to be a burning island, for which they bore, seeing many other islands, two of them pretty high. They passed through a channel about five leagues broad, lying between the Burning Island and the mainland. All the night of the 25th, being still in this strait, they saw the volcano, "which," Dampier relates, "vomited fire and smoke very amazingly."

On the night of the 26th the *Roebuck* had shot to the westward of the Burning Island, whence the fire could no longer be seen, the crater lying on its south side. This volcano lies at meridian distance three hundred and thirty-two miles west from Cape St. George. And now Dampier had attained an important stage in his voyage of discovery. "The easternmost part," he says, "of New Guinea lies forty miles to the westward of this tract of land, and by hydrographers they are made joining together." This he found to be a mistake, and discovered that it was a channel he had passed through here, in which were many islands. Before entering this strait, he named the promontory on the north-east of this coast—part of what was then all named New Guinea—King William's Cape. It is high and mountainous. Smokes were seen upon it. Leaving it upon the larboard side, the *Roebuck* bore away close upon the east land, which ends with two remarkable capes, distant from each other about six leagues, with two fine and very high mountains rising from the sea within these headlands. The country appeared finely mingled with woodland and savanna, as smooth and verdant as an English meadow. Smokes were again seen; but Dampier, who wished to repair his pinnace, which was so crazy as to be unserviceable, chose rather to anchor near an uninhabited than a peopled island, as he wished to avoid the natives. He stood over to the islands, and kept a look-out for land to the north, but saw none. The navigator was now assured that he had passed through a strait, and that this eastern land did not join the mainland of New Guinea. He named this island, which he had now nearly circumnavigated, Nova Britannia, the northwest point of the strait Cape Gloucester, and the southwest Cape Anne. The mountain most to the northwest of the two which rose between those headlands, being very remarkable in appearance, the discoverer chose to give it also a name, and called it Mount Gloucester.

The passage thus discovered is now known in geography as Dampier's Strait. The island of Nova Britannia, in productions and inhabitants, resembled New Guinea. The people were negroes, strong-limbed, bold, and daring. They had been closely observed at Port Montague, and the remarks made on them there applied with equal propriety to the few that were afterwards seen.

Advancing in his course, Dampier fell in with several

islands. One eleven leagues in length he named Sir George Rooke's Island. On the 31st he shot in between two islands,—the southernmost long, with a hill at each end. This he named Long Island. The one to the north was named Crown Island, from its eminences. Both were pleasant, and seemed fertile,—savanna and woodland interspersed, the trees green and flourishing, and many of them covered with white blossoms. Cocoanut trees were frequent in the bays of that island which from its conformation Dampier named Crown Island. It was believed to be inhabited, but thinly. A boat was seen, which just peeped forth from the shore of this island, and drew back; but neither plantations nor smokes were discovered. In the afternoon of the 31st another island was seen bearing north-west by west; and next morning, the ship having steered away north-west to get to the northward of it, lay about midway between it and Crown and Long Islands. The mainland of New Guinea, lying to the southward, was seen rising very high. From this new island, which the navigator named Sir R. Rich's Island, four canoes came off, which from a distance reconnoitred the ship. One advanced within call, but when invited the men would not approach closer. The *Roebuck* bore onward and discovered four more islands, and land to the southward, which might either be another island or part of the mainland of New Guinea. These islands were generally high, full of trees, mixed with clear spots; all, even the Burning Island, were fertile. On the 2nd

April they passed by its north side, and saw that the land near the sea was rich, and good for two-thirds of the height of the mountains. Among this group of islands three small vessels with sails were seen, though the inhabitants of Nova Britannia appeared quite unacquainted with the use of sails. Another island was descried that sent forth smoke, which, however, soon dispersed. This is presumed to have been the Brandende Berg of Schouten. Different observations made at this time showed a variation in the ship's reckoning, for which the navigator was at a loss to account. On the 14th April they passed Schouten's Island, and on the 17th observed a volcano on the mainland, which had either not been smoking or had been passed unnoticed when they sailed round King William's Island. This island, discovered in passing round about two months before, was seen in the same afternoon, and they crowded sail to reach it before dark. But the wind fell, and they were becalmed within two miles of the shore. The night was one of bright moonlight, and a delightful fragrance was wafted from the island to the ship. Next morning they were becalmed two leagues to the westward of the island, and met such whirling tides that the ship refused to obey the helm, and frequently turned round in the whirlpools. A gale fortunately sprung up and carried her off.

The voyage was prosecuted to the island of Ceram, which they reached on the 26th April. Here they obtained a supply of rice from a Dutch vessel, and next went to Timor, from whence Dampier intended once more to attempt New Holland in about 20°. Here he found soundings at forty fathoms, but did not see the land, and steered westward to search for the Trial Rocks,* which were supposed to lie in this parallel, and about eighty leagues westward of the coast. But Captain Dampier was sick and unable to maintain perpetual watch himself, and the officers were inefficient and careless, so that this important point was not ascertained; nor could more be attempted at this time for purposes of discovery, many of the crew being affected with scurvy, and the ship hardly seaworthy. The *Roebuck* accordingly sailed for Java, and on the 3rd July anchored in the road of Batavia, where Dampier supported the dignity of his mission by making the only English vessel found in the harbour strike her pendant. On the 17th October they sailed for Europe, and without any remarkable adventure, having touched at the Cape of Good Hope and St. Helena, approached the island of Ascension on the 21st February, and stood in for it, now reckoning themselves almost at home. On the evening of the 22nd the ship, old and damaged before the voyage had commenced, sprung a leak, and it was with difficulty that the pumps kept her afloat till daylight, when they made for the bay and came to anchor. Every exertion was made to stop the leak and save the ship, while the pumps were kept

---

* So named from an English ship called the *Trial* having been wrecked upon them many years before Dampier's voyage.

hard at work. The carpenters showed great want of judgment, if not want of skill in their business, and in spite of all the ingenious contrivances resorted to by Dampier, their improvidence and the damaged condition of the ship rendered every effort abortive. Dampier remained on board till the very last. He had to regret the loss of many of his books and papers, and a collection of shells gathered at New Holland. The plants he contrived to save. The condition of the party was more fortunate than that which generally falls to the lot of shipwrecked seamen. They were most happy to discover a spring of good water, though eight miles distant from their tents and across a very high mountain, and Dampier thankfully relates that "they were now by God's providence in a condition to subsist for some time, having plenty of good turtle by their tents, and water for the fetching." Here Dampier and his company remained for about five weeks. During that time they had seen several ships and fleets pass; but none touched till the 2nd April, when an Indiaman and three English ships of war came into the bay. Dampier went on board one of them with thirty-five of his men, and the rest of the crew were accommodated in the other vessels.

Though the purpose of his voyage had been accomplished, and though many important additions were made by it to geography, the loss of the ship and of his papers depressed the spirits of the navigator, and but too probably lessened his merit with those fortunate persons in high places who rarely judge of any undertaking save by its apparent success. He was now to suffer for the ignorance or mistaken economy of those who, projecting a voyage of discovery distant and perilous, imagined that it might be accomplished by a useless crazy ship unfit for what was considered better service. The marvel was that it had not foundered long before.

It is to be feared that neither rewards nor even soothing promises awaited the return of Dampier from his public enterprise. His original patron, or at least the person who officially gave him his appointment to the *Roebuck*, no longer presided at the Admiralty. To this nobleman, the Earl of Pembroke, he, however, inscribed his relation of the VOYAGE TO NEW HOLLAND.

About his own private affairs, and his personal feelings, Dampier is at all times modest and reserved, and we can only surmise his disappointment from an incidental remark into which he is betrayed in the dedication of his history of that voyage, which ought to have been regarded from the first as useful to science and honourable to the navigator. "The world," he says, "is apt to judge of everything by success, in so much that whoever has ill-fortune will hardly be allowed a good name." "Such," he continues, "was my unhappiness in my late expedition in the *Roebuck*, which foundered through perfect age, though I comfort myself with the thoughts that no neglect can be charged against me." Justly, no neglect could be charged against him. On the contrary, he was entitled by his conduct of this voyage, independently of his other merits, to future employment; but we hear no more of Captain Dampier in the public service. His voyage in the *Roebuck* is the last of his published writings, and the history of the remainder of his eventful life, which we gather from others, as it is painful, may be brief.

Captain Dampier had not been long at home when the death of King William III. took place, and was followed by the war of the Succession. Among the private enterprises attending this war with France and Spain was extensive privateering; and he obtained the command of the *St. George* and *Cinque Ports*, two vessels equipped by a company of English merchants, and intended to cruise against the Spaniards in the South Seas. The *St. George* left the Downs in April 1703, with Captain Dampier on board; but it was September before both vessels left Kinsale. The basis of the expedition was the old buccaneer maxim, *No prey, no pay*, —a principle ill adapted to the maintenance of discipline or order in a ship. In this voyage Dampier had in view three special objects,—namely, the capture of the Spanish galleons that sailed from Buenos Ayres; and, failing that, to pass the Strait of Magellan, or double Cape Horn, and lie in wait for the ship that carried gold from Baldivia to Lima; or, finally, the oft-attempted exploit of the seizure of the Manilla galleon. The *St. George* carried twenty-six guns, and a crew of one hundred and twenty.

The character of Dampier has been subjected to many rash and unfounded imputations drawn from histories of this voyage published without his sanction. The principal one, written by Funnel, who, till he deserted, sailed as Dampier's steward, is full of evident misstatements regarding the navigation, as well as the private transactions in the ship. So far as these misrepresentations regarded geographical and nautical facts, Dampier afterwards corrected them, though he took little notice of the allegations against himself, further than in one or two instances to point out their glaring falsehood. Before the voyage was well begun quarrels broke out among these irresponsible officers, and some of them quitted the ship; while the commander, without being invested with salutary power to restrain them, was left to bear the blame of the misconduct of the whole company.

The ships doubled Cape Horn, and reached Juan Fernandez without any remarkable adventure. While lying here a strange sail was seen, to which both ships gave chase. She proved to be a French ship cruising in these seas, and so strongly did the old buccaneer associations influence Dampier, that he acknowledged it was with reluctance he attacked a European vessel of whatever nation. He, however, engaged, and after a fight of seven hours, in which both ships suffered considerably, they parted.

Before the proper latitude was reached, the Baldivia treasure-ships had sailed. Though Dampier was the nominal commander, Stradling, in the *Cinque Ports*, acted independently; and as they differed about their future operations, the ships parted company. A design to surprise Santa Maria in the Bay of Panama failed; and though Dampier captured a few small vessels, he obtained no prize of any value.

While lying in the Gulf of Nicoya, the commander and his chief mate, John Clipperton, quarrelled, and the latter, with twenty-one of the crew, seized the tender, in which were most of the ammunition and stores, and put out to sea. It is alleged that Clipperton at this time stole his commander's commission. No captain ever sailed with a worse disposed and more turbulent set of men and officers than those whom Dampier now commanded. They had all the bad qualities of buccaneers without their bravery, experience, and hardihood.

The *St. George* bore northward, and on the 6th December, while only a short way beyond Port de Navidad, descried a sail, which proved to be the Manilla galleon. The Manilla ship had no suspicion of any enemy being on this coast, and she received several broadsides from the *St. George* before being cleared for action. Even taken thus at disadvantage, when her guns, which were of far heavier metal, were brought into play, they at once drove in the rotten planks of the *St. George*, and obliged Dampier to sheer off. The galleon also held on. It is presumed that the number of her men quadrupled those of the English ship, and her guns were eighteen and twenty-four pounders, while those of the *St. George* were only five-pounders.

This proved a bitter disappointment, and the men became more and more impatient to end so profitless and fatiguing a voyage. In hopes of better fortune, they were, however, induced to continue the cruise for a few weeks longer on the coast of New Spain; but this produced nothing, and it was agreed to part company. One party, instigated by Funnel, the mendacious historian of the voyage, resolved to sail for India, and by this route return home. A brigantine of seventy tons which had been captured was given up to him and the thirty-four men who chose to follow his counsels; and the stores, small-arms, and ammunition were divided, four of the *St. George's* guns being also given to this party. Dampier's crew was thus left reduced to twenty-nine. After refitting his crazy, disabled ship, he returned to the coast of Peru. They plundered the town of Puna, and cruised along till their ship was no longer fit to keep the sea, when they abandoned her riding at anchor at Lobos de la Mar, and, embarking in a brigantine which they had captured from the Spaniards, crossed the Pacific.

Of this voyage, and of the subsequent misfortunes of Dampier in India, there remain no certain or distinct accounts. It is, however, known that, not having a commission to show, he was thrown into prison by the Dutch. Before he obtained his freedom and got back to England, Funnel, his unworthy subaltern, had returned; and a London bookseller, named Knapton, the publisher of Dampier's former voyages, had been induced by their popularity to print this person's narrative of the voyage of the *St. George*, under the false title of the fourth volume of the works of the celebrated navigator. Dampier, on coming home, published a few pages of explanation, entitled " Captain Dampier's Vindication of his Voyage in the Ship *St. George*, with some small Observations on Mr. Funnel's chimerical Relation." Funnel's account, however, as no other was ever published, keeps its place as the history of this voyage, though its palpable misrepresentations, and the bad and malevolent spirit in which it is written, have drawn upon the writer the reprobation of every lover of justice and impartial inquirer after truth.

The fortunes of Dampier must have been at a very low ebb when he returned to England after this disastrous voyage, and it is with pain we find this veteran navigator, as much distinguished by superiority of understanding as by nautical skill and experience, obliged, in 1708, to act as a pilot under younger and very inferior commanders. This, which was Dampier's last voyage, again proved to be one round the world, and was undertaken in the *Duke* and *Duchess*, two privateers fitted out by several Bristol merchants.

Copious narratives of this voyage are written by the commanders, Woodes Rogers and Cook; but it is only incidentally that we learn anything from them of their distinguished pilot.

At Juan Fernandez, Woodes Rogers, on this voyage, brought off the celebrated Alexander Selkirk, who had been left or rather abandoned here by Dampier's violent and tyrannical consort, Captain Stradling, four years previously. On the recommendation of Dampier, Selkirk was made second mate of the *Duke*.

The cruise of the privateers was successful. At Guayaquil, where Dampier commanded the artillery, they obtained plunder to the value of £21,000, and 27,000 dollars as ransom of the town. They afterwards, off Cape Lucas, captured a Manilla ship richly laden with merchandise, and £12,000 in gold and silver. They brought their prize into Puerto Segura, and prepared to look for the richer and larger Manilla galleon; which they encountered, but, after a protracted and severe engagement, were beaten off. In this fight the *Duchess* alone lost twenty-five men. The natives of Puerto Segura were blacker than any other people seen in the South Sea by Woodes Rogers. They were of disagreeable aspect; their language harsh and guttural. They carried bows six feet long, strung with the silkgrass. Their arrows were of cane, tipped with flint or bone.

The privateers now turned their thoughts homeward, and, keeping the usual track of the galleons, reached Guahan on the 10th March, after a run of exactly two months, and anchored under Spanish colours. Apart from this venial deception, employed to facilitate the purchase of supplies, the conduct of the English privateers was unexceptionable. They rested for ten days, and made the north of Gilolo in about a month afterwards. At Bouton they stopped to take in provisions and water, and next sailed for Batavia, where they experienced those noxious effects of climate from which hardly any ship's company escapes at that most unhealthy station.

They sailed from Batavia in the end of October, waited long at the Cape for a homeward-bound fleet, and coming round the north of Scotland, five and twenty sail, Dutch and English, anchored in the Texel in July of the following year, and in October 1711 came to the Thames with booty in money and merchandise valued at £150,000. From this date we hear no more of Captain Dampier, whose name appears less frequently in the narrative of Rogers than, from the eminent nautical abilities of the man who bore it, it ought to have done. In difficulties he was, it appears, constantly applied to, and his former knowledge and experience were taken as guides. At Bouton, where he had been in the *Cygnet*, he was intrusted to carry the present to the sultan; and, from respect to his judgment and integrity, he was also chosen umpire in the very delicate affair of deciding what was plunder for immediate division, and in allotting the respective shares.

Dampier was of the number of those men distinguished above their fellows, " who are not without honour save in their own country;" or if at home his merits were appreciated, wanting the most worthless quality of success, the glare and show, they failed of their reward.

By French and Dutch navigators and men of science he has been uniformly regarded with the warmest admiration, as a man to whose professional eminence his own country has scarce done justice. They delight to style him the "eminent," the "skilful," the "exact," the "incomparable Dampier." Humboldt has borne testimony to his merits, placing the buccaneer seaman above those men of science who afterwards went over the same ground; Malte-Brun terms him "the learned Dampier;" and the author of the "Voyages to Australia" inquires, "*Mais où trouve-t-on des navigateurs comparables à Dampier?*" The acuteness, accuracy, and clearness of his nautical observations, and of his descriptions and general remarks, have made his voyages be assumed by foreign navigators as unerring guides and authorities in all subsequent expeditions; and his rapidity and power of observation are fully as remarkable as his accuracy. His hasty glance at the places of New Holland where he touched has left subsequent voyagers little to do save to verify his descriptions. Dampier's veracity has in no instance been questioned, even by those most disposed to cavil at facts which, being remote from their limited experience, appear extraordinary or impossible. Other writers, combining into one the relations of many different travellers, have amplified his descriptions; but there is no detached account of the countries he visited more full of vital interest and exact information than the voyages of this wandering seaman.

The succession of brilliant discoveries which illustrated the early part of the reign of George III. for a time threw the adventures of Dampier, and of every previous navigator, into the shade; but they are again emerging into popularity. Compared with the voyages of recent navigators, his long solitary rambles are as the emprises of the single knightly combatant, bearing no proportion to the magnitude and splendour of a regular battle-field, but, from their individuality, often commanding a more intense and powerful, because a more concentrated, interest.

The cloud which rested on the personal character of Dampier from the ignorance or misrepresentations of envious contemporaries, and the carelessness and haste with which writers for the press copy from each other and adopt current statements, is fast clearing away. By Pinkerton he is termed "the Cook of a former age;" and Burney has taken a generous pleasure in doing justice to his professional merits, and shown a more generous indignation in rebuking the thoughtless repetition of unfounded calumnies. "It is," he says, "matter of regret, and not less of dissatisfaction, to see that some late writers have been so little conscious of the merits of Dampier as to allow themselves to speak of him with small respect, for no other cause than that it appears he had disagreements with some of his shipmates, the particular circumstances of which are not known, further than that he had to deal with a quarrelsome and mutinous crew. Such petty considerations should never have been lifted up against the memory of such a man as Dampier." " It is not easy to name another voyager or traveller who has given more useful information to the world, or to whom the merchant and the mariner are more indebted." To these Burney might have added the philosopher and the naturalist, who have rarely been so much indebted to any adventurer whose pursuits were so entirely remote from their subjects of speculation. This honourable testimony will remain to the credit of the writer, when the vague statements and unsifted calumnies, which other authors have allowed themselves to repeat to the disadvantage of Dampier, are for ever forgotten.

Though the life of this navigator was spent in incessant action, his natural genius appears to have been rather speculative than enterprising. He liked to reason and to scheme, and lost sight of present small but certain advantage in extensive and brilliant plans for the future, which his evil fortune forbade him to realize. If, indeed, there be such things as good and bad fortune in human affairs independent of skill and exertion, Dampier may be pointed out as an example of what the world calls an unlucky man,—one to whom every event proves adverse,—who seems singled out for misfortune. Except the capital error of the mode of life upon which he entered, none of his misadventures can be traced to himself; and this lawless life enriched many of his contemporaries, while it kept him in poverty and left him a beggar. In relating its incidents, he has never once attempted to justify or palliate his manner of existence for so many years. Amidst the vicissitudes and temptations to which it exposed him, his excellent understanding, and the principles he had imbibed in the virtuous household of a Somersetshire yeoman, preserved him, if not entirely spotless from evil contagion, yet from that decay and deadness of moral feeling which are among the worst consequences of vicious companionship. He was humane, just in the most strict and also in the most liberal sense, candid and charitable in his judgments, and—rare virtues in a buccaneer— orderly and temperate, detesting the riotous excess of his associates. Get over the stumbling-block of his early life being squared by "the good old rule," and Dampier the buccaneer was a virtuous man. In the South Sea, and afterwards in the *Cygnet*, he might have obtained command, such was the respect his shipmates entertained for his abilities; but the love of adventure was his strongest passion, and his sole ambition the acquisition of knowledge.

He appears latterly to have deeply felt the disgrace and galling servitude of his lawless life; and serious reflection and remorseful feelings pressed upon his mind with great force long before he was able to get free of his wild associates in the *Cygnet*.

By the time that Dampier returned to England with Woodes Rogers, he was far advanced in life; and his career for forty years had been one of unremitting hardihood and professional exertion. It is therefore probable that he never embarked in any subsequent voyage; and as the remaining part of his life, whether long or short, is involved in complete obscurity, there is but too much reason to believe that it was passed in neglect, if not in poverty. Of this eminent seaman and traveller, though little more than a century can have elapsed since his death, no one is able now to tell how the evening of his life was spent, when he died, or where he was buried. Had he expired in some remote island of the Pacific, or perished in the element on which so great a portion of his life was passed, some imperfect record might have remained to satisfy our natural desire to know the last of the worn-out and veteran navigator; but it was his fate to sink unheeded amidst the conflicting waves and tides of society, and no memorial or tradition remains of *his* death in whose remarkable life the adventures of Selkirk, Wafer, and the buccaneer commanders of the South Sea appear but as episodes. So much for human fame!

THE END.

www.ingramcontent.com/pod-product-compliance
Lightning Source LLC
Chambersburg PA
CBHW020738020526
44115CB00030B/158